Literary Cubism

Geography and Plays

Selected Works
of
Gertrude Stein

Edited and with an Introduction
by
Laura Bonds

Cover Art
by
Juan Gris

Traveling Press
Special Edition Books

Literary Cubism – Geography and Plays
Selected Works of Gertrude Stein

Edited by Laura Bonds, Shawn Conners
Cover art by Juan Gris
Violin and Checkerboard, 1913

First Printing – January 2011

Published by
Traveling Press
Special Edition Books
El Paso, Texas USA

ISBN10: 1-934255-76-9
ISBN13: 978-1-934255-76-6

Printed in the United States of America

Introduction

Literary Cubism

> *"A writer should write with his eyes and a painter, paint with his ears."*

Gertrude Stein was at heart an artist's writer. She became well-known to the literary mainstream with *The Autobiography of Alice B. Toklas,* and was at her most accessible with her speech and autobiographical writing of later years. It is with collections such as *Geography and Plays*, however, that Stein showcased the possibilities of the English language to transcend beyond literature into the realm of modern art. The page was her canvas, and as the Cubist painters of her time treated their subjects, Stein re-assembled words in an abstracted form to present them in a greater context, a context un-tethered by a singular viewpoint.

This push to make words on the page strike the reader as "painterly" or as portraiture should come as little surprise, considering Gertrude Stein's fascination with the modern art movement of the early 1900s. Indeed, before she made a name for herself as a writer and a poet, Stein was most famous for garnering, along with her brother Leo, a world-renowned private modern art collection between the years 1904-1913. At age 29, Gertrude followed her art critic brother and moved from the United States to Paris in 1903, where together they began collecting pieces through a well-maintained family trust fund. Among their first purchases to adorn the walls at 27 *Rue de Fleurus* were Paul Gaugin's *Sunflowers*, Paul Cézanne's *Bathers*, and two works by Pierre-Auguste Renoir. By 1906, the collection had expanded to include paintings by avant-garde luminaries: Pablo Picasso, Honoré Daumier, Henri Matisse, and Henri de Toulouse-Lautrec. Art critic for the New York Sun Henry McBride brought the world's attention to what he considered one of history's most important art collections through a series of widely circulated articles. He also made the observation that Gertrude *"collected geniuses rather than masterpieces. She recognized them a long way off."* It was as if Stein realized she was at the threshold of a new, unmatched age in art, and somehow knew too that she would have a hand in it.

By the midpoint of the first decade of the 20th century, Gertrude Stein was in her thirties, and she and Leo were entertaining the likes of Picasso and Matisse in their Paris home. These two artists soon became integral parts of Stein's social circle, spending regular Saturday evenings with her, along with countless other contemporaries in the arts and literature. In 1906, Picasso painted *Portrait of Gertrude Stein*. When someone commented that she didn't look like her portrait, Picasso replied, "She will." It is perhaps in this prophetic statement Picasso foresaw Stein's growth in her writing as she lived and socialized among the day's cutting-edge artists.

Gertrude began writing for publication in these early years in Paris. Inspired by the artwork that surrounded her, she sat underneath a portrait of Madame Cézanne and began to develop her writing style. Stein took the artist's method and employed it to words. Much like the modernist painters, carefully applying layer by layer of paint upon canvas to gradually unveil the composition, Stein put pen to paper with the same exacting care, building pattern upon pattern of repetitive sentences and phrases to ultimately reveal her works' meaning.

It was during this time, in 1904, that Stein realized her experiences and passions had inexorably led her to writing. In a later autobiography, she commented:

> *...all the forces that have been engaged through*
> *the years of childhood, adolescence and youth in*

*confused and ferocious combat range
themselves in ordered ranks (and during which)
the straight and narrow gateway of maturity,
and life which was all uproar and confusion
narrows down to form and purpose, and we
exchange a great dim possibility for a small hard
reality.*

*Also in our American life where there is no
coercion in custom and it is our right to change
our vocation so often as we have desire and
opportunity, it is a common experience that our
youth extends through the whole first twenty-
nine years of our life and it is not till we reach
thirty that we find at last that vocation for which
we feel ourselves fit and to which we willingly
devote continued labor.*

In short, the "small hard reality" for Gertrude Stein would now be, at age 30, to devote her life, however it would evolve, fully to the written word.

The relationship between Gertrude and her brother Leo had always been an intense and complicated one. From her childhood to well into their time together in Paris, Gertrude looked up to her older brother immensely. After an unsuccessful turn at studying medicine at Johns Hopkins University and leaving the United States in her twenties, Gertrude in many ways depended on Leo for guidance in her youth. Both Steins were deeply insecure and highly intellectual, and they dealt with these shared facets of their personalities in disparate ways. While Leo was reclusive, Gertrude's magnetic personality drew people to her. Leo was self-critical and reflective, Gertrude was assertive and outgoing. As Gertrude doggedly pursued her writing and grew in celebrity, Leo seemed to withdraw under her shadow, and their relationship became strained. Ultimately the rift became permanent in 1914 when Leo moved out of their Paris salon and moved to Italy. Gertrude effectively excised Leo from her life, and the two siblings never spoke to each other again.

While the exact circumstance of their split remains unknown, there are two widely acknowledged factors that contributed to the dissolution, not the least of which was Gertrude's unrelenting allegiance to Pablo Picasso. Picasso's 1906 portrait of Stein was just the start of an ever-deepening alliance between artist and writer, one in which the two entrenched themselves in dialogues about abstraction in art. Leo was dismissive of Picasso, aligning himself more with Renoir and the Impressionists. Gertrude was so enamored of Picasso and his emerging Cubist movement that by 1910, she began to apply the basic principles of Cubism – ideas of simultaneity and the shattering of a single perspective – to her writing. By this point, Picasso had taken Leo's place as her mentor, and Leo had stopped reading Gertrude's writing altogether.

The other cause of rift between the brother and sister was Gertrude's budding romance with Alice B. Toklas. While it is unclear if Leo was morally opposed to the two women's love relationship, it is clear that Leo certainly disapproved of Toklas as an individual. He saw Toklas as opportunistic and unable to resist inserting herself in the limelight of Gertrude's work, once describing her as *"a kind of abnormal vampire."* Whether or not Leo's perception of Toklas was valid, it is true that the women's romantic partnership soon took precedence over any other for Gertrude. Once she moved in with Stein at the Paris salon in 1910, Toklas' influence permeated every aspect of Gertrude's life. She served as Stein's lover, confidante, muse, editor, and critic until Gertrude's death in 1946.

Stein seemed to realize and accept she was a lesbian early in her life, but in the beginning, she tended to struggle with the social dynamics of romantic friendship and any moral dilemmas regarding it. In 1903, she wrote *Q.E.D.*, a novel that was based on a romantic triangle she entered with two other women while attending Johns Hopkins University. *Q.E.D.* is widely regarded as one of the earliest coming out stories, but Stein decided to suppress its publication at the time, perhaps due to her discomfort associated with what she saw as a failed romantic turn. The novel was posthumously published in 1950 under the title *Things as They Are*. As Stein's relationship with Toklas developed, so her acceptance of her homosexuality took a more positive route. The essay *Miss Furr and Miss Skeene* characterizes Stein's growing involvement with the homosexual community and, like *Q.E.D.*, is credited as being one of the first homosexual revelation stories to be published. The word "gay" is used over 100 times throughout the short work, and perhaps because its prevailing meaning at the time conveyed happiness rather than homosexuality, the double-meaning that Stein employed was lost on most readers.

In addition to the daring and cheeky *Miss Furr and Miss Skeene, Literary Cubism – Geography and Plays – Selected Works of Gertrude Stein* contains many of her most radical and influential works. There is *Ada*, one of Stein's many word portraits of famous personages, this one written of Toklas. There is *Every Afternoon: A Dialogue*, a conversation between two unnamed people that highlights the writer's playful, often humorous style. Then there is *Sacred Emily*, in which the reader finds Stein's most often quoted line, *"Rose is a rose is a rose is a rose"* (p.189), a line that employs her trademark use of repetitive language to express that things are what they are, but at the same time, so much more. In Stein's view, the simple naming of a thing already invokes the imagery and emotions associated with it—the writer does not need to manipulate the word any further.

All of the works in *Literary Cubism – Geography and Plays – Selected Works of Gertrude Stein* reflect the main influences that typified Stein's idiosyncratic writing during her early years in Paris: the intellectual distance of her brother Leo, the self-affirming nature of her relationship with Alice B. Toklas, and most importantly, the impact of Pablo Picasso and the Cubists. Stein treated her written work of this period exactly the way the Cubists treated their art. As the Cubists believed the whole of the canvas was important to the meaning of the piece, so Stein believed that every element of text mattered as much as any other on the page.

"The important thing is that you must have deep down, as the deepest thing in you a sense of equality," she is quoted as saying. It is this sense of equality among words, as well as her belief that each word contains within itself its own essence, that gives Stein's work an amazingly objective tone. Indeed, like the innovative artists who inspired her, Gertrude Stein does not produce a mere story, poem, or picture. She conveys instead a mental impression of moods and emotions devoid of judgment, giving the reader the power to decide how to think and feel about the writing, and then allows the words to speak for themselves.

Laura Bonds
January, 2011

Content

Content

Susie Asado

Sweet sweet sweet sweet sweet tea.

Susie Asado.

Sweet sweet sweet sweet sweet tea.

Susie Asado.

Susie Asado which is a told tray sure.

A lean on the shoe this means slips slips hers.

When the ancient light grey is clean it is yellow, it is a silver seller.

This is a please this is a please there are the saids to jelly. These are the wets these say the sets to leave a crown to Incy.

Incy is short for incubus.

A pot. A pot is a beginning of a rare bit of trees. Trees tremble, the old vats are in bobbles, bobbles which shade and shove and render clean, render clean must.

Drink pups.

Drink pups drink pups lease a sash hold, see it shine and a bobolink has pins. It shows a nail.

What is a nail. A nail is unison.

Sweet sweet sweet sweet sweet tea.

Ada

Barnes Colhard did not say he would not do it but he did not do it. He did it and then he did not do it, he did not ever think about it. He just thought some time he might do something.

His father Mr. Abram Colhard spoke about it to every one and very many of them spoke to Barnes Colhard about it and he always listened to them.

Then Barnes fell in love with a very nice girl and she would not marry him. He cried then, his father Mr. Abram Colhard comforted him and they took a trip and Barnes promised he would do what his father wanted him to be doing. He did not do the thing, he thought he would do another thing, he did not do the other thing, his father Mr. Colhard did not want him to do the other thing. He really did not do anything then. When he was a good deal older he married a very rich girl. He had thought perhaps he would not propose to her but his sister wrote to him that it would be a good thing. He married the rich girl and she thought he was the most wonderful man and one who knew everything. Barnes never spent more than the income of the fortune he and his wife had then, that is to say they did not spend more than the income and this was a surprise to very many who knew about him and about his marrying the girl who had such a large fortune. He had a happy life while he was living and after he was dead his wife and children remembered him.

He had a sister who also was successful enough in being one being living. His sister was one who came to be happier than most people come to be in living. She came to be a completely happy one. She was twice as old as her brother. She had been a very good daughter to her mother. She and her mother had always told very pretty stories to each other. Many old men loved to hear her tell these stories to her mother. Every one who ever knew her mother liked her mother. Many were sorry later that not every one liked the daughter. Many did like the daughter but not every one as every one had liked the mother. The daughter was charming inside in her, it did not show outside in her to every one, it certainly did to some. She did sometimes think her mother would be pleased with a story that did not please her mother, when her mother later was sicker the daughter knew that there were some stories she could tell her that would not please her mother. Her mother died and really mostly altogether the mother and the daughter had told each other stories very happily together.

The daughter then kept house for her father and took care of her brother. There were many relations who lived with them. The daughter did not like them to live with them and she did not like them to die with them. The daughter, Ada they had called her after her grandmother who had delightful ways of smelling flowers and eating dates and sugar, did not like it at all then as she did not like so much dying and she did not like any of the living she was doing then. Every now and then some old gentlemen told delightful stories to her. Mostly then there were not nice stories told by any one then in her living. She told her father Mr. Abram Colhard that she did not like it at all being one being living then. He never said anything. She was afraid then, she was one needing charming stories and happy telling of them and not having that thing she was always trembling. Then every one who could live with them were dead and there were then the father and the son a young man then and the daughter coming to be that one then. Her grandfather had left some money to them each one of them. Ada said she was going to use it to go away from them. The father said nothing then, then he said something and she said nothing then, then they both said nothing and then it was that she went away from them. The father was quite tender then, she was his daughter then. He wrote her tender letters then, she wrote him tender letters then, she never went back to live with him. He wanted her to come and she wrote him tender letters then. He liked the tender letters she wrote to him. He wanted her to live with him. She answered him by writing tender letters to him and telling very nice stories indeed in them. He wrote nothing and then he wrote again and there was some waiting and then he wrote tender letters again and again.

She came to be happier than anybody else who was living then. It is easy to believe this thing. She was telling some one, who was loving every story that was charming. Some one who was living was almost always listening. Some one who was loving was almost always listening. That one who was loving was almost always listening. That one who was loving was telling about being one then listening. That one being loving was then telling stories having a beginning and a middle and an ending. That one was then one always completely listening. Ada was then one and all her living then one completely telling stories that were charming, completely listening to stories having a beginning and a middle and an ending. Trembling was all living, living was all loving, some one was then the other one. Certainly this one was loving this Ada then. And certainly Ada all her living then was happier in living than any one else who ever could, who was, who is, who ever will be living.

Miss Furr and Miss Skeene

Helen Furr had quite a pleasant home. Mrs. Furr was quite a pleasant woman. Mr. Furr was quite a pleasant man. Helen Furr had quite a pleasant voice a voice quite worth cultivating. She did not mind working. She worked to cultivate her voice. She did not find it gay living in the same place where she had always been living. She went to a place where some were cultivating something, voices and other things needing cultivating. She met Georgine Skeene there who was cultivating her voice which some thought was quite a pleasant one. Helen Furr and Georgine Skeene lived together then. Georgine Skeene liked travelling. Helen Furr did not care about travelling, she liked to stay in one place and be gay there. They were together then and travelled to another place and stayed there and were gay there.

They stayed there and were gay there, not very gay there, just gay there. They were both gay there, they were regularly working there both of them cultivating their voices there, they were both gay there. Georgine Skeene was gay there and she was regular, regular in being gay, regular in not being gay, regular in being a gay one who was one not being gay longer than was needed to be one being quite a gay one. They were both gay then there and both working there then.

They were in a way both gay there where there were many cultivating something. They were both regular in being gay there. Helen Furr was gay there, she was gayer and gayer there and really she was just gay there, she was gayer and gayer there, that is to say she found ways of being gay there that she was using in being gay there. She was gay there, not gayer and gayer, just gay there, that is to say she was not gayer by using the things she found there that were gay things, she was gay there, always she was gay there.

They were quite regularly gay there, Helen Furr and Georgine Skeene, they were regularly gay there where they were gay. They were very regularly gay.

To be regularly gay was to do every day the gay thing that they did every day. To be regularly gay was to end every day at the same time after they had been regularly gay. They were regularly gay. They were gay every day. They ended every day in the same way, at the same time, and they had been every day regularly gay.

The voice Helen Furr was cultivating was quite a pleasant one. The voice Georgine Skeene was cultivating was, some said, a better one. The voice Helen Furr was cultivating she cultivated and it was quite completely a pleasant enough one then, a cultivated enough one then. The voice Georgine Skeene was cultivating she did not cultivate too much. She cultivated it quite some. She cultivated and she would sometime go on cultivating it and it was not then an unpleasant one, it would not be then an unpleasant one, it would be a quite richly enough cultivated one, it would be quite richly enough to be a pleasant enough one.

They were gay where there were many cultivating something. The two were gay there, were regularly gay there. Georgine Skeene would have liked to do more travelling. They did some travelling, not very much travelling, Georgine Skeene would have liked to do more travelling, Helen Furr did not care about doing travelling, she liked to stay in a place and be gay there.

They stayed in a place and were gay there, both of them stayed there, they stayed together there, they were gay there, they were regularly gay there.

They went quite often, not very often, but they did go back to where Helen Furr had a pleasant enough home and then Georgine Skeene went to a place where her brother had quite some distinction. They both went, every few years, went visiting to where Helen Furr had quite a pleasant home. Certainly Helen Furr would not find it gay to stay, she did not find it gay, she said she would not stay, she said she did not find it gay, she said she would not stay where she did not find it gay, she said she found it gay where she did stay and she did stay there where very many were cultivating something. She did stay there. She always did find it gay there.

She went to see them where she had always been living and where she did not find it gay. She had a pleasant home there, Mrs. Furr was a pleasant enough woman, Mr. Furr was a pleasant enough man, Helen told them and they were not worrying, that she did not find it gay living where she had always been living.

Georgine Skeene and Helen Furr were living where they were both cultivating their voices and they were gay there. They visited where Helen Furr had come from and then they went to where they were living where they were then regularly living.

There were some dark and heavy men there then. There were some who were not so heavy and some who were not so dark. Helen Furr and Georgine Skeene sat regularly with them. They sat regularly with the ones who were dark and heavy. They sat regularly with the ones who were not so dark. They sat regularly with the ones that were not so heavy. They sat with them regularly, sat with some of them. They went with them regularly went with them. They were regular then, they were gay then, they were where they wanted to be then where it was gay to be then, they were regularly gay then. There were men there then who were dark and heavy and they sat with them with Helen Furr and Georgine Skeene and they went with them with Miss Furr and Miss Skeene, and they went with the heavy and dark men Miss Furr and Miss Skeene went with them, and they sat with them, Miss Furr and Miss Skeene sat with them, and there were other men, some were not heavy men and they sat with Miss Furr and Miss Skeene and Miss Furr and Miss Skeene sat with them, and there were other men who were not dark men and they sat with Miss Furr and Miss Skeene and Miss Furr and Miss Skeene sat with them. Miss Furr and Miss Skeene went with them and they went with Miss Furr and Miss Skeene, some who were not heavy men, some who were not dark men. Miss Furr and Miss Skeene sat regularly, they sat with some men. Miss Furr and Miss Skeene went and there were some men with them. There were men and Miss Furr and Miss Skeene went with them, went somewhere with them, went with some of them.

Helen Furr and Georgine Skeene were regularly living where very many were living and cultivating in themselves something. Helen Furr and Georgine Skeene were living very regularly then, being very regular then in being gay then. They did then learn many ways to be gay and they were then being gay being quite regular in being gay, being gay and they were learning little things, little things in ways of being gay, they were very regular then, they were learning very many little things in ways of being gay, they were being gay and using these little things they were learning to have to be gay with regularly gay with them and they were gay the same amount they had been gay. They were quite gay, they were quite regular, they were learning little things, gay little things, they were gay inside them the same amount they had been gay, they were gay the same length of time they had been gay every day.

They were regular in being gay, they learned little things that are things in being gay, they learned many little things that are things in being gay, they were gay every day, they were regular, they were gay, they were gay the same length of time every day, they were gay, they were quite regularly gay.

Georgine Skeene went away to stay two months with her brother. Helen Furr did not go then to stay with her father and her mother. Helen Furr stayed there where they had been regularly living the two of them and she would then certainly not be lonesome, she would go on being gay. She did go on being gay. She was not any more gay but she was gay longer every day than they had been being gay when they were together being gay. She was gay then quite exactly the same way. She learned a few more little ways of being in being gay. She was quite gay and in the same way, the same way she had been gay and she was gay a little longer in the day, more of each day she was gay. She was gay longer every day than when the two of them had been being gay. She was gay quite in the way they had been gay, quite in the same way.

She was not lonesome then, she was not at all feeling any need of having Georgine Skeene. She was not astonished at this thing. She would have been a little astonished by this thing but she knew she was not astonished at anything and so she was not astonished at this thing not astonished at not feeling any need of having Georgine Skeene.

Helen Furr had quite a completely pleasant voice and it was quite well enough cultivated and she could use it and she did use it but then there was not any way of working at cultivating a completely pleasant voice when it has become a quite completely well enough cultivated one, and there was not much use in using it when one was not wanting it to be helping to make one a gay one. Helen Furr was not needing using her voice to be a gay one. She was gay then and sometimes she used her voice and she was not using it very often. It was quite completely enough cultivated and it was quite completely a pleasant one and she did not use it very often. She was then, she was quite exactly as gay as she had been, she was gay a little longer in the day than she had been.

She was gay exactly the same way. She was never tired of being gay that way. She had learned very many little ways to use in being gay. Very many were telling about using other ways in being gay. She was gay enough, she was always gay exactly the same way, she was always learning little things to use in being gay, she was telling about using other ways in being gay, she was telling about learning other ways in being gay, she was learning other ways in being gay, she would be using other ways in being gay, she would always be gay in the same way, when Georgine Skeene was there not so long each day as when Georgine Skeene was away.

She came to using many ways in being gay, she came to use every way in being gay. She went on living where many were cultivating something and she was gay, she had used every way to be gay.

They did not live together then Helen Furr and Georgine Skeene. Helen Furr lived there the longer where they had been living regularly together. Then neither of them were living there any longer. Helen Furr was living somewhere else then and telling some about being gay and she was gay then and she was living quite regularly then. She was regularly gay then. She was quite regular in being gay then. She remembered all the little ways of being gay. She used all the little ways of being gay. She was quite regularly gay. She told many then the way of being gay, she taught very many then little ways they could use in being gay. She was living very well, she was gay then, she went on living then, she was regular in being gay, she always was living very well and was gay very well and was telling about little ways one could be learning to use in being gay, and later was telling them quite often, telling them again and again.

A Collection

My Dear Miss Carey: A Story

There were little places to see Fernville, the town, the hospital, the lying in hospital, the sea-shore and the city.

Once we met my brother he was ringing a bell. He needed an umbrella but he would not buy it. I sent him one not prepaid. Oh yes the people are kind they all drink together. Even now. No not now. We are late.

Did you see the pear tree. It resembles the figs. They are often ripe. They grow in great abundance.

We like milk. My father likes milk and coffee.

Whenever there are flowers my mother is angry. She is even angry with me. That is to say she is generous enough and wishes everything back. We are all that way. My brother takes coal away in a little bag for use. All dark days are necessary. No permission is asked and it is given. For all day. For all day. Whenever it is needed. Not whenever it is needed. We do as we say it is best to do. Even religious people do so.

Come together in Fernville. Not I I thank you. My brother finds handkerchiefs there. For men. For men and for women. So does his wife. Many. Not very many. She brings them with her. Is that so. Many handkerchiefs are not necessary in Fernville. No indeed. We dismiss the church. We separate it. We have it to-day. A great many people call. On one another. Not altogether that. The post-office. The post-office of my brother. Now. Not now. Yes he is there now. Since the war. Yes since the war.

I remember when I was a b of c. I did not speak to old men then not when I was busy. I waited until I was tired and then we all sat down and had a cup of coffee. Coffee is very nourishing. I am very sensitive to the influence of coffee. So are we all.

Do you think that we are married. That we are all married. Mr. Weeks is married. He is going to be able to follow my advice. I advise him to go to my country. There he will do very well. The only advice I have to give him is never to live in the city. His wife does not like the city nor does she like a sunny climate. She is not able to go about with him. We are all of us leaving the end of the month.

Do not be angry.

I was very much surprised that water was the same color.

As what.

As the sun.

I feel that I must go at once.

Did you entirely forget about the other.

Drowning in water.

This is a question that I have never asked about because in the summer one does not think about it. Now it is winter but it is as warm as in summer.

Dear friends have a way of relating themselves to a town. We find in some districts that there are better ways of investing money. Some find that at the end of the war they are not able to continue paying on their houses.

Does this affect you.

Oh no because even if the father of my child is killed his sister will continue to give the money. She is obliged to by law.

This makes the whole matter very simple.

Not to me I have always been accustomed to it and have had some difficulty.

Yes we know we know that it is suddenly cold.

You are not pleased to see the sun setting. Indeed I cannot blame you.

Polybe in Port: A Curtain Raiser

Polybe in Port.

A hunter. He was not a hunter. He had a gun. I do not know whether they have permission to shoot.

Of course he must have if he has a gun. In this country they have a great many dogs who hunt rabbits. They run quicker.

We are surprised to see him.

Polybe is an ornament.

He is not thinner.

He likes the water now.

This I do not believe.

Neither do I believe there was any intention to go that way. Which way do you mean. Polybe does not remember. Me. Yes. The house. Yes. The servant. Yes. You are not mistaken.

We are not mistaken.

A great many shrubs every one of which are labelled.

Scene II

A credit to me.

The cares and duties of a mother had been denied to Carrie Russell.

Polybe silent.

He said earnestly that it didn't matter.

Spanish Chattings

Do you keep books.

All weddings are back.

Pigeons.

Pigeons recognise persons. Do they. We saw them. They flew around.

Shooting pigeons is necessary. For what. For the sea.

I see old peppers that are dried. We do not complain. We say winds are violent and I do not wish them. Wish for them. I do not wish to see the stars. Call it out of here. You mean that pole. No indeed I don't mean Inca.

Oh yes certainly.

They Came Together

I can tell a little story. I cannot describe the character nor the color in the street nor the kind of a stone. A great many people have silver purses.

Wild Flowers

We collected wild flowers. We enjoyed it very much. In a window we saw exhibited the things that can be found in the country.

There was a satisfaction that we had the temporary installation which made it possible for us to ask another servant not to visit our servant. We did not do so. We were not neglectful of our best interests.

Will They Crush Germany

They will crush Germany. There is no doubt about it.

France

Likely and more than evenly, unevenly and not unlikely, very much that and anyway more, this is the left over method. There is nothing left because if it were left it would be left over. This does not make music. The time to state that is in reading. There is a beginning in a lesson in smiling.

What is up is not down and what is down is not reversing and what is refused is not a section and what is silenced is not speaking. This does not make the rude ones murmur, this does not make a penny smaller, this does not make religion.

All the time there is a melodrama there is monopoly and all the time there is more there is no excuse.

A luck in breaths is more to be denied than music, much more. The only long string is that which is not twisted. All the same there is no excuse.

A sight is not a shadow and a whole rise in a cry is not more piercing than danger of being mixed into an affair where there are witnesses. If writing is in little pieces and little places and a little door is open, many little doors are not open and writing is not surreptitious, it is not even obliging.

To show the difference between an occasion and merit and a button it is necessary to recognise that an honor is not forced so that there is no question of taste. To exchange a single statue for a coat of silk and a coat of wool is not necessary as there are appliances. A somber day is one when there is no pleading.

Made in haste, not made in haste, made in darkness, not made in darkness, made in a place, made in a place. The whole stretched out is not part of the whole block, the whole stretched out is so arranged that there is not stumbling but what is just as remarkable, pushing. An easy expression of being willing, of being hunting, of being so stupid that there is no question of not selling, all these things cause more discussion than a resolution and this is so astonishing when there is nothing to do and an excellent reason for an exchange, and yet the practice of it makes such an example that any day is a season.

To be sure that the trees have winter and the plants have summer and the houses painting, to be sure of this engages some attention. The time to place this in the way is not what is expected from a diner. The whole thing that shows the result is the little way that the balls and the pieces that are with them which are not birds as they are older do not measure the distance between a cover and a calendar. This which is not a question is not reverse and the question which is a question is at noon.

To question a special date is not mercenary. To answer a single servant is not obligatory. To be afraid is not nearsighted. An exclamation does not connect more grass than there is with any more trees than have branches. The special scenery which makes the blameless see and the solitary resemble a conversation is not that which resembles that memory. There is no necessity for furthering the regulation of the understanding. One special absence does not make any place empty. The dampness which is not covered by a cloth is not mingled with color. And it comes. There is no astonishment nor width.

Education, education, apprenticeship, and all the meeting of nephews and trains and changing papers and remaining when there is no chance to go there, all this occupied a whole sentence. It is a shame that there is not such an only use for that, it is a shame and there is no indignation more indignant. Everything is an indication of the simple remedy that is applied when there is no refusal and no application. Every thing which shows that is not tied with a string or any little string. All the same there is not much of a remedy.

Alarm over the action of the one who when he sees the light rise and the sun set and the stars shine and the water flow alarm is the same alarm as any alarm.

In all the same ways that pieces are separated in all these ways there are those placed things which are not pieces. They are not pieces and there is reason, there is reason in it because the whole thing shows such dissociation that all doing it for that purpose and together there can be no question but that they succeed.

A tobacco habit is one that a leaf does not enlighten and yet carelessness is so extraordinary. Supposing that the arrangement had been made and that it was agreed that no separation between any one being one and being another one could be established, supposing this were agreed and there was no conversation, would this enlighten any one, if it would why is the result so ambiguous. It is not ambiguous because the authority which does not authorise washing does supply soap. This does not make any change.

It is sensible to be around it is very sensible, it is so sensible that there is every way of stopping a selection, and then there is selection, there is a respect for resignation, there is no disturbance in a disappointment. The question is is there more urging than satisfaction, is there more distribution than renewal. This is not a question, it is a relaxing. And then the time comes for more noise. Is there then more noise. There is then reestablishment. Does that mean return of a price which is plentiful. Nobody knows. All this shows something it shows that there can be suspicion.

There is no separation in majesty. Terms, lines, sections, extra packing, nothing shows that confidence. All the same there is news. The time to stay away is in vacation. Why is there no place chosen. The answer is simple it consists in explaining that there has been given the use of all that will be used. This does not show feeling.

A curtain is not crazy, it has no way of being crazy, it has hardly a way of enraging a resemblance, it has no resurrection. Indeed the chances are that when there is seen more astonishment than anything that is placed it is very likely that the whole system will be not so much estranged as devastated and yet supposing they do not mean that, supposing they do say that it will be a success, supposing they do say does that mean that oration is contradiction, it does not.

Just a word to show a kite that clouds are higher than a thing that is smaller, just that word and no single silence is closer.

Suggest that the passage is filled with feathers, suggest that there are all together, suggest that using boxes is heavy, suggest that there is no feather, suggest all these things and what is result the result is that everything gets put away.

All the silence is adequate to a rumble and all the silliness is adequate to a procession and all the recitation is equal to the hammer and all the paving is equal to summer. All the same the detaining most is the reason that there is a pillar and mostly what is shocking is a rooster. This is not so easily said. There is no occasion for a red result.

Laugh, to laugh, all the same the tittle is inclinable. What a change from any yesterday.

A period of singular results and no gloom such a period shows such a rapid approach that there is no search in silence and yet not a sound, not any sound is searching, no sound is an occasion.

A fine fan and a fine closet and a very fine handkerchief and quite a fine article all these together shows where there has been plenty of rebuke and plenty of expectation and plenty, plentifully reduction of suspension, and so the season is the same and there is every corner.

No chance shows the rapidity of exchange, no chance and this which means one is the same as any two halves and this is not outrageous, not a bit outrageous it is simply the sign of splendor.

All the tempting and the chewing and the cloth all of it shows no sign and no symbol it does not and that is no disgrace.

If standing is an illusion is it necessary to be pressed to bend in that direction is it necessary and if it is necessary is it polite and if it is polite is it urgent and if it is not urgent is it an impulse.

No question has so much disturbance as the principal reunion. This is not so distinguished when there are no ties in the window. This is completely changed, once there were none and now there are none. There are no rebukes. A privilege is not painful. A recurrence is not artificial.

It is not separating that which satisfies no finger, it is not fading. What was it that was not wished. The reason is that the section is there and no reflection makes abundance. The only tangle is when there is abundance and there is abundance when there is pulling and piling. Does this seem to scream, it does not there is not even clustering and yet not hampering not singling everything does not make sorrow, it makes no plant grander, it does make a plant slender, it does not make it so slender that there is every size. All privilege and all practice, all suspicion and grandeur, all the timber and a little wood all this makes silver, paper is chosen and gold is cheap, does this make a little salt, it does not, it makes copper.

Little frame if it is cheaper than a big one is a different size. There is no use disputing as memory is a reminder.

Not to pay for a conversation, not to pay anything for any conversation, not to throw away paying, not to pass paying, not to pay anything this is not being a victim. What is victory, victory is that which eschewing liberation and a girdle and gratitude and resignation and a choice display and more flavor shows a strange reluctance to have a maritime connection. This is victory.

A license, what is a license, what is a license.

An angry coat, a very angry coat shines.

Butter is not frozen, this does not mean that there is no bravery and no mistake. This does show a conclusion.

Difference is no excuse, grain is no excuse, even the remains of a pear is an excuse and yet is there graciousness, there is if there is generosity. There is so much fruit. This is kindly a mistake. No misunderstanding is insurmountable.

Cage no lion, not to cage a lion is not dirty, it is not even merciless, it is not malodorous, it is not virtue.

To surround a giraffe, what does that mean. To surround a mixture, that means something.

Solid, what is solid, is more solid than everything, it is not doubtful because there is no necessity.

Haughtiness, there is haughtiness when there is no tape and no billiard rooms and no need to be secured from wet. There is certainly some selected obstacles.

The certainty of a change in the parts that speak, this uncertainty does not show as it does not fashion speech. All union is in the widow and all menace is in the band.

Any way to bend the hat is the way to encourage vice. Virtue all virtue is resolved and some and any hat, every hat is identical. A shadow a white shadow is a mountain.

Kindness what is kindness, kindness is the necessity of preserving of really preserving all the parts of speech and teaching, not music so much as trimming and a costume, and sincerely most sincerely shoving regions together.

Notice a room, in noticing a room what is there to notice, the first thing to notice is the room and the windows and the door and the table and the place where there are divisions and the center of the room and the rest of the people. All this is necessary and then there is finance.

Heavy where heaviness is and no mistake plentifully, heavy where the breeze is and no darkness plentifully, heavy where there is a voice and a noise and singling out a company, heavy where there is a sale of accents and raisins and possibly more ways of not being heavy. Certainly there is no peril and yet think, think often, is daintiness and a collar heavy is it and what is the disturbance, is there not more registration.

So there is not coming anything. There certainly is no single space useful and betrothed and vulgar and not pretty. There is a sign in placing nothing. This changes from day to day any day. Surely no change is a blessing. All the search is in violation and yet a single search is a single search willing. It is cautious. There is riot.

The likelihood of dipping and drawing and digesting and drinking and dirtying not dirtying smoking, the likelihood of all this makes such an order that every discussion is simultaneous. A large increase in beer, any large increase is here, some large increase is clear, no large increase is dear. A lily a very lily lily is accurate and described and surrounded and so venturesome that there is risk and writing, there is even inlaying.

Darkness, there is no darkness in extremity and in mixing and in originating scattering religion. There is no darkness in designing.

A group a single group proceeding show the necessity of the distribution of the same organization as there is if there is, assuming that there is, if there is reorganization.

Flower, flower and water and even more even a gram of grain and a single little blister, very likely the chance is not perfect and the exquisite arrangement has lace, very likely there are no stains and more likely there are ruffles. In all of this there is no use in practicing medicine. Quinine any quinine is useful and more there is more, there can be more, there is an apartment.

A sign of saving consists in spending the late morning in the morning and in urging in certainly not urging a calculation. A sign of saving is so simple if there is enough handed about, and surely no pains in piling are more shown than when everything is in dishes. This does not happen in an asylum, it does not even happen in the hay and in the double shapes that shelter cooking.

A top a tiny little top that sits and spits and shows the courage calmly, this this is so soon an exasperation and a piece of lightning, it is so ordinarily just that occasion, it is so kindly dispiriting, it is so haughty if there is pushing. There is pushing, this is what makes it repetition.

A long, what is a log to do when it floats, it is to do nothing as it floats but certainly it would be best that it should adjust that to itself certainly. This alone does not make an explanation.

A degree of resorts and a shining wave all this together does not make a regulation and it does not make that irregular, it sustains mischief and an order and it even enforces the likelihood of the season and some color. So sustained is a paragraph that a sentence shows no staring and some noise. This is so simple in the size that is medium and is medium sized sentinel. There is no kilometer. That does not make a sample.

Keep the place that is not open, close the place that has one door, shut the place that has a cellar, suffer where all suffer more, argue, and shelter the understanding orphan, and silence that is silence is not sufficient there must even be sleep.

Puzzle is more than a speck and a soiled collar. A pound is more than oat meal and a new institution. A silence is no more than occasional. It respects understanding and salt and even a rope. It respects a news-stand and it also it very also respects desert. All the ice can descend together.

Was there freedom, was there enchaining, was there even a height rising from higher. If there was what is a coat worth and by whom was it made when.

A lining any lining is a trimming. More trimming is extra.

A sort of arranging, a kindling of paying a shilling, does that mean another extravagance and more candles, no more candles. It does not show.

A famous single candle has a chance to shine so that glaring meant that no more would be reversed by lightning. The safe lamp and the bright lamp and the dirty lamp and the long lamp were all not the lamps that were attending baptism. Why is the baptism patient, baptism is patient in the first place because there is no coarse cloth, in the second place because when there is nothing taken enough is left to give every reason. A practice which engaged more attention than the rest was that which shaved a tame stopper and did not even end that. Supposing crossing a street is necessary, supposing it is, does that show more of such occasion. It does and it does.

A lime is in labor, a lemon is cooler, a citron is larger, a currant is redder, a strawberry is more vexed, a banana is straighter.

A little thing is a little thing, a single point is bigger, a bigger thing is a bigger thing, an older thing is older, an older thing is an older thing, a station is a station, a station is a station and a station is a thing and stationary only that is a stationary thing.

A blind being blind and deaf and deaf being deaf and blind and blind and deaf and a coat with a cape and more use in all than in any shape all this makes a reason for criticising the use of machinery and paper and even a pen and even a stamp and even more flags than ever.

In the pin in the picking of a pin, in sewing a little feather and avoiding deserting a pin, in retaining the feather and arranging to rank the pin as a pin and to hold it there where if it is seen it is found and if it is found it is seen, to not mark a pin and select a pin all this is a reason for using that way of waiting.

A standard blessed is a standard that is blue if it is blue and blue and white when it is blue and white. Supposing there is no money, supposing there is no dress and no skirt, supposing there is no window and no bed, supposing there is no more distribution and not any more violence, supposing there is not even arithmetic and intelligence, supposing there is a light and a round hole, does that mean that there is no success suggested. It does not. A little bit of choice makes a color regular. A little bit of black makes dinner necessary.

If there is a shape a real shape prettily, if there is and there is no wonder does it happen all the time, if it does not is there a certainty that there is collusion. These interesting questions crowd the house, they crowd, they do not crowd everywhere. They crowd separately.

All there is of more chances is in a book, all there is of any more chances is in a list, all there is of chances is in an address, all there is is what is the best place not to remain sitting and suggesting that there is no title for relieving rising.

An excursion, what is an excursion, an excursion is a picnic if it is recurrent, it is a picnic if there is no absence, it is a picnic and not necessarily, it is a picnic.

Black horses, very black horses are not peculiar, very large horses are not peculiar, very splendid horses are not peculiar, horses are peculiar regularly and with an awake resemblance to the best the very best description and regret. The kindness of this is mentioned and very often quite often the same rebuke is outrageous.

Not allowed, not only allowed to eat, to ache, to resemble, to project, to make a motion, to study preaching, to stumble on anything, to stretch audibly.

Not allowed a prize or a couch or even what is not necessary a searching, not allowed more formerly, not allowed more entirely, not allowed a dispensary.

It is a custom, it is a custom when it is not undue, when it is not undue, when it is not. It is a custom. It is a custom when it is more due, when it is, when it is an angle, it is not a custom, it is a custom altogether.

In cross and across, in that show and wide there is the sensory statement that there is night rule and a winter rule and even the chamber is empty and watches why are watches lighted.

What a day to pay to stay, what a day. When the work is done too soon and there is a crossing of hands and even of heads entirely when there is and when the rest is so awake, is there any slept out sleeping, there is not gradually, there is more chance than there would be in a colored collection. There is more chance certainly.

What is the resolution between a cutlet and an ingredient. It is mentioned and made in paper and floating.

What is the example of a miner. A single example is in the best of cups and also in the rest of the places and also in the show that is there.

After a mixed cloud is there any use in a trimming, there is, there is. There is a trimming behind in. There in no use. There is the case.

Calm, a calm, that calm, along the calm. This which is in the ell is so much are so. When and when and when is there. When the rail is the passage to. Through and so and much orderly.

Beginning to twining and sudden girls what is mended in a street, what is a rut in finnish. What is it in a market.

A considerable engagement, a considerable engagement.

Excuse the point that makes a division between the right and left that which is in the middle in between. Surprise an engagement, surprise it so that an agreement is all the time.

This is a way, this is a trout, this is the succession.

To linger in the pale way and not to show spots to be greener to do this means that all the references are what they are.

A pedal a pedal is that which when examined is made and this is no mistake in regularity it is a splendid thing.

Covering in and covering, covering with inside covering. Covering a lion with the same shape as the bear and yet what is the best measure for a tiger, what is the measure steadily.

A half safe wife and a whole safe wife and a half safe wife and a half safe wife.

A bet and sugar and a bet and within, a bet and within and a bet in within.

Cut a slice to show a pear, cut a slice to show a row, cut a slice and there is visiting. An angel is in the exchange.

Suppose that there is a cost, suppose that there is a beggar, suppose that there is a powder and a powder suppose there is a real gold mine.

A curly fate and a household fact and a gloom too soon, and a couple of necessary pockets.

Explain, explain why there is a shell fish and an oyster.

A pleasant little spot to have gold. The same spot is used for silver. The gold is the best way to keep it. The silver is the way to keep silver.

A cloud of white and a chorus of all bright birds and a sweet a very sweet cherry and a thick miss, a thick and a dark and a clean clerk, a whole succession of mantle pieces.

Conceal a nose and climb, counsel a name and shudder, believe a glass and relate, cool a pound and put in that.

Wednesday is a day and a closed begging is reasonable, reasonable, is reasonable, reasonable is reasonable.

Piston and clothes, consider the wet sack, coal hack, hack a piece of gum.

Americans

Eating and paper.

A laugh in a loop is not dinner. There is so much to pray.

A slight price is a potato. A slimness is in length and even in strength.

A capable extravagance that is that which shows no provision is that which when necessity is mild shows a certain distribution of anger. This is no sign of sin.

Five, five are more wonderful than a million. Five million, five million, five million, five are more wonderful than two together. Two together, two together.

A song, if a sad song is in unison and is sung, a sad song is singing. A sign of singing.

A gap what is a gap when there is not any meaning in a slice with a hole in it. What is the exchange between the whole and no more witnesses.

Press juice from a button, press it carelessly, press it with care, press it in a storm. A storm is so waiting and awful and moreover so much the worse for being where there is a storm that the use the whole use of more realization comes out of a narrow bridge and water faucets. This is no plain evidence of disaster. The point of it is that there is a strange straw being in any strange ice-cream.

A legal pencil a really legal pencil is incredible, it fastens the whole strong iron wire calender.

An inherent investigation, does that mean murder or does it only mean a railroad track with plenty of cinders.

Words that cumber nothing and call exceptionally tall people from very far away are those that have the same center as those used by them frequently.

Bale, bale is a thing that surrounding largely means hay, no hay has any more food than it needs to weigh that way henceforward and not more that most likely.

A soap, a whole soap, any piece of a whole soap, more whole soap and not mistily, all this is no outrage and no blessing. A precious thing is an oily thing. In that there is no sugar and silence.

A reason is that a curly house an ordinary curly house is exactly that, it is exactly more than that, it is so exactly no more than more than that.

Waiter, when is a waiter passive and expressed, a waiter is so when there is no more selection and really no more buckets altogether. This is what remains. It does. It is kindly exacted, it is pleased, it is anxious, it is even worthy when a material is like it. It is.

What is a hinge. A hinge is a location. What is a hinge necessarily.

When the butter cup is limited and there are radishes, when radishes are clean and a whole school, a real school is outrageous and more incensed, really more incensed and inclined, when the single satisfaction is so perfect and the pearl is so demure when all this is changed then there is no rattle there is hardly any rattle.

A and B and also nothing of the same direction is the best personal division there is between any laughing. The climate, the whole thing is surrounded, it is not pressed, it is not a vessel, it is not all there is of joining, it is a real anxious needful and it is so seldom circular, so more so than any article in the wire. The cluster is just the same ordinarily.

Supposing a movement is segregated and there is a piece of staging, suppose there is and the present is melted does that mean that any salt is bitter, would it change an investigation suddenly, when it would would it mean a long wide and not particular eddy. Would it and if it did would there be a change. A kind of exercise is hardest and the best excellence is sweet.

Finding a best hat with a hearty hat pin in midsummer is a reason for being blindly. A smell is not in earth.

A wonder to chew and to eat and to mind and to set into the very tiny glass that is tall. This is that when there is a tenement. All weights are scales.

No put in a closet, no skirt in a closet, no lily, no lily not a lime lily. A solving and learned, awake and highing and a throat and a throat and a short set color, a short set color and a collar and a color. A last degree in the kink in a glove the rest.

A letter to press, a letter to press is not rowdy, it is not sliding, it is not a measure of the increasing swindling of elastic and breaking.

The thread, the thread, the thread is the language of yesterday, it is the resolution of today, it is no pain.

What is pain, pain is so changing the climate and the best ever that it is a time, it is really only a time, it is so winding. It is even.

A warm banana is warm naturally and this makes an ingredient in a mixture which has banana in it.

Cooling in the chasing void, cooling more than milder.

Hold that ho, that is hold the hold.

Pow word, a pow word is organic and sectional and an old man's company.

Win, win, a little bit chickeny, wet, wet, a long last hollow chucking jam, gather, a last butter in a cheese, a lasting surrounding action.

White green, a white green. A looking like that is a most connected piece of example of what it is where there is no choking, no choking in any sign.

Pin in and pin in and point clear and point where.

Breakfast, breakfast is the arrangement that beggars corn, that shows the habit of fishes, that powders aches and stumblings, and any useful thing. The way to say it is to say it.

No counting, no counting in not cousins, no counting for that example and that number of thirty and thirteen and thirty six and thirty.

A blind hobble which makes distress. A place not to put in a foot, a place so called and in close color, a place best and more shape and really a thought.

Cousin why is there no cousin, because it is an article to be preparatory.

Was it green told, was it a pill, was it chased awake, will it sale per, peas are fish, chicken, cold ups, nail poppers, nail pack in hers extra. Look pase per. Look past per. Look past per. Look past fer. Look past fer. Look past fer.

No end in yours, knock puzzler palers, no beast in papers, no bird.

Icer cream, ice her steam, ice her icer ice sea excellent, excel gone in front excel sent.

Leaves of wet perfect sharpen setters, leaves of wet purr feet shape for seal weight for shirters.

Leaves of wet for ear pole ache sold hers, ears for sake heat purse change to meeters, change to be a sunk leave to see wet hers, but to why in that peace so not. Knot lot.

Please bell room please bell room fasten a character fasten a care in apter buttons fasten a care in such, in such. Fasten a care in, in in a in.

A lovely life in the center makes a mine in found a lovely pond in the water makes it just a space. A lovely seat in a day lump makes a set to collapse, a lovely light in a grass field makes it see just the early day in when there is a sight of please please please.

Due tie due to die due show the never less more way less. Do, weigh the more do way less.

Let us call a boat, let us call a boat.

Leave little grace to be. Leave little grace to bea, live little grace to bee.

Leave little grace. Leave little.

Leave little grace to be.

Near red reserve leave lavender acre bat.

Shout us, shout horse curve less.

Least bee, least bay alter, alter the sat pan and left all, rest in, resafe in article so fur.

A cannon ball a cigar and a dress in suits, a cannon ball a cigar and a dress suit case, a cannon ball a cigar and a dress suit case, a head a hand a little above, a shake in my and mines.

Let us leaves, moor itch. Bars touch.

Nap old in town inch chair, nap on in term on chain, do deal sack file in for, do bale send on and for, reset the pan old in for same and chew get that all baste for, nice nor call churches, meet by and boot send for in, last when with and by that which for with all do sign call, meet with like shall what shirs not by bought lest, not by bought lest in own see certain, in own so same excellent, excellent hairy, hairy, excellent not excellent not knot excellent, excellent knot.

B r, brute says. A hole, a hole is a true, a true, a true.

Little paper and dolls, little paper and row why, little paper and a thin opera extra.

No use to age mother, no whole wide able recent mouth parcel, no relief farther, no relief in loosens no relief abler, no relief, no relief pie pepper nights, no relief poor no relief or, no relief, or no relief.

America a merica, a merica the go leading s the go leading s cans, cans be forgot and nigh nigh is a niecer a niecer to bit, a niecer to bit.

It was a peach, it was a long suit, it was heavy harsh singes.

Leave crack his leave crack his eats, all guest all guest a stove. Like bit.

Nuts, when and if the bloom is on next and really really really, it is a team, it is a left and all it cut, it is a so like that between and a shun a shun with a believer, a believer in the extra, extra not, extra a rechange for it more. No sir.

No it sir.

It was a tame in, it was a tame in and a a little vent made a whole simmer simmer a wish.

What is it not to say reach house. Coal mill. Coal mill well. It to lease house. Coal mill tell. Coal in meal tell.

A pill shape with a round center.

Color Cook color him with ready bbs and neat show pole glass and nearly be seen every day more see what all a pearly little not shut, no rail see her.

No peter no rot.

Poles poles are seeds and near the change the change pets are swimming swimming and a plate all a plate is reed pour for the grammar grammar of lake.

Lake in a sad old chimney last and needs needs needs needs needs needs needs, in the mutton and the meat there is a change to pork walk, with a walk mean clean and butter and does it show the feather bench does it mean the actual and not or does it light the cylinder. It is in choice and chosen, it is in choice and knee and knee and knee and just the same two bay.

To irregulate to irregulate gums.

America key america key.

It is too nestle by the pin grove shirr, all agree to the counting ate ate pall. Paul is better.

Vest in restraint in repute.

Shown land in constate.

I am sorry I am awfully sorry, I am so sorry, I am so sorry.

No fry shall it see c bough it.

Nibbling bit, nibbling bit, may the land in awe for.

It is not a particular lamp lights which absolutely so far pull sizes and near by in the change with it not in the behoof.

It was a singe, it was a scene in the in, it was a singe in.

Never sink, never sink sinker, never sink sinker sunk, sink sink sinker sink.

A cattle sheep.

By the white white white white, by the white white white white white white, by the white white white white by the white by the white white white white.

Needless in pins.

In the fence in the for instance, in the fence or how, hold chirp, hold chirp her, hold your paper, hope hop in hit it.

Extra successive.

Little beats of long saturday tileing.

No neck leg ticking.

Peel more such wake next stir day.

Peel heaps pork seldom.

Coiled or red bench.

A soled in a light is not waver. There is for much ash so.

In the second, in the second second second.

Pour were whose has. Pole sack sirs.

A neat not necklace neglect.

A neat not neglect. A neat.

A neat not neglect.

Put a sun in sunday. Sunday.

Italians

Some of them were where some others of them were. Some of them were where no others of them were. One of them was where not any other of them, of that kind of them, had been, and it was a thing that was important to any one to have seen that one, to have heard that one. It would have been discouraging to see more of them. It was disillusioning to go to the place where there were many of them. If there were many of them then there were more than one. If there were more than one then there were many of them and if there were many of them one could know any one of them and if one knew any one of them one knew all of them. And if one knew all of them then one would be beginning again, one would be beginning knowing them. One would be beginning knowing that kind of them.

There are enough of them and most of them are where the others of them are. There are enough of them but certainly not too many of them, certainly not, too many of them. There are many of them and most of them are where the others of them are. They have a way of doing what they are doing, they have a way of not doing what they are not doing. They have a way of having some feeling about them that they are ones doing what they are doing in the way that is a thing satisfying the desire of having anybody do anything. They are ones that give to some feeling them a feeling of knowing that they will not do in a way that is satisfying anything they are doing. They are ones talking, they are ones doing something, they are ones waiting quickly waiting very quickly waiting for anything to be happening and easily going on with waiting, with waiting for anything to happen, to not happen again. They are ones talking and talking and they are ones quick in talking and waiting for something to happen and they are ones who are not so quick, not quick enough not to be slow ones, quite slow ones. They are ones very many are seeing. There are very many of them. There are quite enough of them. There are not too many of them. Certainly very many are pleased at their being completely existing, certainly very many are completely pleased by their being completely existing.

There are not too many of them. They have something growing on them, some of them, a good many of them, and certainly very many others would not be wanting such things to be growing out of them that is to say growing on them. It makes them, those having such things, makes them elegant and charming, makes them ugly and disgusting, makes them clean looking and sleek and rich and dark, makes them dirty looking and fierce and annoying.

They are not peculiar ones these, they are very many of them, they are a kind of them, they are natural ones for any one to be knowing, there are many kinds of this kind of them. They are talking, often talking and they are doing things with pieces of them while they are talking and they are then sounding like something, they are then certainly sounding in a way that is a way that is a natural way for them to be sounding, they are having noise come out of them in a natural way for them to have noise come out of them. There are very many of them, not at all too many of them. Very many hear them, quite enough hear them. There are not too many of them not at all too many of them, they are talking, they are moving their fingers and their arms and their hands then and they have noises coming out of them and some are hearing them, quite a number hear them and some like them, very many like them, very many tell about liking them, some do not like them, some tell about not liking them.

Some are smaller than others, some are darker than others, some are harsher than others, some are sweeter than others, some are queerer than other, some are older than others, some have more hair on them than others, some are softer than others, some are quicker than others, some have longer nails than others, some have one longer nail than others, some look longer at some than others, some wear more things on them than others, some wear more kinds of colors than others, some are stronger than others, some are noisier than others, some are more respectful than others, some are braver than others, some are quieter than others, some are not lovelier than others.

There are very many of one kind of them and they are not all the same, certainly not all the same. They are in a way the same and yet not so much so that some of them are not altogether like some who are not at all of that kind of them. When there are very many of them together they are more like each other, they are and they seem to be and that is natural. They are, that is natural because they are together. They seem to be, and that is natural because what is in one is carried over to the other one by it being in the feeling of the one looking at the one and then at the other one.

There are a good many of that kind of them and it is a good thing, certainly it is not a bad thing. Certainly not any one is really objecting to their being ones being existing. They are ones who are being living and then they go on being living and some of them are not then being living, and they like it being living and they can bear it to be not being living. It is not a sad thing that they are not being living those who are not being living. It is not a sad thing that they are being living those who are being living. It is a gentle thing. It is a lively enough thing. It is a pleasant enough thing. It is an important enough thing. There are very many of them who are not any longer being living. It is an accepted thing. It is a quiet thing. It is a pleasant thing. It is a certain thing. It is a thing not remembered, not forgotten. It is a thing existing. It is a thing persisting. It is a thing contenting any one. It is a thing disturbing some. It is a thing any one can have had happen in knowing any place where some of this kind of them have been living.

It is a kind of them who are existing who are ones very many are visiting. Very many always have been visiting them. Very many are going on visiting them and that is a natural thing.

They will do something and they do do things and they will offer to do something and they will then not be surprised if they are not succeeding. They will expect something and they are surprised if they are not succeeding and some of them are surprised and are quick then and some of them are surprised and are slow then and they are surprised and really then being surprised is not existing in them, really not, they are not surprised that they have not been succeeding. Certainly some of them are surprised if they are not succeeding but certainly being alike all of them is in not being surprised that they are not succeeding.

There are very many of them. And they are alike, all of them. Certainly they are not alike all of them. Certainly not. They are certainly not alike all of them. They are alike all of them. They are expecting something, they are doing some things, they are offering some things. They are not surprised that they are not succeeding.

It is not a melancholy thing being one of them. It is not an interesting thing being one of them. It is not an exciting thing being one of them, it is not an important thing being all of them. It is an important enough thing being all of them. It is a pleasant thing being with them. It is not a pleasant thing expecting anything from them. It is not a disconcerting thing expecting anything from them. It is an agreeable thing knowing about them. It is an exciting thing first hearing about them. It is a delightful thing coming among them although it is a frightening thing the first seeing of them. It is a very pleasant thing living where they are living. It is a completely pleasant thing living where they are living. It is a troublesome thing waiting for any one of them. It is a troublesome thing waiting for them to go on finishing anything. It is not an exasperating, not a disconcerting thing waiting for any one of them.

They are certainly ones deciding something. They are certainly ones expecting anything. They are certainly ones not despairing in being ones being living. They are certainly ones not certain that they will be expecting anything. They are certainly ones deciding something. They are not ones deciding that they will be ones expecting something. They are not ones despairing. They are ones expecting something. They are ones deciding something. They are ones not deciding that they will be expecting something. They are ones not certain that they will be expecting something.

It is a pleasant thing to be living among them. They are not interested in this thing. They are not at all interested in this thing. They are smiling. They are not interested in this thing. They are expecting something. They are interested in this thing. They are not certain they will be expecting something. They are feeling this thing. They are then deciding something.

They like being living. They are not interested in this thing. They are quickly being existing. They are interested in this thing. They have been existing. They are not interested in this thing. They are going on being living. They are not interested in this thing. They are deciding something. They are not interested in that thing. They are doing something, they are going to be doing something. They are interested in that thing. They are going to be doing some other thing. They are interested in that thing. They are quicker than others who are slower. They are not interested in that thing. They are slower than others who are quicker. They are not interested in that thing. They are quicker than others who are slower.

That is astonishing but not to them. They are slower than others who are quicker. That is not astonishing and not to them. They are quicker and they are slower and certainly this is in all of them and certainly this is astonishing to some coming to understand this thing. They certainly are deciding something. They are not interested in this thing. They are interested in everything. They are expecting something. They are not certain that they will be expecting something. They are deciding something then. They are not interested in this thing in deciding something, in having been deciding something.

There are a good many of them. They are certainly different one from the other of them, quite different one from the other one of them and this is quite a troublesome thing and quite not an interesting thing to some. There are quite enough of them. They are certainly each one of them quite different from the others of them. There are some of them like others of them. This is a pleasant thing to some. There are some who are like others of them and some of such of them are ones who are completely being that thing being a kind of one which is a kind of one that is one giving to some a feeling of being an arranged one that is in the whole of them a thing not exciting, not disconcerting, that is a thing that is a thing that is growing in a certain arrangement that is a solid, unexciting, definite, beautiful enough thing, that is a thing that is something that each one being that one is in some way knowing, that is a thing that some are admiring, that is a thing that is not intensely interesting any one, that is a thing that is a beautiful thing in being a beautiful kind of existing thing, that is a thing that is a very agreeable thing and one is liking and one is noticing that thing.

There are very many being existing who are ones who are talking quite often and they are sounding as they are looking, as they are acting, as they are being. They are certainly sounding very pleasant when they are not sounding harsh and terrifying and unpleasant. They are certainly sounding pleasantly and that is sometimes a surprising thing and it is sometimes a surprising thing that they are not always pleasantly sounding. It is quite a serious thing deciding if they are pleasing to one or not pleasing to one. It is quite a serious thing coming to a decision. If they are pleasing to one that is an important thing. If they are not pleasing to one that is an important thing.

If some of them were different, not so very different, they would not be so willing to go on being living. If some of them were different and not so very different they would be certain to be expecting something. If some of them were different, quite a little different they would be winning something. If some of them were different, not really different, they would be quite certain not to go on being living. If some of them were different, just a little different they would be doing something that would be making some other one decide something.

If some of them were certain that they would go on being living, they would decide something. And really they are certain, in a way completely certain, all of them, that they are going on living, that not any one is going on living. They are all of them quite certain that every one who is not coming to be a dead one is going on being living. They are all of them quite certain of this thing. They are all of them in a way always saying such a thing. They are all of them in a way patient with this thing. They are all of them certain that not any one is going on being living. They are all of them quite patient with this thing. They are, very many of them, very lively in this thing. They are, very many of them quite quick in remembering, quite quick in not living in this thing. They are then ones, all of them certain that any one not coming to be a dead one is going on being living. They are all of them quite certain that not any one is going on being living. They are all of them quite patient with these things. They are all of them quite quick and they are not forgetting anything of these things. They are living and they are quite quick and they are not remembering and they are not forgetting anything of these things.

When they are young they are quicker than when they are old. When they are quite young they are very much quicker than when they are old. When they are young they are quicker than when they are old but not really quicker, they are not slow when they are old. When they are very young they are very much quicker than when they are older. They are quicker when they are young, when they are very young, when they are old than it is ever natural for them, for any one to think them. And certainly this is a very natural thing, a very natural thing. They are quick and certainly they have very much time to be quick in, and they are using very much time for this thing. And certainly any one can know this thing that they are using very much time, a great deal of time. They certainly have been, they certainly are using very much time, any one can know this thing, any of them can know this thing. Every one knows this thing, knows they are using very much time, that they are all of them using up very much time. Every one is naturally certain of this thing, that any of them, that all of them are using very much time. They are then quick ones, quicker when they are very young than when they are older, a little quicker when they are young than when they are old.

There are quite enough of them. They are different enough each one of them from the others of them. They are different enough each one of them from the others of them and it is easy enough to know this thing to know that each of them are different enough from the others of them. It is certainly easy enough to know this thing to know that each of them are different enough from the others of them. They are different enough each one of them from the others of them. In a way it is completely easy to know this thing to know that each of them are different enough from the others of them. They certainly can show this thing, any of them can show this thing that they are different enough from the others of them.

There are enough of them. There are not too many of them. There are quite enough of them. Each of them is quite different enough from the others of them. They do each one of them easily enough show this thing, quite easily show this thing that they are different enough each one of them from the others of them.

In a way they are completely simply showing this thing that each one of them is different from the others of them, from any of the others of them. They can very simply be showing this thing and certainly then it is a thing to be pleasing to any one to be knowing that each one of them is different enough from any of the others of them and is simply enough showing this thing.

Certainly any one can be completely showing this thing, any one of them, that they are different enough from any others of them and they are, any one of them, completely simply showing this thing. So then it is a pleasing thing, this thing, and again and again and again it is a pleasing thing, and certainly each one of them is showing such a thing, showing they are different enough from any other one of them, simply enough showing this thing. So then it is a simple enough thing, being different enough from any other of them, this then is a simple enough thing. In a way then it is a pleasing thing, certainly this thing is a pleasing thing, it is a simple enough thing, it is a pleasing enough thing. This thing, completely this thing, this thing a completely simple thing, a completely pleasing thing is a thing existing and certainly every one is knowing it in all of these of them knowing it so as to be quite certain.

Being different enough from any other one is a simple enough thing in all of these of them and certainly very many are being completely content with this thing, with these being completely expressing this thing, with these having been completely expressing this thing. Some then are knowing that certainly this is completely pleasing, this thing, this being different enough from any other of them, this being simply enough in all of them and certainly then every one has been certain that such a thing has been completely pleasing. Certainly all of them and there certainly are enough of them and not too many of them and very many of them are each one different enough from any other one of them, and are simply enough such a thing are simply enough different enough and certainly such a thing is pleasing and certainly it is completely enough existing to make them being ones being, having been completely pleasing, and certainly having been completely expressing such a thing, being different enough each one of them, being simply enough such a thing, having been completely enough expressing such a thing, being so simply that thing different enough each one of them, has made then ones certainly having been completely pleasing, having been completely expressing a thing being completely pleasing. Certainly it is not a complicated thing, being different enough from any other one, being simply enough different enough and certainly these then are expressing this thing, and certainly this has been completely expressed by them, and they are expressing this thing.

Some are needing that not any one is one some are not wondering about and then again and again finding that they are knowing everything that that one is ever doing. Very many are needing this thing and these then are ones being living and these then being ones being living are ones sometimes singing and sometimes making noises in being ones just then not wondering and not knowing anything about any one doing anything. So then all of them all of each of them that are being existing and being ones being such ones are being ones who are ones being ones of this kind of them. This kind then are all of them for all of them are of this kind of them.

Many of them, any of them are ones that are completely not needing going on being living when they are ones any one is hearing. Many of them, any of them are almost not at all needing going on being living if any one has been listening. And certainly very many are listening, mostly all of them are listening, any of them are listening and so not any of them are needing to be going on being living.

Certainly any one of them, all of them are different from any other one of them. Certainly all of them, any one of them, if any one has been listening to them are not needing then to be ones going on being living. Very many of them, almost all of them are listening. Very many of them, all of them are having again and again some hearing them, and so many of them, all of them are not needing to be ones going on being living, they are then not at all needing this thing needing being one going on being living.

There are very many of them, certainly enough of them, certainly not too many of them. They certainly are not completely needing going on being living. Certainly they are not needing this thing if any one has been listening to them and certainly they are, all of them, listening and certainly then all of them have been having some listening to them and so then not any of them are needing are ever needing being one going on being living.

There are certainly very many of them. Any of them are ones having some listening. Any of them are ones listening. There are very many of them. They are, each one of them different from any other one of them and that is a very simple thing and all of them are ones then having some listening and all of them are ones not needing being ones going on being living if some have been ones listening and certainly there have been ones listening and certainly not any of them are really needing being ones going on being living.

Being different each one from any other one of them and this being a completely simple thing, being each one of them not needing being one going on being living if any one has been listening and being all of them listening, and all of them being living is something that gives any one of them gives all of them a way of being one doing anything any one of them are doing so that any one can be quite certain that it is a thing that is being existing and again and again every one can be looking and again and again can be certain that that thing is a thing completely to be existing.

A thing completely to be existing as certainly there is not any reason that it is not a thing completely existing, a thing completely existing as certainly every one can be certain again and again that being completely existing is a thing that thing is certainly being, being completely existing as any one can be certain to be content that any such a thing is completely existing, being completely existing as each one being existing and expecting anything being completely existing is content to be finding, that is certainly being living in all of them and in everything any of them are doing and in any way any of them are living, and in all the place they are all living.

There are then enough of them being living and doing something and living somewhere and dying and being dead there.

Certainly any of them can be expressing completely feeling anything so that they are almost doing anything. Certainly any of them are completely expressing feeling anything strongly enough to be then doing anything. Certainly all of them, certainly any of them, certainly completely some of them are expressing feeling anything, feeling anything strongly enough to be almost doing anything, strongly enough to be completely doing anything.

They all of them and there are quite a number of them, quite a good many of them, enough of them, are expressing, can be expressing feeling everything, feeling everything enough to be ones doing anything, to be ones almost doing everything.

All of them are ones completely expressing feeling everything. All of them are ones expressing feeling anything. All of them are ones completely expressing feeling everything and all of them are ones completely expressing feeling anything.

They could any kind of them be quite different from any other kind of them. They could any kind of them be quite like any other kind of them. They could any kind of them be quite different from any other kind of them. Any one could know this thing that any kind of them could be completely different from any other kind of them. Any one did know that thing, that any kind of them could be like any other kind of them. They were ones then being quite different some kinds from other kinds of them. They were ones then being very different in concentrating this thing in being quite different one kind of them from any other kind of them. They were then some kinds of them concentrating on being that kind of them. They were then some completely concentrating on being one kind of them. Some were completely concentrating upon their being different kinds of them. Some were completely concentrating on going on having been a kind of them. Some of them had been concentrating. Some were going to be concentrating. Any of them had been one concentrating on their being, all kinds of them, one kind of them. Any of them could be concentratedly coming to this thing that all of them could be any kind of them. All of them could be concentratedly coming to this thing that any of them were one kind of them. Any of them could completely concentrate on any of them being all of them.

Some kinds of them had been concentrating and other kinds of them had been concentrating on being that kind of them. They were, they are, all of them their kind of them. They are all of them different kinds from other kinds of them. They are, any of them, one kind of them.

They could, any of them, be ones doing something, be ones doing anything and they were doing it as if they were doing that thing and they were doing that thing. They are all of them doing something and any of them are doing that thing, completely doing that thing as if they are completely doing that thing, and they are completely doing that thing. That is interesting that they are ones doing something, that any of them are ones doing something.

Any of them are ones doing something and any of them are completely doing that thing, they are, any one of them, completely doing that thing, as if they are completely doing that thing they are completely doing that thing. This is quite interesting.

They are many of them completely different from any other one of them. They are, any of them, completely different from any other one of them, and this is a thing that not any one is finding interesting. It is a very simple a very easy thing that this is in them that any one of them is completely different from any other one of them. Any one of them can easily completely be that thing can easily complete being completely different from any other one. Any one of them can easily complete that thing complete being a different one from any other one.

Any of them can easily do anything in being one being completely different from any other one, any of them can easily do something.

They are each one being one and they are, enough of them, they are each one of them being one and any one can see by looking can see that they are different from any other one of them, that it is an easy thing this thing that they are one each one different from any other one of them.

Any one can see that there are very different sizes among them. Some of them are taller, are very tall and some of them are smaller, are exceedingly small. Any one can see this in them, they are, all of them are where any one can see them. Not all of them are always where any one can see them. Certainly all among them that are men are always where any one can see them, and they, all of them, stay where they are long enough so that any one can see them a very long time, and they are, all of them, there very often so that any one can see them again and again. They are, all of them, that is all of them that any one can always be seeing, that is any of them that are men, they are all of them being ones doing all their living in being ones being where any one can see them. Any one can see all of them, all of them that any one can see, any one can see all of them a long time and again and again and again.

They are all of them ones that any one can be certain are ones that will not ever be doing anything. They are all of them ones that are ones not going to be doing anything to make any one certain that they would be afraid again if they were going on doing that thing. They are all of them ones not coming to be doing anything to make any one afraid to be one going to be left alone with all of them, with any of them. They are all of them ones quite certainly being such a one and any of them might have been one not being such a different one and certainly not any of them is one being a different one.

All of them are ones that any one can remember are ones not doing anything to make any one afraid of them again. Any of them are ones being such a one, one that any one can remember, are ones not any one will be afraid of again. Any of them are ones completely interesting, completely pleasant in this thing. Any one of them are ones, all of them are ones being entirely interesting, completely pleasing in being this thing.

Any one of them being one can be completely that one and that is being completely one being any one. Each one of them is completely that one and any one of them is completely that one. Any one is completely that thing that is being that one, is completely then being any one, is completely interesting is completely pleasing in that thing, in being that one, in being one being any one of them.

They are all of them then one of them who are ones being completely pleasing, being completely interesting and this is to them not completely exciting, it is to them stimulating, it is to others not completely stimulating, it is to others quite satisfying.

It is completely satisfying to any one that some one is one completing doing anything again. It is completely satisfying to every one that there are some who are ones who are completely doing everything again. These then are such ones are ones doing anything completely doing anything again and these are then ones satisfying any one. These are not ones satisfying every one, some are not wanting that these are ones being those who are ones doing a thing completely again. Any one is finding it satisfying that there are ones doing anything completely again. Some are not wanting that these, these who are doing anything completely again are the ones who are doing everything completely again. These are ones completely doing anything again. These are ones doing completely doing anything again.

These were not always doing that thing completely doing everything again. These were then completely satisfying, these were then ones not doing everything completely again. These were then more than completely satisfying, they were then completely being that thing completely being ones certainly going on being ones completely satisfying, entirely completely satisfying anything. These were then not ones completely doing anything again. These are ones completely doing anything again. Completely doing anything again is something to satisfy any one. These are ones completely doing anything again. This is satisfying to every one. Some are not satisfied that these are doing that thing completely doing anything again.

Some in doing anything are learning to do that thing, Some in doing anything are doing that thing. Some in doing anything are going on doing that thing. Some in doing anything are doing that thing again. Some in doing anything are beginning doing that thing. These being ones doing anything are ones doing that thing and are ones then not learning doing that thing, not beginning doing that thing, not going on doing that thing, not remembering doing that thing, not doing that thing again, they are ones completely fully doing that thing, they are completely fully doing that thing at any time that they are doing anything that is that thing, at any time they are doing anything. These then are ones completely fully doing something, are completely fully always completely fully having something being done by them. These then are ones being ones having anything completely fully being done by them, are ones always having something being completely fully done by them.

Some are certainly not believing this thing, not believing any such thing, some certainly never have been believing any such thing, some who have been who are completely knowing, certainly are not believing that all of them are ones completely doing, are ones having been ones completely doing something, anything, everything. Some are certainly not believing any such thing. Some have been ones completely loving that these are being existing, some are ones who have been ones almost completely living in being one completely loving that these are ones who are being existing. These then those who were almost completely living in being ones loving that these are ones being existing come then to be ones not loving that these are ones being existing come to be ones not regretting that these are ones being existing but are ones being almost entirely annoyed by such a thing by these being ones being existing and these then are almost completely living in this thing living in being entirely annoyed that these are being existing.

Some know very well that these are being existing, some know entirely that these have been existing. Some of both these kinds of them are completely living in that thing, in these being existing, in these having been existing. Very many know that these have been existing. Very many know that these are existing.

These, these being existing are ones who have been existing are ones who are existing. These are ones who could be ones completely living in the thing that they have been existing. These are ones living in having been existing, these are ones living in being existing. These are ones completely living in having been existing and they are then completely living in being existing. They are ones completely liking this thing completely liking having been existing and completely living in that thing and are completely living in being existing and completely liking this thing. These are ones that are completely exciting in having been ones being living, are completely excited in this thing and are completely excited, excitement is completely in them in their being one being existing. These are ones completely existing in having been existing and are completely existing in being existing. These then can be ones that any one can be certain are ones that are completely being having been and being and this is something that certainly can be quite disgusting to some completely not liking that thing, can be something completely displeasing to some completely not liking that thing.

These are ones liking being living. These are ones quite liking being living. These are ones quite needing being living. These are ones quite needing this thing quite needing being living. These are ones liking being living. They are ones going on doing this thing going on liking being living. These are ones quite liking doing this thing again and again liking being living. They are needing this thing needing being living. They are quite liking being living. They are liking being living.

They are liking this thing, liking being living and they are doing this thing they are being living and they are then not doing anything to be liking the thing to be liking being living.

They are, all of them, being living, they are doing enough of this thing so that any other one will be doing that thing, so that there will be enough of them quite enough of them doing this thing, being living. There are always enough of them doing this thing, being living. There are always enough of them doing this thing enough so that there will be enough of them doing this thing, doing being living. They are liking this thing liking being living so that they can any of them be ones being this thing being one liking being living. They are ones liking being living, they are ones being such ones, all of them being such ones any of them are being such ones, each of them are being such ones, any of them are doing that thing are liking being living.

Any one is such a one and is warmly that thing, is completely warmly one being living, one liking that thing. These are ones warmly being that thing, quite warmly, entirely warmly being that thing and certainly any other thing is a thing that can be too exciting, too wearing, too destroying. These then are ones warmly liking, entirely warmly liking being living and are being living and doing enough to have it that there are enough of them certainly enough of them being living.

These then are ones almost needing being ones being living. They certainly are ones completely doing anything, they certainly are ones completely bringing any teaching to any needing any teaching to be themselves doing quite enough living to be always going to be enough of them to be warmly liking being living.

A Sweet Tail (Gypsies)

Curves.

Hold in the coat. Hold back ladders and a creation and nearly sudden extra coppery ages with colors and a clean voice gyp hoarse. Hold in that curl with a good man. Hold in cheese. Hold in cheese. Hold in cheese.

A cool brake, a cool brake not a success not a re-sound a re-sound and a little pan with a yell oh yes so yet change, famous, a green a green colored oak, a handsome excursion, a really handsome log, a regulation to exchange oars, a regulation or more press more precise cold pieces, more yet in the teeth within the teeth. This is the sun in. This is the lamb of the lantern with chalk. With chalk a shadow shall be a sneeze in a tooth in a tin tooth, a turned past, a turned little corset, a little tuck in a pink look and with a pin in, a pin in.

Win lake, eat splashes dig salt change benches.

Win lake eat splashes dig salt change benches.

Can in.

Come a little cheese. Come a little cheese and same same tall sun with a little thing to team, team now and a bass a whole some gurgle, little tin, little tin soak, soak why Sunday, supreme measure.

No nice burst, no nice burst sourly. Suppose a butter glass is clean and there is a bow suppose it lest the bounding ocean and a medium sized bloat in the cunning little servant handkerchief is in between.

Cuts when cuts when ten, lie on this, singling wrist tending, singling the pin.

Lie on this, show sup the boon that nick the basting thread thinly and night night gown and pit wet kit. Loom down the thorough narrow. It is not cuddle and molest change. It is not molest principal necessary argue not that it, not that in life walk collect piece.

Colored tall bills with little no pitch and dark white dark with rubber splendid select pistons with black powdered cheese and shirts and night gowns and ready very ready sold glass butts. The simple real ball with a cold glass and no more seat than yesterday together together with lime, lime water. This is no sight, no sight suddenly, no supper with a heat which makes morgan, morgan must be so.

If it is and more that call life with show cared beard with a belt and no pin when shine see the coat and left and last with all it was to be there why show could pause with such read mice call it why those old sea cat with a shining not mouth hole if it is a white call with the inch of that sort could see that tie west with loaf which is not the copper lasting with a bright retract lamp call negligence utterly soothing in the coiling remain collapse of this which by there a called which never see and hammer by which basket all that glance zest.

Cut in simple cake simple cake, relike a gentle coat, seal it, seal it blessing and that means gracious not gracious suddenly with spoons and flavor but all the same active. Neglect a pink white neglect it for blooming on a thin piece of steady slit poplars and really all the chance is in deriding cocoanuts real cocoanuts with strawberry tunes and little ice cakes with feeding feathers and peculiar relations of nothing which is more blessed than replies. Replies sudden and no lard no lard at all to show port and colors and please little pears that is to say six.

It can no sail to key pap change and put has can we see call bet. Show leave I cup the fanned best same so that if then sad sole is more, more not, and after shown so papered with that in instep lasting pheasant. Pheasant enough. Call africa, call african cod liver, loading a bag with news and little pipes restlessly so that with in between chance white cases are muddy and show a little tint, all of it.

Please coat.

Way lay to be set in the coat and the bust. The right hold is went hole piece cageous him. He had his sisters.

Like message copowder and sashes sashes, like pedal sashes and so sashes, like pedal causes and so sashes, and pedal cause killed surgeon in six safest six which, pedal sashes.

Peel sashes not what then called and in when the crest no mandarining clothes brush often. No might of it could sudden best set. Best set boar.

Rest sing a mean old polly case with boats and a little scissors nicely sore. All the blands are with a coat and more is coach with commas. A little arrangement is manufactured by a shoal and little salt sweats are to grow grow with ice and let it seat seat more than shadows which have butter.

Suppose, suppose a tremble, a ham, a little mouth told to wheeze more and a religion a reign of a pea racket that makes a load register and passes best. Kindness necessarily swims in a bottom with a razor which needs powder powder that makes a top be in the middle and necessarily not indicate a kind of collection, a collection of more of more gilt and mostly blue pipes pipes which are bound bound with old oil and mustard exact mustard which means that yellow is obtained. Gracious oh my cold under fur, under no rescued reading.

Able there to ball bawl able to call and seat a tin a tin whip with a collar. The least license is in the eyes which make strange the less sighed hole which is nodded and leaves the bent tender. All the class is sursful. It makes medium and egg light and not really so much.

Catch white color white sober, call white sold sacks, crimp white colored harness crimp it with ferocious white saffron hides, hurry up cut clothes with calm calm bright capable engines of pink and choice and press. Peas nuts are shiny with recent stutter which makes cram and mast a mast hoe, luck.

A winter sing, take thee to stay, say mountain to me and alabaster.

Curious alright.

Wheel is not on a donkey and never never.

A little piece of fly that makes a ling a shoulder a relief to pages.

Please putter sane show a pronounce, leave sold gats, less it measles. A little thin a little thin told told not which. Rest stead.

Appeal, a peal, laugh, hurry merry, good in night, rest stole. Rest stole to bestow candle electricity in surface. The best header is nearly peek.

Come in to sun with holy pin and have the petticoat to say the day, the last oh high this that. No so.

Little tree, bold up and shut with strings the piney and little weights little weights what.

Cold a packet must soak sheer land, leave it a yield so that nuts nuts are below when when cap bags are nearly believe me it is nice and quiet I thank you.

Pluck howard in the collided cheese put and not narrow.

Little in the toilet tram.

Seize noes when the behaved ties are narrowed to little finances and large garden chambers with soled more saddled heels and monkeys and tacts and little limber shading with real old powder and chest wides and left clothes and nearly all heights hats which are so whiled and reactive with moist most leaves it sell to apart.

Sober eat it, a little way to seat. The two whiskers.

All chime. So be eat hit. No case the lines are the twist of a lost last piece of flannel.

This beam in which bought not a hill than store when stone in the point way black what slate piece by all stone dust chancely.

This wee did shut, about. A land paul with a lea in and no bell no bell pose with counters and a strike a strike to poison. Does a prison make a window net does it show plates and little coats and a dear noise.

This is a cape. A real tall is a bat, the rest is nice west, the rest in, be hine with a haul a haul not. Knot not knot. A vest a voice vest. Be able to shave, shave little pills in steady, steady three, coal pied. This is hum with him, believe hit believe hit page it.

Is it necessary that actuality is tempered and neglect is rolled. A little piece. The blame which makes a coping out of a cellar and into a curtain and behind behind a frontyard is that then. Please dust.

It is so thick and thin and thin, it is thick. It is thick, thin.

A spoon, thick ahead and matches, matches wear sacks.

Stew, stew, than.

I Must Try to Write the History of Belmonte

If Maddalena comes I am going to be asleep. You can entertain your enemy much quicker. If a servant is your friend there is no getting rid of her.

Belmonte is a bull-fighter. I have not seen him. He is sick. He had bronchitis and now he's wounded. They put him in a specially prepared place and they say the wound is serious. He will recover. It is said that the Queen hit the King. Not here. In Greece. So be it.

This is going to be the story of Cook. Oh yes that will be alright.

The story of Belmonte is that we know he is hurt in the leg. A Mexican is to take his place. The man at the Cafe Artistos after much experience likes him better and says that though not good looking has better technique.

The dog. He thought he wanted it at once. The curtain. They wanted it and liked to look with a telescope. First he came that way then the same women had places. They can read.

Cook does and he says and he is kind to all. He has french as a friend and he speaks Mallorcan. He understands all. He is so kind.

Continually fatten. They continually fatten. She is so. She likes it. She says she is dreadfully bitten.

This is the way they met. He was abroad and he was used to English. Not to speak but to be disappointed. He was never disappointed. He spoke it. He called it. He spoke in a low tone. He said I am sorry I have no faults I am without fear but I have no money, I am not afraid of that and I am not reckless. I am very careful. I always pay back.

He does. He never said I said so. I said Mrs. Hardy was right when she said he had honest eyes. He is fond of swimming.

We saw it. She could not go because it was hot. The one who was advertised was a failure. The other one the one we had seen had learnt how to do somethings very nearly and he did it using all his old vigor and carrying it successfully. A man of talent and plenty. He had blue eyes. He was carried away. By whom. By many men. They were really there. The other one is one one is not sorry for. He is too old for yesterday and we remember him. We remember him at the same time two years ago and he was not the strongest man or even the good one. I do not understand why they speak to him.

Belmonte.

We have not seen him.

After all he doesn't talk french very fluently and so perhaps it would be better if only you came to dinner. Of course you know best.

The moon.

The moon rises more to the left every night considerably more.

I remember how I felt about it, we began on top and slowly came down and this time we were down but there was no liveliness in it. Even if there had been anything delicate it would not have been pleasurable. That's how I felt about it.

Don't listen to her.

In places they go to see their husbands. They wait until he is off the boat. Then they rush.

It is a sweet story.

Don't come up after ten. If you want to come come alone that's alright but don't come with Fanny after ten.

I love you Fanny Fanny is your name isn't it.

This is they way they disturb him.

Belmonte Belmonte.

They are going to have an opportunity at night. Not he. Horses. They are going to do it in the way we have not seen. It is not right to wear those clothes made by a dressmaker who eats lunch. No.

All men are dark and women white.

We went out and saw six soldiers and a woman.

A little boy Bartholomew goes to school in the hot weather August and June. Also July. July and August. His father is proud. He says he does not eat too much. He does not eat enough. He learns English french spanish and Arabic. Arabic is for the Arabs. He learns it so that he can speak it. He is not a son of a baker. He is the son of a hotel keeper. A small hotel. Nobody sleeps there.

Capable of studying. He is capable of studying. We were not sure that she was french. We thought she spoke it. How do you know how to say we do not care about lemonade.

We have not yet mentioned that on the twenty-first there will be an opportunity to see fighting when it is lighted by electric light. We will certainly go by this means. They say that the effect is not interesting.

This is not the history of Belmonte because there are so many mounted men. We said we did not admire them here but we have admired them. We said this instructedly. Today we were pleased to see our servant. He said that electricity does not work on Sunday.

Cook works.

He said he asked every one about Guano and they said he worked better than Belmonte. If so they are both of the school of Gallito, in the manner of Gallito who does continually what he does a little. He is no doubt incorrect in what he had heard. He often is. He does not understand. Nevertheless there are horses and electric light. We will see.

Today we walked. We walked up and around the hill. One would speak of this as not having taken a very long time. We were full of discussion. We were frightened that evening. No we weren't. Certainly we said we were plain. Dear things. What is it.

This is not like his painting. Talk about Mathilda.

Grief for Belmonte.

He did not hurt his foot. It was Cocherita of Bilbao. who hurt his foot. He hurt it so badly that he cannot walk.

Tonight it is very different.

Cocherita de Bilbao. He is not an American. Torquito is. He reminds us of it. He is very successful. He is intelligent and he is strong and he has blue eyes in the distance. I saw him very near.

Horses. Why are horses blind. They are in one eye.

What does a lizard want to get. He wants to get Polybe. Who will train him, who will wash him. Who is beside him. Where is he. We do not know.

Cook is such a believer in parent's age. He says it all the time he is certainly or thirteen or fourteen plus seventeen. I mean it. I think he is older. We never hear about Belmonte.

When they gave a dinner the other day Belmonte was not there.

Plan this. You meant to walk up to the horse kneeling on one knee throw your weight on the barrier and relieve the attack relieve it by planting sharp stars into his shoulder relieve it by stroking the horn, by hurrying. This was the plan and he did it again. He continued to assure the attack by not being quick. He was very quick. This is the way to pursue it. Follow it about and have the understanding with the uncertainty. Nothing is uncertain to him. He is a wretch. We can be angry. We were disappointed Belmonte was not there and we had paid as if he were.

I remember long dashes. Mr. Kitchener said that he was to go and he would meet him. Mr. Potter he said if you will go later I will be there. Mr. Potter did not go or he would not have met him. Mr. Kitchener did not go neither did Mr. Potter. Belmonte had his foot hurt. He is still in the hospital.

They were here to eat their dinner. They ate their dinner and they advised us to get sea-weed. They said seaweed. He said seaweed contains iodine which is very important for medicine. It is very important in medicine. Belmonte uses it for his foot. He uses it to put on his foot. Belmonte uses it on his hurt foot. It is put on his foot a great deal. They use it often. They use it on his foot whenever he is hurt. He has been hurt.

Belmonte was hurt. His foot was not hurt. It was just above his foot and there he was seriously hurt.

Necessarily the secret of Belmonte. I do not wish to weep. I forget war and fear and courage and dancing. I forget standing and refusing. I believe choices. I choose Gallo. He is a cock. He moves plainly.

In the Grass (On Spain)

Occident all Spain the taste.

Milled cautious and plaster and with the heat her trimmed white. Seat silver, seat it next. Poor it in gold hot hoods.

Be cool inside with a monkey tied, with a monkey tied. Be cool inside the mule. Be cool inside with a surrounded tied, a cast, before, behind again, indeed, many.

What in the cut with any money and so, and so the climate is at stake, all the circular receipts are pears and linen is the stall to peep, likely and more the season's chair and little grasses with a pole all the occasion is the wreath and many houses are baked. Many have the same in came and all the light is many wet all the burst in in the man and best to hide is only sweet. All is that and a little haste, a little pleading with a clouded pup all is chance to be the curl that sets and all the winding causes. All of it cucumber.

Cup of lather and moan moan stone grown corn and lead white and any way culture is power, Culture is power. Culture.

Clambering from a little sea, clambering within bathing, clambering with a necessary rest for eye glasses, clambering beside.

A little green is only seen when they mean to be holder, holder why, coal pepper is a tissue.

Come up shot come up cousin, come up cold salmon pearly, come up, come in, nicely, nicely seen, singing, singing with music, sudden leaves loaves and turtles, taught turtles taught turtles teach hot and cold and little drinks.

Colored huts, cold to din acres of as real birds as stole when. Stole when, it is a lie. It is coming to the seal, it is coming how is it. Language of the hold of the sea sucking dart belt and no gowns in, no gowns in pelting. This is the cane that is short and gold more.

Cold not coin in the ground be sour and special and settled and soiled and a little reason. Come then to sort the kinks in how surrounded is a limb.

Cute numbers, cute to be so bold and so sallow and so in the cream and furled, furled with chalk and lights and high bees and little legs heady and little least little cups, least little cups bellow, bellow electric shadows, real old teachers with a private cake of bean and numbers those numbers. Do they pack.

Spanish cut that means a squeeze and in place of water oil and water more. Mine in the pin and see cuttle cuttle fish call that it is that it is sardine, that it is in pelts and all the same there is paper in poles paper and scratches and nearly places.

Guess a green. The cloud is too hold, collected necessary pastes in that shine of old boil and much part much part in thread and land with a pile. The closeness of a lesson to shirt and the reason for a pale cullass is what is the revolution and retaliation and serpentine illustration and little eagle. A long little beagle, a long little scissor of a kind that has choice all this makes a collation.

All winter is dutiful. All the short stays are digestion. All lines are cylindrical that means that there is leading.

Any roast is not leading. Enough pale ways are scratched.

Spend a height all up and only pup, spend it with the soon. And this when. More call. Cane seat in bottom choice makes a melon within. A melon within then.

A little return bitten with a cake set white with ink and size and little parlors healthy with a coat. A keen glance wet with accustomed perspiration. No need to dry, no need to current a sand paper with white seams and long shoals. No more mail in splendor and shape to set sights and little steaders in so hat shoot, shut toes, shut toes with a rid of not that, no that, not that.

A peach a peach pear which means a pear early and looking and near near there, exactly pass the light hall where there is no cover no cover to what.

Suppose it is past the mouth which is peculiar and nervous and left and argued and whiled whiled with a tree.

Less a chain than a loss and pieces of pearly paper that means blue not all and the best choice is moreover.

Naturally lovey naturally a period which is regulated by a perfect beam of carpet and more boats does mean something. It is enough.

A handsome beam a handsome beam is quite like the standing of a little peak shut up and needles all not needles. Rest and zest and powder to shout and color and ball and sweet word black.

Believe, I believe you restruck my cold wet and the dun hit it back choose it set.

Come to why, sit in oil save the sos, all the gone sing in a pin save sit it kit, kit all.

Suppose a little chance to hold a door would leave the door closed would that mean that the sun was in, would it mean messages and a kite, would it mean a sold bone and little pies. The necessary shakes makes a whittle. This is not none.

A little pan, that is to please it, a little which is a point to show that co-incident to a lively boat there is nearly places. That is nobody touching. All the plays garden. Little screen. Not collected and spacious not at all so old. And more places have the behold it. The best example is mustard. A little thing. A little no old shut.

Lot in that which is a place surrounded by a fence. A fence is small it is a wall, a wall is tall it is a tunnel, a tunnel is not necessary to a city. A city is celebrated.

Leave piles steady, show it the moon.

Not cut loud and teasing I bleed you, not quite shadow and niece it lises. This is mike when the land is shooken and left peel short is most to sake and not sublime is moist to ramming and leave it whet is most in chance. Nest bite is way back in the clam of dear gold weights with necessary williams williams wild williams with lamb laden twitches and new-casts and love boosts and most nextily.

Reason with toil and a mark upside down and left boils not knealed with close cracks and moses. A real plume with a no less boiled collander and share.

This is the sport.

Leave it to shut up the right nasal extra ollofactorising sea lights and nearly base more shall sees to the place of the best.

We wide lade the tall tack which squeeze load the no sire and leave more in church maid than rest so to streak.

Mow chases in a spoon and tub, big clam, mow places in a boil a piece. No gas bests.

Look it to peas, loaf it in both spats mean a glass mean in passes in passes a poke and a chair and little cries and a bottle.

A veil and a place seater and a peanut which makes throws so grand.

Never pet never pet a gallon because there is a trunk. A trunk has a bosom. Lead less. Lead prosper pour, poor gold wax and much much tower.

Please place what, place a colored glass. This shows two three eight three nine. This is not sunday. A trouble home.

If a wake means bounded numbers eighty and lately. This is three, show shine five, leave it pare. All that. Seven rough state.

No nuisance is in a married widow with a collection of dear ones in one room nicely. Why is black cooler, black is cooler because spread in makes a little piece of pillow and a coal black lace. This is so best shown.

Suppose it is a parcel of oats and no fat, suppose it is a drill, suppose even that it is a winning centre, this means five and five and five.

Let let let a chief go.

The reason why a laugh is laughed after is that a shed and a shawl and little onions and keys and keys are after all a dog and a curtain and a little less.

Please please please please please.

The more the wet is water the more lilies are tubes and red are rice rows. A little scene and a tall fanner and a flower a hair flower and a shoes and a shoes boots and rubbish all this makes raising please tease and a little likeness noises.

A gain again pounds. Agate in pets, love biscuits, a time.

Again in leaves of potatoes and cuts, cuts with, with in, in him, a length.

A little belly a little belly cold, speed out stuff, stuff alike, alike shirts and goats and get ups and laid car cases.

All a bill, a bill boaster. Suppose it happened when, when a little shadow was a tail and a can a can was gathering. Gathering then.

Suppose a clandestine roof had tires and could neglect a blue spot suppose it was the end and three places were necessary a like view would be charming charming, charming weather.

Cries is, coming, a leg, all a leg, two utter, more children, no narrow, read a little.

If a horse and a bat and a gathering bleed stir and a chin and a cloth and early ear marks and then such such raiding and little lives and a multiplied purple, all the spool all of it cloth and gets gets out and a piece of reasonable white jacket and a hair a long pail and all bone some binding and a little season silk.

Grand mutter grand mutter shell, real core, real oak plate.

Lara Lara Psyche, Lara Lara three brothers and a mother, sister sister and a new year a new year not christmas, christmas is off off of it. Really.

Three brothers and mother. Leave it fit to a string and there is a ball a ball a hat, a hat a special astracan, a kind of loaf, a real old seventeen checkers. Come to be in, see the table and the look and the little day tomorrow, it is Thursday Friday, Friday, Friday in a day to Sunday, Sunday Sunday, Monday Monday Monday Wednesday and seventy failing out sights.

A son what is a son, a son is in the sitting room and in a central carry ball. A son is not a sister diamond, it is so noted.

Whispers, whispers. Whispers not whiskers, whiskers, whiskers and really hair. Hair. Hair is when two are in and show gum.

Kiss a turn, close.

Suppose close is clothes, clothes is close.

Be less be seen, stain in burr and make pressure. This is bit.

Excel a line, a line is in end purple blue, yes guess show packets and it it it.

Spain is a tame name with a track a track so particular to shame, a track a little release in sold out casts a little next to saleable old cream. Able to pass.

A land steam, a cold cake, a received egg check, an oleander.

Lessen pay a corridor, meal passes.

Necklace, strings.

Necklace, strings, shoulder.

Newly set tea, tea be hold.

Tea behold.

If the soiling carries the head, if the baking measures the pint, if the rudening leans on a strand then shutters.

No need to say a little deaf way is a goat, a goat has a pin in him. Leave glasses, glasses are so cactuses.

Able able ever grass her, get up fern case, get up seize.

Noble and no noble and no next burr, net in and bee net in and bee next to shown miner. Next to beat bean, next to beat bean next to be blender, next to between, next to between in intend intender. In tender.

A laugh in cat, coal hot in. A remembrance of a direct realteration with no bust no buster, no bust here.

Suppose it a glaze a glaze of curtain a fetch in pots a news camper, supper the next old meat oak and kneel kneel with excellent excellent least sands and neck stop. That is.

What you call them what you call them say butter butter and let us leaves and a special a realteration lace a realteration lace.

Next all, next all, inks.

It was a strange name that which when a record of a lucine and naughty bent made it by that that nearly any excellent shade of night glasses made a pleasing and regular hair.

A wet syllable is we are, a wet syllable is we are we in.

A Spanish water and a coop shape mine and legs and reed ridiculous red, and little lively hue, little lively hue and copper, little lively hue and copper up.

England

Leave off more time than the hope which assures the rent of a custom, the sweetness is not only there it is the reason left and monkeys are not merry. If you do have the eyes blue and the hair the color then it is easy to see the hands.

All along and the day, the prize is not driven and the selecting of all the coal is that.

All the while is light and cleaning is not repetition. If you see the chance then spring again and if not be extreme, be certain that the show has that line in line and do not, never, see the patent desert the measles.

So the cloth is alright and the carpet is English. Pink and the moon, that sweet sugar is brown.

Cane sour asparagus and do not season with reason. Certainly the union of oxygen with ostriches is not that of the taught tracer. It is not a window that has an elastic it is planted gutta percha.

The change is not plain seeking, the hills are not dislocated and the cluster has not the name of the intermediate beginning.

To paste more attention on a bridge is not the path that is taken. All of it is planted. The blossom is pealing, the tender dew is green, the presence is in the time in between, the sacrifice is that that the bell which rings has a clapper. The pleasure in the use is not so dreary but that there is an exchange.

One sees a custom, one sees a date, one sees a potato, one sees a caterpillar, one sees more particulars than kissing, one sees the blame distributed, one sees more than any one.

Powder and food, union and despatch, so that there is no pale color, so that there is black, so that there is much preperation of a return to the same.

If a little meadow and a tree have that use and a morning and the west wind have that use and the evening and the continuation have that use then there is no use when the sing song ends rising.

Yes there is the same. There is all of that which makes it certain that something is what is there and not misplaced. This means that to be different there is not any place that is the same and if the whole place is there then it is not alarming it is confirming. This is so shrewdly what is proven.

Bailing the center of a spot and not having an embankment is not the only way to flirt. So soon, so left without a spoon, so august and so strange and taller than every other, it is not astonishing that some one is older.

There is not a seed and an orange. An orange is red and yellow. A seed has only a little way to grow and there is not any palm that grows larger. It is the same. It is astonishing, it is the same. The sweet spread of the union with intuition and every anger is so certain that there is no bloom. There is red feeling and the color is deeper. Blue is of some use. There is more place for weather.

A pigeon is a bird and flying it is not widening the piece that cooking makes duller, not at all, it does not taste that way.

The cause and any effect this does not make the smell stronger, this does not make what is pie.

To change any sigh, then to place all of that hope, to destroy dancing and to make a lovely turn that is not the season of every day, that is not the season of Monday, that is not the season of Sunday.

A pleasant taste and plenty of butter, a pleasant drink and plenty of water, tea and more fruit than in winter, bread and more eaten than ever this is so sad and every one sees that it is to be cheerful. Any one sees cheerful weather, every one eats cheerful potatoes, they are large and there is water and there is butter, a whole city is not subdued it is iniquitous, it is so soon to see the plant that is not buried showing more white tail than ever. A little thing is never tender. The size is there.

In the moan where there is no groan, in the noise where there is no presence, in the palm where there is the range of the seed and the light of more, in the room where there is all there the place where there is every chair, in the hall where there is steam-heat all about there is union in the height of some. So then there is no prayer where the use is more strange than none. This does not make for cheese and the rest are the same every day.

Butter which is every where has a little table, fish is all the time of day when the silver is away and there is more there. All the daylight makes for meat and the washing has that price, every price is cheaper. All the finished way to treat everything there is to place is not the only way to shape the standing heating. All the day is every day and exercise is made that way and piling plates where there is grass is something that is neater. To originate a smash means more tasting than there is when there is no use in stewing more than has been put in there to stay. So comes more length and some more weight and the bestowal of that piece is not astonishing.

The lantern of blinking is not lively and this is distracted by quick ways of winking. There is so much use. The line of the rise is afternoon sunrise.

So the main is seen and the green is green. Pleasure the rotten winter when there is a rotten summer. There are some things a place can not show.

So there is no end to a name and there is no end of likelihood. A darling makes no noise and a spoon makes nothing pink.

Return the whole special short sentence and then say that he will be pleased. To say that in that result is so much more particular. The cleanliness comes from washing the little pieces at the center and not making them have the sparkle in black. This is not all of a windy day. So much more that is green and not gold makes the bottom have that form. The shapes are there. They are not there when they are the same. A reason is given. It has a whole name.

Soon the Susan is all past, the land is clean and the green color is not singled with more yellow than some. This shows in the catalogue and in the hair.

All the plate is glass and cleaned with white which are hanging, the whole is spent and there is more than the size.

All the long way to be in that length which makes no more of some cuckoo is not shown by the intermission of every reply. It is so cheerful and the breath which is not all of a response is used some more. There is a sound that came and made the agreeable deplacement of no sign. If it is to be had there is a way to surround the time of day. The sooner sand is not the smell of heating and this more ancient than the day does not mean all the noon.

He can be pleased in the same time as a bright Sunday. He can be dancing so. He can be and he is somewhat. He is altogether.

He and there are the patience, he and all the whole way is uplifted with that and surely the simple thing is to neglect that and to do so.

Soon to have an eye, soon to have plenty of them, soon to have a nose, soon to have plenty of them, soon to have a light soon to have plenty of them.

The argument is that if there is a way there is no need to say that separation means more use than all the cake. That is true, that is a belief. A thorough substance is one that has no particular caterpillar, a caterpillar has no color, this is no loss, there is no less more than there is clothing, it shows that much and anybody can say no, anybody has a hat, a hat has no use, that does not mean that it does shine when there is a plain sight.

All the heavy weight is that color and nobody is more famous than an oaken piece of wood, not any body and every one is famous, every one, when there is no lavender.

Peace to more calm, and rest to more regret that selling is not burdening buying.

Still so many change, the time to say that the change is not a meadow is not to all the same and anyway all have nothing bare. They season their chocolate, they partake tender, the rest is the finish of the street, the houses are adjusted and adjoining. The conclusion is no veil, the breeze is taller and surely walking is something, there is any occasion, there is no pink appurtenance, so much suit, so much harbor, so much that is described in response.

A land is not more seen than a beefsteak and a beefsteak is wasted. All the roast has a sale and all sale is varnish. The section that has the twin set of notwithstanding are all suited with the linen, and more camps are made to fit than there is hair on a peninsular. The reason is so just that a question has that right and a belief is universal that is to say there is no doubt of something.

Drafts are not dark nor is the sea and livelier are the seven months of warning. All the perils are serene, and laughing is not stranger.

Piling for a witness means the boat and all the floating places are so searched, tighter and more of the breathing there makes any swelling so much simpler.

A plain tie makes a connection on Saturday and they are the first. They have that reason, no one can oppose visiting, there is no use in obtaining a station. Time to go away is October. That shows more winter than weather. This does make a written reason.

A bloom on a red thing means that there is a single country. An apple offered means that there is no disgrace. A single thing that has no seeds means that there is land. A same joint and no appetite means that there are no sandwiches.

Like the mantle and the light and the crackling underwear, like the colors that are dark and the mixtures that are bright, like them all there is no destruction, there is no analogy, there is a dislocation, there is no disturbance.

Startling and true the same are few. The presence of many is acute. The death of more is arduous. The relation of all that is in that language. So simple a date makes no hard singing. If it is a wild cow it is tame. The single hair shows the reason in a precise ham. It is a dinner. It is leaning.

Kindling is wood and coal is tonny. That is the blame and a blower is funny. The time comes to state that. There is seriousness.

Blame is not forecast it is a sunrise, how soon is there more shade than light.

A bang is the sound of water, a simple string ties it together. It is so struck that there is water, moisture has a sample of more. There is no sympathy. There is no educator. If the width is more the wider is wider. The width is not a wayside it is the block. There is the color soon. There is no shade. Shadows are a sampler. There is no sampler. The width is precious. It is wading in length. The wide angel has no wet winter. It is not drained wetter.

Bursting no more and being the sample of more of it is not so much simpler than it was. It was so sudden. It was suddenly so much more safer. Then there came the same time and there is analysis, there is the whole time and there is no more simplification than there is. There is very much more. There is that there. There is there more than that. There is.

To avoid a shot means that there is no way to jump. Why should an engagement fit two. There is no cause in despair. The darkness that makes a mind show dirt is that which is practical. The union of all that is wetness, the change is underweight and yet the practical use of length is the same as width. There is that belief.

Ink is black. That is brutal if there are fish.

A church is so enchanted that there is hymning. This makes the question safer.

All the peals that were ruined were those that were stumbling and if these were in the way they were a shop. That means that selling is an obligation.

A clamp is that which when attached has a pin. This keeps it from coming more to say less. This does not show wagering. If the time is between then there is no certain wisdom and yet there is no denial. Why should there be. What is the taste. It is not so painful to see hanging. Hunger is more perforated. That does not mean that there is a change in weight.

No powder, pink is not a color, any color is an order that is to say if a window is not the same every one has that resemblance. Saving no soap and coming in, coming right in means that there is that action. The tone of surprise is uplifting but there is not that disgrace, there is down, that is sinking. Coming in, that is coming and rinsing, that which is used is the room, that which is used is washing, that which is used is not preventing anything resembling any soaking. So much substance, so much receipt, so many more cakes of wintry dancing. Is it astonishing. It is. There is every disturbance. Why is there whether. Why is the Thames warmer.

Packing and not mentioning being adjoining does not mean eye-sight. It does not mean a release from an operation. It is not destroying a button.

So then the price is the same and the size is dependent on the whole piece. It shows no holes clearly. There is no use in scissors.

A kind of wading is not so poisonous as wiped water. The length of a street is not disturbed by the use of slippers. Not at all.

Loud and not louder and the time is stouter and the width is wider and the selection is thicker. No time to be tall and small no time to prick a finger, no time to surprise a noise in the sides and yet all that is used by there being more time there every birthday. Every birthday which is not yesterday has an occupation. An occupation is that which when there is the time shows the center of that which is the lamentation and lamenting does not destroy that use, it does not fulfill a judgement, it does more, it is relined. The same shows more when there is no date. Any reading is simple. The use is all day. A response uses words. They mean that full. The length is more than the joining. There is that reestablishment and no violence. The time is more so than peculiar. There is nothing to see. Reading is action. There is a swim in a way. All the time is an accident. There is a reason. There is that experience of detraction. There there is expression, there is a blame not intending disturbing unattaching unintelligent attention to extreme intention.

Payment and subjoining sin, the length of death is not between, the tooth and the age and more than all, the salt, and more than all also the hard bed and no petition. There is the use in pointing harder than no wind and no other.

This is not white, there is no cream any kind color, there is the time to grow longer and all the same if there is no paper it does not show in the print and pen-wiper. It does not.

It can see more than what, than then. Henry and a doleful danger. There is a sending of a principle line of unpointed apples, and a target, a whole thing is no example. And the caneseat joint is so soundless in quiet cushions. There is no more pen-wiper.

Anything that is everything and everything that is anywhere and everything that is everywhere has no special singular purpose. If purpose is intellectual then there is a garden, if there is a garden there is a fountain, if there is a fountain then there is an intellectual purpose. No respect is resembling that more than the mischief.

To choose more is to choose something. That choice which is admonished is not more dated than that which is remembered and there is a fine display of zeal there certainly is and nothing is more orderly nothing and when there is washing there is interlacing. This means so much cleaning and cleaning which has that sign is the same as the whole time of being peculiar.

Any one is older. Any one is a sight for a beholder. Any one is saved a sickness. And any one is a particular substitute for remaining undetermined and seeing a clean collar. All the same the full service is in the height of a rich thick sandy sticky silence. There is no dispute when there is harmony. All the date is in the place. There are such red ones when they are pretty. A color which shows is one that is not seen anywhere. This will happen. This does not start a subject.

To be reckless and rejoined, to be sad and not forsaken, to be earnest and awake, to be sure that there is freedom, all this makes no difference at all. A sight that disturbed was not that after all there was restraint and to look differently shows that there is a resemblance and that the nation has partaken. The nation has partaken and there is no pleasanter reunion.

To be forced to say that there is no denial, not to be forced but to be rejoiced that comes from the time when there is no hesitation and much ease. Very much ease is more ease than much ease, much ease is more ease than the ease which is not that ease. That comes to be said. That comes to be so said that there is no individual reunion between the first second third fourth and fifth.

A cause for disturbance rests in the fact that more time is used in a long time than in a short time. There is no criticism when the time is long. The time is so long that an answer comes promptly. This is so much the more satisfactory as the occasion for an answer is whenever there is cause for a question. The difference between this and no elaboration is extreme. No elaboration is not achieved in a question nor in an answer and this which is so eminently satisfactory is that there is no doubt that there will be no reason for the occasion. To be faithful is to be accustomed and the custom which is without that reservation has no circumstance to replace it. The time to state that is when there is no reason to doubt a result. There never is a reason to doubt a result if there is a promise. If there is a promise it means that idleness is only another name for a thing.

The whole place is so large that there is no dust and so there not being that there is every occasion for no difference to be noticeable. This makes reading so necessary.

Nothing is perplexing if there is an island. The special sign of this is in dusting. It then extends itself and as there is no destruction it remains a principle. This which makes that reveals that and revelation is not fortuitous it is combined and ordered and a bargain. All this shows the condition to be erect. Suppose that there is no question, if there is no question then certainly the absence of no particular is not designed. And then when it is astonishing it is not liberty. Liberty is that which gathered together is not disturbed by distribution and not given without remark and not disturbed by frugality and an outline. All this makes the impression that is so disturbed that there is no question.

There is no use in denying what any one hearing reading is hearing, there is no use and doing it every day is not tantalising, it is not a bit more tantalising than exaggeration, not a bit and the whole result is spoken out in the best time and place and moment. This increases daily and all the time what if there is meddling, meddling is not automatic, and if it is automatic why should it not be obligatory.

A candle light does not mean that there are candles, a candle light means arithmetic and training and ways of stating a question and it means much more, it means that every night if there is moonlight there is that light, and light has so much place in a lighted place that every one is accustomed to it.

It is so wintry and hair is blowing and all the slippery slides have water on them, it is so summery and wind is water and all that is red is what is burning, the whole excitement, all the wedding shows the spring to be the place where water springs, all the horizon, all the dwelling shows that escaping is not an escapade that is in a suggestion. So to reason and so to eclipse and so to redden the western sun, so to accept and so to annoy and so to have no piece of money, so much so is not a tangible substance, it is intangible and therefore it is sliced.

A toil that has no frozen dish-water, a trembling that has an appetite, a refusal that has a nervous extremity, an expression that has a direction of disregarding, all this shows the essential use of a minority, they show it and they caution it, they do not outrage giving it credit. The time does not come to any one who is pardoned, it comes and then when there is patience when there is use, when there is talking and a table, when there is even a slice of ham, it comes then to be announced that certainly understanding is what is not partial, it is so kind and strong and lengthy that certainly there is no disgrace.

A goose girl is no goose girl when there are geese. A church is a church. A ship is a ship. Thunder is thunder.

Silence which makes silence give that sense to all there is, silence which has light and water and unison and appetite and result and a motion and more exaggeration and no recklessness, silence which is there is not disturbed by expression.

There is no doubt of one thing there is no doubt that the real rate of establishing frequency is that which is used when there are numbers.

What comes out of silence. What comes out of silence is that which having that usefulness, that nature, and that fashion is not shown to be managed by the combination.

Surely silence is sustained and the change is sudden.

Supposing that there was no use for that which there is use for, supposing there was a bridge there where there is what there is, supposing all this and suppose that the enlightenment of everybody consisted in everybody having that condition, supposing all this, this is then the answer that silence gives in answer. The silence that is not preserved, the silence is the same as the characteristic which is not finished.

A pound of paper and no more string, a pound of string and no more leather, no pounds of anything else, does that make indifference, it does, it does make authority. All the calamity that shows origin and design is that which when it is understood is redetermined all this is entitled readministration. There is no use in a pencil, there is no use in any direction of succeeding in experience, there is not one single objection. The wholesale cloth is not handled with a sprinkler, it is so handled that when there is no obligation there is every inducement it is so handled that pathways are mended, it is so handled that there is a single sound. All the same there is no such language, it does not mean by that that the letters are smaller it does not mean that at all.

The strength of purpose which joins resignation with neglect and action with reducing and interpretation with resignation, the strength of purpose which connects distribution with desertion, and pink coloring with bathing, the strength of purpose which does not deny reddening, which does not authorize forbidding which does not disturb utilizing, the strength of purpose which adjusts desertion and exercise and resolution, the strength of purpose which organizes recognition and the disturbing of a perfectly satisfactory reception, the strength of purpose that withdraws no application and registers no reaction and suggests no opening, such a strength of purpose is resolute and reliant and reestablished, such a strength of purpose has the same service as the expression of recognition, such a strength of purpose has the borrowing of relaxation and the neglect of retardation, such a strength of purpose is selected selecting articles for recollecting, such a strength of purpose has origin and unison, such a strength of purpose has the surface of differentiation, such a strength of purpose has the organ of rehabilitation, such a strength of purpose is not pasting, it is not nailing, it is not swinging, it is not fighting, it is not saving, it is not utilizing the origin of sewing, all the same the strength of purpose is something, it is there, it is worried, it is in the precise situation that nothing shows, it is displaced, it is practiced, it even has a little place to spread a certain kind of preparation, it even is the kind of thing that has celebrations and bursts and specks and a kind of thing that has no particular name but is useful when it is not used in the end, in every way there is adaptation and that does not mean the same as the use of no excuse it means something that any one can see is opposite, it means what is coming to be realized as the intended metal to make nothing of and not be wasted. All the same there is that idea and if there are no more pieces why then there is a difference, there is a kind of way of saying that, there is no doubt that any one can join in with some member and surely if the rest makes no matter what is there any use to say there is no difference. There is none and so the whole thing shows that there is no pot and no dirty winter, all the same it does sound that way.

The shed and the house and any shelter shows mud in winter, it does and it shows in summer as well, it shows it in summer and in winter and it shows so well that anybody says something different, anybody shows something when something is showing, and something is showing whenever there is sauce and there always is that to save and put around. There always is some way to be reconciled to a difference. The whole thing is just shown in their being no celebrated invalid.

Mallorcan Stories

Romanonos no.

Maurer see.

Sun never sets.

Napoleon the third, cathedral.

McKinley's eagle.

Pope's prayers for peace.

Pins and needles ship.

Mallorcan stories.

Scenes. Actions and Disposition of Relations and Positions

Keep away and visit every Saturday. That is the only way to resist carrying all the attention when there is enough time. Time is not the thing any evening. Time is not the thing in the afternoon. There is not such a morning.

Not a time when there is occupation not such a time is the time that is not used and a knock that has no intention has some hope. It is not open to stay. There is a way to go away. That is not the use of that way. There is every return.

That which is not used is not a word it is enough. That which is asked is not a conversation, it is a piece of typewriting. And so there is no choice and yet if there were not would there be the exchange of everything. There is enough of that which is admitted often and sometimes to make any difference there comes to be of returning receiving. This is not what is kindly.

To keep on is to use what there is when there is enough of what is in daily use. That is not the medium that has that renewal.

It was the time of day to fill all day. The steadiness of that and that which is useful is the thing that is individual and a refusal to sing is one thing, to go on with a song is not wrong, to say that a use is not passed away when what is not said is not useful is one way to say that the quality that is the same has any experience.

Winter in a room and living there and many rooms and some air and all the same breath when food is not scarce and enough to eat if boiling is neat, all of that which does not pass away stays to place the work that has that presentation.

It was not dark and the light was not lost as that which was finishing the condition was the same if it was wood. It had not the same description. There are ways of admiring something.

There is a regular way of having that position that entering is not permission if there is no need of question. All the time that the talk is done there is a way to stay. To use anything is not the best way to have the right answer. All of the time is so placed that an awkwardness does not mean a pleasant entrance and there is the presence of that which is not necessary which induces a reception.

There is no dreariness in success and selling a picture and arranging an exhibition. There is no dreariness in four galleries and five cities and a packer. There is no dreariness in charging a direction and using up a special expression and seeing that sustain reorganisation. There is no dreariness in having some reception. There is no dreariness.

The time has come when seeing a different coat reminds some one of the time of the year and this does not make the same difference as a strong nature. This makes the particular use of some understanding and loss of hope and change of face. This does mean that the pleasant time has been near.

A darker day is not darker and the reason of that is that the impression being made it is continued until there is that change and the change is not coming, it has not that complexion.

The whole time is occupied when there is no place where the effect of that impression is not wearing into some shape and then when the copy is not perfect it is not prettier and the thing to show is the intention and the way to spend the whole piece is to move away and explain that in a letter. If there is a faithful action then belief is certain if there is no change of reputation. All that is received is answered when any subject is open and there is no place to sit and talk.

There is a way to say that the thing there is not in the square and when it is in the square if it is there then seeing it is enough if going into it is to be put there and there is a way to go in, the way to go out is if it is the same is the same. The whole of that time is not used when a little thing that remains has no meaning. Any little thing has that meaning. There is another way of being a dirty fellow.

If the effect of a defect is to allure and to change the base of any recognition then it is a wonderful way that makes a vision and that is what is if no one is the same and the one is only that one and is not any different. It has not any meaning that which is so plain that a screen keeps nothing clean. The air is not there. If there is no surface then the only way to choose is by example and there is not a way to compliment, there is a way to try any way and to have had no resolution and to have been received by some. To come into the relation means that if there is a response something has been said. This is not too exact. It does not exhaust a preparation.

Not lading the leaning and not exhilerating the creation and the tending of the flowering is practically all of that thing. Arranging the renewal of refusing by accepting is the only sweetness succeeding is not subduing. Succeeding is not staggering when it is not proceeding and the best plan is the day that has less provision. The whole place is one place and the place that is that place is the place where the hope is that which has no time. The only withdrawing of nothing that has longing is the time that it takes to say that there is joining.

Arrive and wait and say to no other that there is no deception when there is relaxation. Not to say anything is obliging.

To have that position and to meet that destination and to show the way which is not changed as a pleasant greeting and that reception is all there is of all reunion. It does not copy the relation and it does have that movement.

To see no harm and to see all the charm and to have possession and to defend permission if there is any way to ask it is to despise one another if there is the same reason. What can be used if all that is held is supported by everything. What can be some change. The whole place is there to see and to go there means that the same thing is begun. The regard is different.

Leading in hearing, that is to be tired, that is what is the way to hear more and always then there is that result, there is a change. Leading in hearing and then that is being tired and being then staying and being remaining and exchanging that for that thing.

Not feeding eating, that is eating in feeding, eating is what eating is and feeding is what feeding is and eating and feeding that is the use of that receptacle which is not empty. Nothing is empty and open and everything is full when it is opening and closing. Closing is nothing.

The open way the open way and the closing way, the open way is not the origin of that which is interesting, the parts of speech are not the same, they have some origin.

The whole place has that which it has when it is found and it is there where there is more room. Room has not that expression. It has no change in a place. It is not dirty, there is no cleaner passage and the best way to have it all express that is to cook a dinner. There is enough to get a suit that is not had when there is no hope. That is the difference if there is much and there is much more.

To place one by the side of another and they both have something that is their color to do that and not languish is to look then and see that relinquish what it will have when it remains where it is to be. This is not foolish, it is a part of all distraction. It is the intention of all dissension. It is the measure of all language.

To see that a piece is used where there is no receipt is one way to express that things which are different have that resemblance and this does not mean that there is not a denial, this means that the same room is different when the furniture is colored. To color furniture is to say that the furniture is wider and the walls are taller and the light is clearer. To change often is to say that the use of something is the same.

To answer when there is no question, to intend to follow when there is no plunging, to embody that which has that knowledge, all that is the way to remain with the little button that has a button-hole. This is so attached.

It is not there to squeeze that which has no meaning, it is not there to squeeze. The order that has not been begun is the one that sends ten away. The ten stay some where and the time is longer. The use of it is that there is more in any long way.

The distaste for cold meat does not lead to eating. It leads to everything. This is not all of a feeling. It is enough to suggest any little thing.

The way to thank is to respect the whole opening and the way to despise one apple is to choose another. This can be done by weighing. It can also be done by looking.

The way to use a quotation is to hope that it will be heard when it is spoken. That is the way to make that sound.

It is not the same that which is not sad with that which is repeated. It is not the same and the sight is so different that there is that hope and no more excitement. Then the change is there and there is all the comparison. The rising of the wedding is not the same as one child if there are no children but one child has that to use and there is enough to give it a cold. This is not seasonable. This is not the way to despair.

The heat of hearing is not the silence of answering and nothing is produced when the question is the same as the name. That is one way to answer and there might have been more but it was different, it was the same.

The whole district was not used when a place was borrowed and the pleasure in that union is the same as giving permission. The hope of that intention is what keeps the answer from being prepared and if it is prepared then it is printed. There is enough intermission.

To cause a special heat and to be colder is not the way of having any custom. There is no irregularity in that. It is too plain. The time for that grief is not in the head it is in the origin of salvation. So there has come to be no neglect and there does not waste any order when the time which is all day is the same time and if not older then not that difference in spending. It is not all the same if nothing is spent. It is not all the same because then there are all the things there that have come to be gotten by searching and finding something. This which happens often uses the time that is not plain to see. It is not so discouraging and the whole thing is not so full as it would be if there was not another. The resemblance is there.

There is no paint when there is nothing to dirty. There is never any change in that and the silence is not there when it is empty and there is no intention to show more than enough. All the time there is the exact way of changing it a little and not mixing more and that is not the origin of industry, the origin of industry is the evening of recitation. There is some past playing of singing every past evening. This is not more than the future.

A pleasing way to use a broom is to lean upon the wall and not do more than make any one who is the one welcome. This if it is pleasing is pleasing and working is industry. That does not change everything. Intending to remove the dirt does not destroy the variegated color. The color is not a stain. It shows what glass is when there is a reflection. This peaceable pursuit is so earnest and so steady that there is no remark made when all the time there is that description and the way is that way as there is what is said as the way that is that way. The door is not so open.

It was not dark and the weather was not clear and the sunshine was not gloomy and the color was not red, it was not dusty and the window was not open and the stove was not shut and the table was set. There was no pepper and there was some salt and there was more chicken and there was more sweet. There was cauliflower and there was cake and there was no steamer and there was butter and there was potato and there was cucumber. There was no cream and there was banana and there was cream later and there was orange mixture. All the potato that was eaten had been roasted and the pigeons were kept and the fruit was finished and there was another platter.

All the time is dark and there is a light and the time to think is the time to paint and the grey blue purple is the red rose color and the pink white cover is the fine broken china. The object of more is to stay that way and the use of the present is to mingle that future and the presence of all is the use of that and the pleasure of that date is to separate in weight. The time to express is to receive that attention and the change in tone is not the disgust. The dwindling of more is not to show that wear, the spring of the change is the loosening of that. The mingling of this is not the spurt and the winning of the white is not the soiling of the black. The tin that presses has not a hollow sound and the color blue is not so pure and true. The best of all is the presence of the best and the way to stay is to sit long in that way. No way to stay is a way to go away. No way is a way. No way is way. There is enough to sound the note and the little flute is there where there is no air and the blowing is strong and the blowing is long and the air is there where there is no air. Solemnly to stay is not a sad way. To stay away is not the glory of that day. To begin the time is not the time to dim the evening and enough decision has no origin. This is that result.

Labor and not long makes a sad song and that is not true when the name is short and the preparation is the same. There was a particular time of day to hope more and this was not all of the morning and the evening and the beginning of the afternoon. This was after finishing a piece of the copying that gives splendor to any situation and this was also the time when having stayed long enough there was no more explanation. All the best permission lies in correspondence and more permission is not used when there is no distance. This does not disentangle vice. This makes a season last longer and the cold weather which is not such very cold weather has the happiness of expecting to rain. This does not warrant all that intention.

In the time to wait and tell the truth there is no more dispute than if there had been more time. This does show the antiquity of acknowledging that a morning is used for something. To deny that is to deny everything and to determine that would need no hesitation. This is not what there is to think. This is more of the presence of witnesses.

This which is assured would make the nervous one not so worried when the answer is not coming. A great many risks need that advice. A dash of the following is so distinct and the time to send more is what is not hopeless. All the time and all the date and all the superfluous wood and porcelain show the mark and the use and the continuation of retention.

Patience is not plenty and waiting is not abusing the intention. Any little thing is more than a question. Any attempt is a return of a permission. To be attentive and intended and make that mistake is not more deceptive than anything.

Present the detachment and have the words continue to come there and this will not make a tune slower and destroyed, this will not at all be that. To put that question does not mean the mention of an author. To repeat the name is not the same when there is no chair. To draw it in is one way to approach the place that was not there to intrude. This does not make the objection clearer it just makes the same tune.

It was thought that as the mountain of something which does not grow does not grow, it was once thought, it was thought that the change was not so old and the age was older. It was thought that the same thing pressed would be put on there where there was no custom. It was thought that there would be some more age. It was intended and there was that which was earnest, it was intended that the obligation which was not climbing would lead to the showing of anything and it was there where there was hope that the time was. The whole thing was not the same.

To open a door and turn in the direction that the one entering will bow shows so little quick movement that there is a way to advance. And so to be timely, to have that hesitation, to bring a chair up and to enter into standing does not occupy the whole evening if there is some singing.

That is settled that which needs some introduction. It is not necessary to refuse it. Any evening there is more hesitation. Any thickening of the coat shows something and there is a use of that word.

It was all right, there was that hesitation, there was the time of the afternoon and there was one evening of some which were those which were evenings. There was that and the best way to show that is to have more than each little piece not used as a question. This can commence that. There is no perplexity, there is that abuse, there is more, there is something. There is no bit of more than was used by any writing. There can be more printing. There can be intending lending. There can be that interest.

A peculiarity of the steps and the entrance is that it is not so peculiar as there are more calling out something. This would change a beginning if there had not been a setting. This which was was the time to do that and the result is different.

So the whole thing means this that if there is a continual use of it all there can be and there is the expression of that emotion.

The pleasantest anticipation is that reaction and more time is then spent and the whole place is lonely. There are four in it.

If the cleverness of that copy means that a voice is louder then certainly there is not that connection that there is as there is what has been lasting. This is not so dirty. Cold water is not cleaner.

Pound the little time-table and then spread it so that reading it is not any more simple than it was. This has that charm and every little quality has that intensity. It is not more distinguished to be whiter than to be redder, to be taller than to be shorter. The meaning has more necessity.

A beaming expression does not mean that the eye is so clear that there is no fatigue.

The drag that keeps that important is not spread out. This is a reason why if that which is left to do is done there is no admission. All the same there could be more if the direction was necessary and it is so full that there is always that hope and that room.

Blessed are the patient particulars manifesting that hesitation so that when there is no hope there is always a guide. In the languages that one used and sung some words are longer than others and this has so much seasoning and so strong a fence that certainly the tangle is not made by more than the three words that come being divided by there being no more. This does take the time.

All the beginning has that intelligence and certainly a useful time to make requests is when there are any addresses and there are always addresses in places. This does mean that need and that use and that return and that plentiful remorse. There is so much to say.

A timidity that has no use in a boast is not that which tells about drawing. The continuance of that is not more than promised, it is continued.

To have the land behind when there is no sea has that to do which is not settling that which is more than free. It is so natural that the opinion is there.

To detail more is to ask that question, it is to refuse to answer, it is to add that to it. That is some excuse and more would not be enough and certainly that way is that authority. To control the time is where there is an impression.

About the time when a book is borrowed is the time to return it and leave it. This makes any one having that light not need to put it where it is to be put.

Adding any more to a change is to occupy what is offended and the refusal to go together may mean that. This when there is a song does not make a choice depend upon meaning.

That rising and falling which singing is doing means that drawing a chair closer can be repeated. This would be more than that interruption. There is no place for that time.

To sweeten a lucky star means that a sad way to sweep together the leavings is the one way to continue favor. And that which is most active is more active as industry has that meaning. It has. It has that meaning.

The surplus weight is inside and when it is put into the pockets it is not heavier, this gives some feeling of not lingering. The authority that makes that lonesome is not the same as disgust. It is always different sometime.

This makes an attempt more tedious than it would be if the change were coming and the presence of that is some little quality. There can be agreement and the spectacle is the same.

Then this which is not too much is often and so there comes to be that time and certainly that which was spent was not wasted as waste has not that meaning.

So there is no empty place. All the time the chairs are there and there are enough tables. Wood has not that meaning.

This is not a slice and all the juice that is dry is not so dry when the hair and all is fair. This does not make a greeting any less pleasing and certainly that which is done is not so discouraging. There is no hope to use.

Paint the little piece of wood more and there is no way to know that which is sore. This does not mean more rarity than an exception. This does not displace waiting for a wedding.

To ponder and not plaster any section is so long to stay in the house where the meals are given if there is food provision that enough of it means something. It does not mean a color in a symptom. That is not the only way to hope.

See Thomas bring the grain, see the grain have the color that grain has when grain is growing in any winter which is any summer. See Thomas bring the rain and see that the thunder is not the thunder that any rain raining longer is having thunder when having thunder. See Thomas bring what Thomas is bringing and the load is not lighter as Thomas turns the shadow darker. Thomas has no spring of water, Thomas has the color brighter. Thomas is the time to stay. Thomas hears what any source can supply. Thomas not darkly not lightly, Thomas does the chamber over.

The ruling of the pencil and the farm, the ruling of a shadow and the grain, the ruling of the woman who gave away what was not there to stay, any ruling is the same and the line is there and has that prospect.

So closely was it passed that there was not more space than there was and so sweet are the pleasures of the rest that a quarrel with a cousin has the same result.

Pass it on to the bottle, houses in the corner have shutters, a little tree is not lonesome because the leaves are not bright.

The presence of the necessary question does not mean that a kiss is to be given. The sweetening of chicken is not all that is remembered when the form was such that buttons were plentiful and the surroundings were there. That was not any way to say that the change was the same.

All the long expression that means a longer state of natural example is not so pardonable as everything that is in some instant. The back and the waist and the presence of not any splinter, the sundown and the kitchen and a table with a window and a napkin ring in winter, all the presence of the most, all the longing of that summer, a pleasure and a sign and there is no chance to refuse any chair.

To the rug that has that hole and that color, to the wood that has that color and that white, to the table that has that carpet and that erection, to the bed that has that shade and that carving, to the lantern that has that light and that cover, to the shapes that have that decoration and that derivation, to the floor that has that surface and that meaning, to that light that has that look and that garden, to that wall that has that line and that concentration, to the best that has that choice and that color to all and there is something sounding, to that and there is no witness signing, to more and the explanation is not a mistake, to less and the time is when there is that to pass, to all the length and there is more of that then, there is not any refusal to resist a smell.

This is not the compliance of the teeth and there is no more force than that out loud. A plain paper is often used.

Pasting nothing in a little book is the way to use the paper and nothing is then lost and that is such a collection. The season that weather is colder is that when there has been that change. If all that is full has that liquor then the time to drink is in the beginning and the beginning has the complete return of the use of handling. That is the kindness of September and October. All the months that are the same have this in common.

To desert the red beard and to have no change of color means that the beard is all the same age. There can be more shaving than illumination. This does not change every red color.

If the shape is the same and the use of the evening is not much then a dress has that meaning and closing it is not music. Something is not quiet then.

All right where the well is shining and the waves are never higher than the water, cover the slipping ocean and do not mingle more smell. See the remaining accentuation and explain more and more and not more so. See the rattle that was not eaten and use a pen-wiper soon too.

The patent that was taken did mean more than all the work that was spent every day in the morning. No grief means time and no change means divorce, and no pleasure means all eaten, and no birthday has meaning. This which has a pain in that nose means the left when the right is mentioned. All is not darkness when the lights which are out are burning. The tall cat has so much particular face that the garment is not more beautiful than a great number. Pain and particular pleasing pleasure and more than particular plain explaining weather all this is more than told and a past violin is not remaining. And yet the last little Monday is not every Sunday and the whole cheese is not frightened and the question is not all considered and more aid engagements were not special. All this and no more is so much more and the language and all the kernel was the time that solitude changed in going to another dinner. Lunch was often.

To be the article of the wound and to have no purser is not any more of a delight than is mutton. This was so fully eaten that every day there was cooking.

Not that startling sage-brush, not that mortal melodrama, not any fluent symptom, not more simple feather sofa, not more cloud than most of the members of the breathing place, not a joiner and not a retroactive syndicate none of all the powder was more blue than a yellow plant.

This was not that memento, this was not that parallel syncope, this was the half curve of the splinter, this was not every mounting, this was the perfect parliament, this was no dope.

Show the place where the reproduction has that ease and drowning has a figure. The lovely lane is not in sight where the hair is yellow. If the change comes sooner and there is no stroke then the time of day has that to recommend it quite.

So then the platform which is not raised is occupied and that means that if there is a meeting a delay is offered and surely the use of that is not long when there is no question. If there is a little quality and any quality is that then the whole hope is so arranged that a cloth has that short length.

And so there is no excuse, there is every mistake there is every position. An earnest protection has some meaning and the same thing has the charge of the place of no exchange. And still it does happen, it has happened and there is more of that. There is no such expression.

A tomb and the time is not Christmas, the time and the way is not a carpet cover, the leather and it is not water and the window and it is not a silk mixture, the bright season and there is a composition, all the moon has not pain in a conglomeration.

There is none, there is no preceding catastrophe, there is no period and there is no preparation. There is not much when all is not the same and the change has not been indicated.

Why is a sour pear-tree in a blossom bee, because it is so pleasant to remain in the summer detachment. That is not the excuse for the box and the opening. That is not the way to refuse that gesture. So then the union has a widow and the mother has a father and littler and there is no length much longer.

Jumping is not anything if a little way is behind the elbow and the knee. This is the season of rejoicing and the moment to have a denial of advice. If it is a pity it is not the same pity as more toast. It can be so warm that there is sunshine and it can not be what is helped by appetite.

Telling the last time that a green and mixed repeater was not lost and bought for more did not pass as it was not told. So the beginning was made and there was some use. They would not leave the thoughts together. This did not make enough separation. There was still more to behold and the time that was so frequent was any afternoon. This came to silence any day and the single attention was such that any candy was the same as eaten. This was not the whole school. There was more copying of drawing.

So the tune and the light was not the light of any moon. The rain was the same and the stairs were cleaner. There was an exchange and this did not borrow trouble.

Settle and there will be dinner ready, settle and return the cake today, serve the chicken and have cream all ready, season everything and pour the oil away, have the salad and the cheese between, see the cream and love the candy there, pass the day and eat the rest away, stay away and do not shed the tear.

If a duty is so done that there is a chance let no one who passes any way engage a room. Let them do so, show them that direction, have the language and do not distribute more than all of that selection, this makes knowledge all increasing and makes the return of patient splendor show the shadow that there is in that intention. This is not a dream. This has the same thing as the pleasant conversation and request. A song is not more than necessary.

If the message is sent and received and if the tunes have words then certainly there will be soon the center piece which has not been removed. Every little flower has a number. There is that way to question.

A regret with more comes when the tickets which are not serious were written and the same time was stated. Then there comes to be not a surprise but a result. There is no more than any enquiry.

A walk is not where the door shows a light, a walk is where there is a request to describe a description. A walk is when a place is not to be exchanged. There is a respect in every walk.

There is a result in every walk and the turn is there, the foot and the boot have that union that there can be slippers. Talking of the return of that shows that there will not be an opening. There is no reason to exchange the joke.

No mending, no mining, no motto, no mine, no pin, no purchase no salad no oyster, no practice, no more, no thought, no happy day and the best is there and there is everywhere. Say it all in the morning, put it off in the day, have it come in the evening, use the tune every day, say it and please the organ, laugh and remain the same, coughing goes by favor, and coming has a day to stay any way some way that way.

Full and the tune, a shaking of the ends is not paling in the more and then if there is no exercise there must be that and anyhow why should there be an implacable substitute. There is no exaggeration.

All and one and any place to make a gold color show on paper, that is not the evening, that is what is heard. Any pleasure is the one and every evening is no matter. All this does not make that weigh more than again. There is no patient perfume. This is not the sign of release.

Blame no more than the mouth and this makes that regulation. There is that use and there is no way and there must be that and there shall be a disposition. That is the sign. Any language cannot be foreign.

Lumber is not brick and brick is redder. The path of a rug is that which is not returned. Enough has been put that way.

Pile on more potatoes than corn-meal and more sausage than chicken and a little more tender oil than egg and all the eggs are fresh. So fresh and fair is no behaviour when the whole thing has disappeared. A taste and a branch and a sucking of the day and the calm and the man and the noise so wettingly. This which sees that which mourns that which colors any moon all the paste is so straight and a scissors has a pleasing line to measure and there is no hidden treasure.

See that painful delivery of a portion of more that has squares, see it and emphasize more than any afternoon, emphasize a special rate.

Please all trembling when there is a time to rise, please it all and do nothing nicely. So serene, so much a moon, so white and always plain, a sensation is not altered by more being mentioned.

A time to stay is when there is the feeling in it and it has been done. Why should no hope be more. Why should it. It does show faces and if there are there one is smaller, there is no reason why a beard should be there. It is mostly in sight and blindness is satisfying. There is no blindness where the talk is cheap.

Laugh the basket into a little glass and all the point is painted. So soon is the jewel and so dirty the splinter that any march is a distinction. There is that way. If and there is no accusing, if the sight means that surely the illumination is incandescent then surely something is expected of the direction which is opposite. There is that union and the face is there. So soon does a cork mean closing and the belt open. This is no time to stay. A time for splashing is not ever with a brick color. No shaking is too great for a head. This does not mean coming after. It means that that is never over. It means more and it has no splinter, it does not mean samples.

A pale rose is a smell that has no fountain, that has upside down the same distinction, elegance is not coloured, the pain is there.

It is so clearly pleased that which is benumbed and articulate and if in replying there is the indication of a sentence then surely the whole thing is hurled. The house has that patience. The story is in the evening. A single recital makes a hat, more makes no more cloth than pleating.

All the same there is silence, there is uneasiness, there is an appetite, all the same there is silence, there is the tune, there is the birthday. All the same any Christmas is nearer. All the same more talk is solemn. All the same there is a special way. All the same there is left a pint. All the same the fruit is quince. All there is is that shape. The return is extinguished.

A life-long dismissal means an admission to each one. This passes more places and not any more faces. This does show the joint when there is chicken. The salad has cheese and there is no more added table. It is so large that there is a window seat.

So much persistance, so much elbow place, so much single authority and able china, so much more and a cold bigger, that means that there is thieves. Staining anything is not underwear. So soon there is more motion.

Plead the use of a magazine and send more card paper, this is so tiring and reading a letter is the same as writing an answer. Something was handed to some one.

A dark tunnel has no open shelter and to be dark is to be left lighter. This does not mean that there was a shadow, it does not mean that a shadow has a painting or a passage it simply means that it is unique and that there is an explanation.

Keep a pint which is not fuller, keep it and throw away everything, a little gain means that wood is not burning, a little gain means that there is no answer, a little gain is a little gain.

To see a sample of cheese means that the authority which mingles excellence with scratching is such that a new beginning has no swelling. All the tunes are played and the voice is louder. There is no repair.

Plunder and an appetite, seasoning and sensitive singing all this makes that come back. There is a solemn winter. There is that.

To fit a car to the same stand as the pressing of every button means that there is a decision. So much unity does show friendship. A tangle is no less. There are no narratives.

A plain pet does know how to draw. Drawing is a sin. There is no picture. There is a comparison. All round is the collection. There are parts anyway.

No part and no more, no part and never.

Nicely and the shape and all that section that is the time to use a weeding. A precise desolation is so distracted. All the curtain of river is running to be green and yellow, all the lifting is by sitting, all the time is on the bricks, there is no seat there, there is no church there, there is no church, there is nowhere there. There is no crying. There is no next butter. There is. There is more shape to leave lower.

A lame stool is one that has three lengths and a suspender, there is a collar. There is no disorder.

If the precious sand is rich and there is union then there is something. If the precious sand is poor then there is poverty. If there is more then there is anywhere. What is choosing. It is the predicate when there is illness. There is no sickness there is a package. Are the eyes finer. They are there yesterday. They enter the weather.

Lightning has no meaning, gleaning has choosing descending, bread has origin, a taste is spreading. There was once a made ready lifter. There was once a birthday. There was a saleable afternoon. There was no deceiver. There was none.

A little thing to send in and have a pain from singing, a little thing and no person who is willing is signalling, no person needs a shoe, every one says what they do, this does not mean that hopping is swinging. It does that in the mean time. It does that there heartily. Heartiness is the same principle. It is no challenge. It is not more a church. It is not most a circle. It is not a vestibule. It is a single place of growing grass. Grass is not deserving. It has all that to show. It shows a marked meadow. It is not by the baker. Fishing is sudden. There is a decision. All yesterday is passed.

A page of no addresses does not mean a mistake it means that there are places where the whole family is glad to eat together. This is not a sign of anger it is the necessary sunshine of the country and to be pleasant is so close that there is no change. The last time that there was an address there was no change. If the ones turned away they ate in a little place and ate there. If they did not show that they were enjoying it. They did please that most and they collected that there and it was a hope and a silent time was not present. There was no explanation. There was the hope of the remains being recently for that and best taken nearer and not passed into the same time. This did make the change stationary and really any authority is in the language and singing is not a victim, there is no joke, the time is the same and the place is not let, there is a little square center and no center, there is a simple dessert, any cheese is darker, any fish is lighter, the same thing is the place unset, the same time is tomorrow, there is no date to marry if marrying is replaced by having that having been done. There is no doubt of the mention of that and there is a taste of the meaning which is not a waste. There was an exchange in decision. All the way is plenty if there is the time to choose a pope, there is no choice there then, there is no sense in a waiter. If the time has that note then certainly the choice of a seat means that two are not taken. The time is given and the invitation is not pink when there is water. The little bunch is not known and more is mentioned. All of it.

A dark net is not a veil and a veil is not long, it is not longer than following repetition. Granted that there is an hour that is half after six, granted that does that mean that there is any use in being willing to have no other meeting, and yet it must mean something and almost anything is that and it is very likely, it is most likely that there is the time and the place, it is most likely not often, it is most likely that there is a longer day-light, it is most likely.

Ham and celery and chicken, a roast is frying, the ham if it is thickening is squeezing roast beef into a mayonnaise dressing. There is oil, there is cake, there is chicken. No absence is fonder.

All right to discuss that matter all right and the nature is fonder when there is no choice of kissing. It is fonder and Saturday evening is mingling borrowing some one, not borrowing some one, that is to say there is an offering.

All like a thing, all like winking, all like thinking, all like sinking, all like that, all like a thing, all like massaging, all like thinking, all like that, all like a vision, all like that, all like distinguishing, all like that, all like that thing, all like that, all like thinking.

No old jerks, no old news, all is wet and there is no time in a day. Every day is not away. The morning is sooner. If the morning is sooner then the habit is spread, it is spread and there is a whole row. Every row has an earthquake, every ring has a color, every piece there is is as different as it is when there is a comparison by putting them all together. To be so particular shows that there is a difference in copying and copying is copying a picture, and copying is copying a piece of sugar, and copying is copying china. All copying is so arranged that there is no trembling when joy is filling. All the time that sadness has is the time that sadness is. All the temper is in place, darkness is not looking like this. No sorrow is loaned for the succession of friendly business intervention. A research means more. There is a cause in extreme recognition. No place is taken. Time for bells is ringing and breaking nothing is disturbing urging. There is a piece.

A room, a paper, a fig, a chase, a poison cup, a trace of a hat, all this together is no disappearance. The joy prevails and the season is Sunday. The end is beyond that.

If there is no question and an answer is not a toilet, if there is no question is there any strangeness in a garden. Certainly not, the danger is not any color. It has the bloom and the sign of an early summer. There is no necessity to deface anything. An escape is not needed.

There is one question. In not asking a question the permission which is continued is so courteous that there is no moon-light. The time does keep the rain from startling more than a diary. This shows that there is no question and an answer is no meeting.

The point then consists in there coming to be so much recent relief that the advance is simultaneous and surely if the same step is there there is no treachery. The interchange is worshipped with a boat. There is no time in the use of money. A little means more of that same multiplication and in any case there came that time. There is no worry and this does not mean that there is that absence, it does not even mean more, it does mean that a change is enveloping. It does not mean that it exists.

A tune is splendor and a turn is that which a mark on the floor does not chasten. So much sun is not a sunbeam. So much clarity is not stifling. Surely the representation of an uncherished filling is not more odious than mankind. The thought which determines a flight is the firmness of the plant that is not boiling. All the time which is of use is that which when the change has the same resemblance as some origin shows no mixture of more capping. The necessity is not ungainly and gaining that is what is the obstacle in staging. It is no place when the basket is there and baskets have no pink ribbon, they have glass. A piece of the same is cheaper.

All the same there is an exceptional use of the point of a resprinkler. It does not mean the same as the future. There is that quality.

A pink and that is a flower and smelling, a pink and the name is different and has some when there is intonation, a pink and the rumor has not spread, it is ordinary. If so and the opposition is astonishing then surely there is that destruction and no suspicion is more, there is a report. All the same there is more nervousness than retraction and more in sight than outside and in any case a name is there. Two of them are the same.

Was the explosion that authority, did it succeed more than yesterday, was there tomorrow before, these are not questions asking, they are not existing missing, they are so applied that there is no joke, there is no pleasure. All the same the standard is there and the separation has a position, it has no repudiation, it has no hurrying centralization, it has nothing there. If to be there is mentioned then the whole response is the occasion. It is and there is more. There is no answer. There is turning. Turning is not a victim, it has no protection, it has no authority, it has a receipt.

Time to state and to circle the whole thing to be an island and not water, this is the season of fishing and in and by circling there is no surface, there is all there is and the time to rain is not the time to station swimming. This is no disgrace.

All the same there is a splendid piece of special soft sour and silk lining, there is and there is a mistake. An object is not more used than a mixture and surely if the time was chosen it was not there beside the swift selling mother of colored clothing, and yet there is no sale and there is a reason, there is the reason that anything is the sign of a use and using nothing is not a pointed selection, it is more than that, it is collecting.

This does not mean that antiquity is more antiquity, it means that the origin of eating is eating and the renewal of the wading is not swimming. It does not mean that, it means that the time and place and more is so satisfied that there is no place, and any place is no vacation. And yet that is not so narrow and actual, not at all, if it were and it is, if it were then certainly they would celebrate the result, they do not that is to say one does if there is nothing, the other does if there is nothing. There is that establishment when there is no land and any land that shows the line is that and is one. Any extra way is the way of speaking. There is no use in no more.

The King or Something (The Public Is Invited To Dance)

Letting me see.

Come together when you can.

Have it higher. You mean that lake.

What was that funny thing you said.

I am learning to say a break.

I am learning to say a clutch.

I am learning to say it in french. A house or lions.

A young lion looks like a dog. We laugh. I am not satisfied.

You have to feel what you write.

PAGE II

I hear a noise.

PAGE III

Did I say I was a mechanic and a chauffeur but not of the working classes not of the class of the working classes. I saw a funeral. All along the street. This is not inauguration. It was Sunday. Cook said he was sorry he drove us there.

PAGE IV

Letting me see.

Nellie has a gift.

PAGE V

Do you mind whose presents.

We didn't bring them up.

PAGE VI

By hand.

PAGE VII

Nellie.

PAGE VIII

Now then yesterday.

Now then for today.

Nellie is poor that is to say she is not spending more money.

Josephine and Genevieve.

A cup.

I am so happy.
In counting gifts.

Yes.

And in mixing ceramics.

You don't mean to make them.

Oh no to give them.

Oh yes.

PAGE IX

Were you pleased with this.

Are you fond of blue flowers. Yes if you pick them. We will pick them together.

PAGE X

Not after you learn to drive.

PAGE XI

Not that.
Not that today.

PAGE XII

Next to come.

Next to come to me.
I speak splendidly.

Say it to come Egyptian.

I mean Bohemian.

Birds are not very tired.

Boys are being prepared.

Laugh and see.

Don't try it again.

I wish there was a market for chairs.

Do you mean that by that.

PAGE XIII

I will not say yes.

PAGE XIV

Two cooks.

Any two cooks together.

Dismiss all the servants.

She did.

PAGE XV

We didn't.

Allow me to differ.

PAGE XVI

Did you say it did.

PAGE XVIII

Very likely I missed it.

PAGE XIX

Turn turn.

PAGE XX

You must never hurry yourself.

No indeed.

Now I understand.

PAGE XXI

Think a minute think a minute there.

PAGE XXII

Wait a minute.
When will you remember about me.

Tomorrow.

Yes.

Tomorrow.

Yes.

PAGE XXIII

A splendid instance of good treatment.

PAGE XXIV

There was a little apple eat.

By a little baby that is wet.

Wet from kisses.

There was a good big cow came out.

Out of a little baby which is called stout.

Stout with kisses.

There will be a good cow come out.

Out of a little baby I don't doubt.

Neither does she covered with kisses.

She is misses.
That's it.

PAGE XXV

Seventy figs.

Apples are scarce.

Melons have not a good flavor.

Chickens are very good.

PAGE XXVI

A little inclination to the hotel Alcazar.

A little inclination did you say I am taking lessons for it.

Indeed you are.

Convocation.

PAGE XXVII

Did you want me to mention churches.

If you please.

PAGE XXVIII

Surrounding cities.

Selfish cats.
And birds.

Birds are flying.

So are automobiles.

Listen to me when I speak.

Because I speak.

I dislike even raspberry vinegar.

We used to have it in California.

PAGE XXIX

Lizzie says yes.

She had a child.

PAGE XXX

Are you wretched.

PAGE XXXI

I change the place.

Not at all.

I will sit.

This is the place for me.

You are not insulted.

By any one.

Every one says oh yes.

And I am very well pleased.

PAGE XXXII

Yes oh yes.

PAGE XXXIII

Any place to stay.

Today.

I know what I bought.

PAGE XXXIV

Conduct Mr. Louis.

I say conduct Mr. Louis.

Flat pains.

PAGE XXXV

Neat kings.

Afternoon watches.
Clouds in summer.

Rain.

Boxing flowers.

I do not mean white flowers.

PAGE XXXVI

Credit me with wishes.

I do.

I will.

PAGE XXXVII

Why doesn't he begin.

PAGE XXXVIII

Lots of pages.

PAGE XXXIX

Night today.

Tonight today.

I can sit sinking.

Have a reproach.

PAGE XL

Why do you mean to attack.

PAGE XLI

The Cow.

Yes Caesars.

The Cow.

Oh you blessed blessed blessed planner and dispenser and joy.

My joy.

The Cow.

PAGE XLII

Such a successful morning afternoon.

PAGE XLIII

Just like the prince's.

PAGE XLIV

Pages of eating.

PAGE XLV

Pages of heating.

PAGE XLVI

Not a word of warning to them.

PAGE XLVII

I make feeble crackers.

Strong in birth.

Willful in argument.

Planned to take me.

Soldier wishes.

We wish an automobile.

We have stalls.

Stables.

In weather stains.

Do you mean it. All of us mean it. Call us horses. We are afraid of horses.

PAGE XLVIII

Sing to me resolutely.

Mr. Louis says not.
Joseph.

PAGE XLIX

I have infinite patience.

PAGE L

Count in places.

Why do you need perquisites.

Because furniture is heavy.

It is heavy here.

And light in the hurry of needing water.

Why do you satisfy her.

I satisfy her with holes.

We were wicked on slates.

You mean roofs.

Roofs and nations.

PAGE LI

Can you praise me.

Can you praise me.

PAGE LII

Nominal general.

PAGE LIII

This is a shore.

PAGE LIV

Great civil destinies.

PAGE LV

Come to me Louisa in a limousine.

We were walking.

We were walking and talking.

PAGE LVI

Lift brown eggs.

To me.

PAGE LVII

Have you splendid pearls.

Have we splendid pearls.

PAGE LVIII

I always think it is the best.

This.

And the name.

PAGE LIX

Call me for the chance.

Does the moonlight trouble you.

It troubles me here.

PAGE LX

This is the way to point.

That is the way.

PAGE LXI

Not a Greek God.

How do you say that.

PAGE LXII

I have a name.

She has the same.
Expression.

She looks like the soldier.

And we too are dull.

PAGE LXIII

I can just see them processioning.

I will not write a play.

Thank you kindly for your kind wishes.

PAGE LXIV

Let me see the sloop.

We used to use that word before.

In the evening and they met with attention.

PAGE LXV

I read about a star.

I heard a star.

I saw a star.

I hear a star.

I see it.

Do you where.

There.

Don't you see.

It's an aeroplane.

Oh yes I heard it before.

So did I.

I do not care to bother.

We do.

That is quite natural.

Come again.

PAGE LXVI

Scratching her head.

Marcel.

Oh Marcel.

Spots.

Cleaner.

Nuns.

Wishes.

Does she neglect the subject.

I like what I feel.

Folette.

Hear.

Mrs. Beffa.

What is the name of the girl.

I wish I had such a child.

PAGE LXVII

Can I speak to you for his sister.

This is what I like to think.

Yes of course.

PAGE LXVIII

You do not understand our grievances.

We do not understand their subjects.

They are not annoyed by each other.

We have flights in aeroplanes at Buke. Spell it with a t.

Did you hear me wishing.

I wish to go away.
Expect Muriel.

We expect Muriel

Mrs. Tudor expects Muriel. We have no such wishes. We wish to hear that she has another name, Ethel or Muriel.

PAGE LXIX

Some people are heated with linen.

PAGE LXX

Can you pronounce it.

PAGE LXXI

Can you see why I am inspired.

I can recognise the cause of inspiration.

So can a great many people.

This is laughable.

Come pleasantly.

And sing to me.

PAGE LXXII

Counts and counting.

War liberty and success.

The window says then and there is a refusal.

Let this be a lesson to millionaires.

PAGE LXXIII

Ernest says that they will not give money.

They are not charitable.

PAGE LXXIV

Come Connect Us.

PAGE LXXV

Lead him to me.

PAGE LXXVI

Come to me easily.

Come to me there and tell me about speeches.

Speeches and my cousin.

He will not send the van.

Yes he will send the van.

And when he can.

He can send it.

PAGE LXXVII

When she comes does she leave her kitchen dirty.

When she comes does she wash the silver.

When she comes do they all say how do you do.

This seems very little after it all.

PAGE LXXVIII

When she comes say yes.

When she comes say she is.

PAGE LXXIX

When she comes say he is.

PAGE LXXX

I do not like stories mixed in in a story. This is an instance the colored regiment. Yes I see. Of course you can be angry about it.

PAGE LXXXI

A splendid attraction and a visitor. Was she sorry.

PAGE LXXXII

How much did Harriet pay for her suits.

PAGE LXXXIII

Can you think about me.

PAGE LXXXIV

Do you think about the Chinese.

PAGE LXXXV

Can you eat.

PAGE LXXXVI

Do you eat.

PAGE LXXXVII

Leave them alone.

PAGE LXXXVIII

Can you mean to be sleepy.

PAGE LXXXIX

Can you not neglect to answer.

Yes I can.

PAGE XC

An educated mark.

Educated leisurely.

You can not despise him. Can you despise him.

PAGE XCI

I want to be simple and think.

PAGE XCII

You are very ready to do it. No I don't think so.

PAGE XCIII

Can you be wise.

Can you be very welcome.

Can you be very welcome in mentioning a winter. Believe in a winter.

Yes we do.

PAGE XCIV

Can you establish stations. I can establish stations here.

PAGE XCV

Can you give advice.

Can you give advice to him.

PAGE XCVI

Can you give advice to her.

PAGE XCVII

What does the nigger say today.

FINIS.

Publishers, the Portrait Gallery and the Manuscripts at the British Museum

The answer in the house is that talking is not the same thing as a lamb. So that was the way it came to be and the second answer came before the first.

All the part was distributed and the selection of more was not made before the sight was so particular that any letter had a signature. This which is even is not the whole page, there is more that is even, very much more and any size is larger.

To beam is not to seem to have an eye that is there and a hair that is colored, to beam is not so disturbed that any afternoon is not sooner than the next morning. This was so useful and the excuse was not placed in between the hotels, it was not placed anywhere. This is the date of some days in every week, and the morning is before noon. So simply and so strangely, so much the more advanced, so much the more interior and so much more coughing than learning, so very much more and yet there is no disappointment, not any disappointment.

The cute way that a certain place is open on Sunday and not on Tuesday does not mean that an invitation will not be coming. Not at all, there is more chair than standing exhausts.

So then the whole spring is earlier than February. This was so much the tail of the previous setting of the sun and the moon and some of the stars. Electric lighting is so usual and more weddings are celebrated in the place of thanksgiving.

A target and a round face, a beard that is not whiter, the center of it all is that resemblance and surely there is that to pass away and have the same decision. Surely there is that resemblance and surely the ones standing alone have that copy. Surely there is the safe persuasion. Surely there is danger.

So to move and to faint and to separate the lists together, so to lengthen and to shorten and to curve the same direction, so to measure every daughter and to lessen every sister and to manage every mother and to sever every brother and to undertake a father and to beam upon a lover so to sing and so to talk and so to change the line together, all of this and any show is the way to season nature and to have it all together means the same in every letter.

This which is not so strange is the more used and in there kindly being a face there is more resemblance than if it were written and then comes the time to look and there it is, there is the writing.

So astonishing is it not when there has been preservation. The noise which comes has not any decisive obligation and yet the whole date is just the same. So sweet are the singular pleasures of recognition. The strength of the place does not mean more than all. Some have no distaste.

Link the hat and the coat and the collar, have the hair and the eyes and the color, see the time and the tea and altogether and do not be singular enough, and so there is that to view and the single planter has the rest as history. He did not tell it in giving it more room than cloth. So early is it not.

Saddle the simple sore without a touch of lame despair and do not touch the hair because there is the use of all that pause. So sweetly is it true that neatness does not mean the curls are true and yet there is absolutely none, absolutely no powder. So the place is not used for the tea and the last water is not more boiling than is touchy.

Frown nowhere and do not change that space, that is the way to use the time to purchase mining pictures. The little darkness and no large lamp, all the light being together does not make everything strange. Please the daylight, show the ruins that there is water, do not disturb the lamp, make more noise than resting and more that is changed is changed and an agreement shows the pink not to be redder. All that partial resemblance to a disagreement and a reunion is not more questioned than no answer. Not any more choice is so determined, and yet, why is the season so ingrained in the early morning when noon is no later. There is always a return of any answer.

Peace and the morning and a show of any evening, a reflection and the pleasant state of nature, this does make so much debt that there is no name anywhere. So pleasing is disaster, so ancient is being old enough in the matter.

Bestow a curve in the collapse and there is no withdrawal and that which is secure has some way of preserving any walking. All the time has a finished undertrimming and so there has the approach to a lingering printing.

To place an eye, to set the corner, to make a blessing, and to search a mansion, to persuade the noon and to establish harmony, the cause that is the mention is not more pained than anything. So then there is a memory, there is a stone home, there is no weakness.

Clearly and a gem, singly and all four, the stem, the stone the happy way, the single blessing of the longing soon, the patent habit of the leaving of the room, all this and no white light is not more dim than every candle and many of them make the illumination gentler, they dwindle in large, they season the sun, they blossom the churn, they bestow in a plant. This was no sprain, this was the regal pin.

A broom and a window, both of them uttered are so plain that there is more space and very much more hurry and yet there is a change of address, this is written. So clannily there will not be when the envelope is larger. The same union is stronger. An afternoon is weaker. That was the time and then in the evening there is dinner and later, any time later there is more than one corner, there is a fire, there is that, there is no pleasant place in more fire. Then came that which pushed away a piano, then came that and there was a whole collection. The question was not detained. There was that to do and arranging is done by separation. This is yellow and brown is a color. Peace is rested when it is occupied.

If the three are one they do not have voices, that means no more than that all of them are four. More is not regulated and yet there is an introduction, there are degrees, there is past pressing, there is the change of a pudding. All is not any meddling of a mess and the keen lump is not shadowed by any sun.

Plant the union of a question later, all the time has that change, the pink length and the satin fixture this does not make any question uncertain. A question if there is no answer is a question where there is no answer. To place more is always a way.

Put the partial pleasure in place and do not see more than the town. If the town escapes and sees a building it will be satisfied. It is.

When the speed is there and there is pink color there is a pale pink, there is a color.

All the two baskets and the little apples and any that are the same size in measure have so much hidden that is not paper so very much and they think out of sight. They do.

So plaintive and so careful and so many little spaces and so largely all the time, and so pointed and so half and the whole which is there has the other side of pinning and the time to have the rest is not what there is to leave. A vacation is not needed, a bundle is not needed, a precise result of more than an example is not so different when the division is the same.

Kindle the blame when the refuge is in water, express that excitement when the paint is there to fade, see no more and love the rest, all the tender part is running, all the liquid taste is temperate, all the time and there is that, all the time has only water. This is not the only haste, there is so much of it lonely, water never has so much that a little more is water. No kind lady has the time, no sweet trough is lingering longer.

Any two who see the same time are the ones who do not expectorate and this does not mean it is habit, it means no more than that sometime is included when there is no time to place pottery. Certainly there is a trifle, any one knows what there is when there is all the table, that does not mean that there is a collection, that does not mean more than the place pounded. Not any single little piece of the red makes a yellow color, and yellow is more so than anything. So reasoning are they and they conclude a bottle.

Not so sweetly as a bottle, not so sweetly anywhere.

To see longingly and sharply indicates a predisposition. If there is a memory there is no use suggesting offending.

Pleasant and an interval which is empty and there is no empty way to begin again. This which makes an appetite larger does make travelling easy.

All the account and most of the account is not kept where there is more lightness than there is home. It says more and it does mean that. It certainly does.

So then there is a shade of the pleasure of sensible exclamation. There is, there is the beaming oak and the spending of more money and then the answer, the whole answer, does that mean that the occasion is furnished or does it mean that no auction has any circle. What is it like. It is like the whole reliable point which has no measure, it is the pressed leaf and there is not anything that shows what is obliging, nothing at all and more organs and a little light and so much blending of an industry all that does not lead to a margin, it does, it has the practice and the music, it has no more bent wood than any train that is not burning, it has not, it does make a joy.

Looking in the face of eyes means the strangest elephant. Looking in the same set teeth means the presence of a seat.

All the talk and all the light means the same result of voice and a solid substance then means a tear and then a tear. Choose the money when there is more result and all the plainer staying for the evening. This means that what is curious has more shortness than speech and more hope than dangling. Surely the section is mended and the change has not been made. Surely the name has been mentioned.

He has it, he is the son and the mother, he has it, there is no darker brother, he has it. He has it and the length is not poisoned, he is the ample special principal protector. He sells it cheaper.

He does not deny a shorter letter. He does see the revival of unison. He does decline a match, he does entitle that.

He which is the sense man in the timely story, he and the weaker is fonder, he is the praised and the praiser, he does not speak the waiting the weaker. He does speak when there is a specimen rejoinder. He does play more pastry than the tea-time. He is there for dinner. He does not steam anyway. He has the state. He has the craning care to endure. He is not more particular. He is so tender. He is the link and left light.

The same season makes the moon strange, the same sun light is October, the same piling of the single glass stamp makes no monotony. There is no rejoinder. The end is in the great division between the counting and the bloom of passing a glass covering. If it were left and in a way it was left, if it were left then the meaning would be that there was hope and hope which is active does direct that there is some one to stay there and say it and doing so why should it determine a passage, it should. When it should and there is more there then certainly all of them are the same that is to say there is a difference. Any difference is greater.

Roche

Was one who certainly was one really being living, was this one a complete one, did that one completely have it to do very well something that that one certainly would be doing if that one could be doing something. Yes that one was in a way a complete one, certainly he was one completely listening. Was that one one completely listening, was that one completely listening and certainly it was a pleasant thing if this one was one completely listening and certainly this one was completely listening and certainly it was a pleasant thing having this one listening and certainly if this one were one being one really completely listening it would then certainly be a completely pleasant thing.

Was this one a complete one. Certainly this one was one being living. This one was one certainly going to be quite beautifully doing something if this one really did this thing and certainly this one would be sometime doing this completely beautiful thing if this one is really a complete one.

This one certainly is not one who is weakening, who is not continuing well in working. This one certainly is not at all a weak one, that is certain. This one is certainly feeling, in being one being living. This one is certainly an honest one and it is certainly a pleasant thing to have this one listening. Certainly this one does not do very much talking. Certainly this one is liking very well to be knowing what any one doing anything is doing, in what way any one doing anything is doing that thing. This one is one certainly loving, doing a good deal of loving, certainly this one has been completely excited by such a thing, certainly this one had been completely dreaming about such a thing. Certainly this one is one who would be very pleasant to very many in loving.

This one is perhaps one who is perhaps to be sometime a complete one. This one is perhaps one who is perhaps not to be ever a complete one. This one certainly was often listening and this was then certainly a very pleasant thing. This one was perhaps one completely listening, certainly this one was one who was listening and it was then a very pleasant thing, certainly if this one were one completely listening it would be then a completely pleasant thing.

This one certainly would be doing a very beautiful thing if this one did do that beautiful thing. This one would certainly be steadily working to be doing that beautiful thing. This one would certainly not be slackening, not be stopping going on working, not be weakening in working, in making that beautiful thing. This one would be making that beautiful thing. If this one were making that beautiful thing it would be a very satisfying thing. This one would certainly be one completely making a beautiful thing if this one did make a beautiful thing. This one was not a weak man, this man was not an unsteady man, this man was not an aspiring man, this man was one certainly going to be making a beautiful thing if he did make a beautiful thing. This one certainly was listening and this was a very pleasant thing, this one was certainly one going to be doing a beautiful thing if this one is one who is a complete one.

This one is certainly one to be doing a beautiful thing if this one is going to be doing that thing. It is not disturbing to be wondering about this one going to be doing the beautiful thing, not really disturbing to that one, not really disturbing to any one. This one is steadily working. This one is listening and that is a pleasant thing. If this one were complete in listening that would be a completely pleasant thing. This one certainly is one steadily working to be doing a beautiful thing, this one certainly will be doing a beautiful thing if this one does that beautiful thing. This one is very nearly completely needing to be knowing what any one is doing who is doing something, how any one who is doing something is doing that thing. Certainly if this one is one really completely listening and certainly perhaps this one is one completely listening then that is a completely pleasant thing.

Braque

Cap and corn, auditor, interest and exertion, aim and audience, interest and earnest and outset, inside in inside. Alarm no sun, alarm is thinking, alarming is determination an earth wide moth is something. Price in curving is weeding. There is an undetermined super division. There is the percolating bread stuff, the window is thickening.

Alarm no alarm is standing and holding something. No alarm has a perpendicular position. No alarm is in that position. An alarm which is not a choice shows the necessity of good nature. It shows and the tune which is on any wind the same, that tune is the organization. It has a place, it is a circle and this which is not guarded is not soft, it is softening. It being soft breaking is something and what is round is not widening. It is particular and so much more than the saving of an elimination. Practice is particular. It is recognition.

Silence is not hurt by attending to taking more reflection than a whole sentence. And it is said and the quotation is reasoning. It gives the whole preceding. If there is time enough then appearances are considerable. There are in a circle. They are tendering a circle. They are a tender circle. They are tenderly a circle.

This was not past a future.

If the speck is plain and the tail is there tail is made of hair. That makes that. Any one is no tailor. The curtain is not made of wood and a candle is placed in a candlestick and the whole, the very whole, there is no robbery.

If the pet is whole and the juice is so serene then the salt is pure and there is pepper in between. The harness which is on the stake is used to rubbing on a wheel. There is the complete absence of all reason for an excuse. The time has the wealth of a separation. The season is not that of baking.

Brack and neuresthenia and lean talk with a marvel and make a spittoon clear with a mixing in a mustache. The sense is in that.

Pie is not peeling and the date and the poison and the cake when the pan is a shape is not minus all the practice. The time is not filling.

Brack, Brack is the one who put up the hooks and held the things up and ate his dinner. He is the one who did more. He used his time and felt more much more and came before when he came after. He did not resemble anything more.

The time and place of a corner is no convenience if it has not been filled, none at all, and if it is filled then there is a resemblance, there is some resemblance.

Do not celebrate what is hearty and surely there is no danger in expecting a strong summer. If the place is shown to be damp there is no use in that excuse. Anyway there is no time to rise together. They cannot sit in a seat.

The time came when there was no occasion for geography. This did not mean that there was a change of place, it meant that there was a change of influence. This change was understood, it was no wonder. In understanding the whole thing of precomposition there was no more light than sweetness, there was no more size than bulk, there was no more load than a caravan, there was no mingling of unison. The time did not come any more.

And then the simple way was celebrated by causation and the charge was sweetening, that is to say there was a round mass.

Powder is not brown. The color does not show in the mixture. In curving and not lengthening the disposition there is no meeker feather. To show the wave to be cultivated and to show the suspension of a razor the light does shine directly. It shines and it darkens another, it does not shine and destroy the connector, it does not shine in a color, it does not make a brown tender. Brown is tender, that is no trouble and no appetite.

It follows that when the time is separated that the sacrifice is not the same as when the conversation is sensible and it is sensible to discuss carving and oak-trees and the season and to be disturbed by a mountain and to argue when there is no desertion. It is sensible and to be present is enough to separate the future. If it comes to happen that there is no eraser then certainly there is no cause why there should be. This is the reason. The best shape is that which is pasted without paper. At any rate the paper is not white and brown, it is brown and it is black and white and colored.

The time is not replaced by indicating the reason it will there be resplendent travelling. This is not a question because that is not an answer.

The time which was put to some place was that is so well placed. The question is is there travelling. There is no question as to if there is travelling where which showed solemnity in not turning in turning. This was so put that certainly not any more reception could be astonishing.

To pass away, to choose some away, to object to abhor that and to be not triumphant this is not the splendor of a single standard this is the solemn reverberation of an enlarged and of a small masterpiece.

The way of the man and the way of the lamp and the way of shining and the way of settling all this is in accord with the devastation and destruction which resembling is not disturbing motion. This comes so soon that talking is ennobling. This which is is what comes, that coming is what is come and can come. Coming it comes and is come and there is some mingling and there is more willing than there was when the coming came to suggest and disturb and reassure reason.

A lane is not a hill and a hill is a descent. To explain this it is necessary to practice mending and disturbing and relating. The time to go is not more arranged than the roundness which makes for beauty and to be round is not what there is to height.

The time when selection is vacation is when the perfection is so replaced that there is a premonition. This does make baking so easy and at the same time there is no separation and no disgrace not even desertion. This comes to be so told that any appearance is regal. So then there is no announcement.

A little seat which is not low is not more elevated than a little seat which is low and high. There is no space for more than there is room for. This makes no demand on conscience, this makes no demand on anything, this does not alter an exhibition. The reason that there is no alteration is that in separating spaces they come to show that there is the same space between that there is there where there is the place which is it in it. This shows that there is nothing so clearly shown by the whole exposition. It does show it, it shows the extension of the resemblance and the unification of the differentiation and the extension of the interval and the inhibition of the retention of acceleration. This does show no more than is individual. And yet there is no train that does not go in that direction and to return is not passing that way. Returning is not vagabonding it is a spacious interception. The use of the spread of the arrangement between that and that is not so wide that there are no spaces. There are spaces. They can repose so. They do call whiteness no wonder. They do not shudder together. There is no example in a relation. There is none in saving spacing.

A capable curtain is not used and the meaning of this is that protection on both sides is protection everywhere. The band played longer.

So much sorrow in winter and so much sadness in summer, so much nervousness in the country and so much disturbance in the city, so much counting with a letter and so much writing with no electrician, so much piano color and so much musical permission, so much steadiness in circling and so much singleness in searching, so much bloom in labeling and so much secrecy in enlightening, so much saving in abandoning and so much steadying in remaining, all this and no more, so much and not often, all this and no moment when a monument is not mind and munificent, no time and sweetness and no escape and separation, all this and no obliging desperation, all this and the same moment in particular and if it were in not passing, all and no one never to be satisfied in signalling, no more and the choice is absent, there is a season in the right, there is a sanction in the left, there is a presence in the center, there is an upheaval in the distant circumference, there is a resonance in the special curve, there is a susceptibility in the unperspiring relation. All this nightly and some daily and weakly and more yearly and not certainly and not reducingly.

To be raised and to be so respected that there is no doubt that the lines that are turning are the lines that are turning, to be so respected that talking is not continuous and the presence of nothing is more selected, to be so raised is not an expectation, it is capable of calming.

There has been no doubt. There has not been any doubt. There is not being any surface and there is not that there then.

The strong hold is the mildness of the salutation of the metropolitan. This is not obligatory and it is not capable, neither is it casual. The mint is not where there is no building, it is not any this is never a surprise, it is never a surprise because when the whole thing is considered and the whole thing when it is considered has that beginning, when it is put where there is no selection it is then not made noticeable. To be noticeable is not declared, in declaring it there is no speech, in not keeping on talking there is no silence. This is not heard louder and there is no doubt. There will not be that doubt.

The capacity which makes the size that has that meaning have that meaning, that is what has the sensitiveness which does not make anticipation, there is reality. In that there is touching morning and in touching morning there is no course. There is all there inclines to be. The freedom which has no ornament is not spilled and this does not mean anything not lively, it certainly does not mean an extra. The practice of no pronoun is not audacious. There is no prize in a pocket. There is none there and the circle having a separation makes all that which is not the same similar, it does not make it a circle. A circle has no pleasure, it is not encircled and there is this to say that the white and black are brown.

Portrait of Prince B. D.

A space is not spent, it is not used, it is similar, it is represented. This shows no more than a latitude which running through the center makes the surrounding. The space is not placed, it is presented, that is the relation of the similar settlement. To settle upon and to settle under shows more than the similar circle it shows the degree which makes more similarity than that, it sinks higher and there is no roar. The section and there is a section, the section means that penetration resembles distance, it supplies the drop and it selects no sightless system.

The incident that succumbs is the one that is early. The lateness is not tending to define a definite darkness, it does not shine and since that time there is a large light. The western windless is not the same as the white wind. The white wind has no poise. There is a diamond. A diamond is a treasure. If a treasure is that color then there is a resemblance.

A trade between the one who has a hat and one who has a hat is such that there is no hiatus. The one who has had a hat is the one who adds that. The one who is the one that has that is that one adding that thing. No neglecting and adding, no single safety silent disturbing, no neglect and no glass is there to pass away and stay. It sees the solid sight and that which is not bright is white, that which is single is resembling and so it comes that when there is a show a way to pass into the recent glow means more fire. A fine color is red and green and purple and rose and yellow, a fine color resembles the continuation. Any fine color is in a glass. A glass to resist must be a glass to pass. This shows no shadow. This shows no scratch.

A change is measured, a card is unmeasured. There is a return of much more. Stupor is not in winning a climate. It is lost in the remembrance of poisoning. The list of a result in stretching a building does not make any mark. The wheel is there. The trend is not behind a back. It is in the window of a fenestra. The blending is distinct interspreading. This is not the measure of wind. The return is not so, it is occupied. The rest is arisen.

There is no height. If there is there is wind. There is wind. Height shrinks below and settlement is not soluble. The erection of yellow is no violence. The five are won. Single, same, purple, blue, circle. The last which section has the reverse resemblance has no moment and there is a tendency which in the rising of the setting sun means new arising.

To shine and whine, to shatter and shrink, to collect and settle, to stir and suck, to lose violence and select simultaneity, to see that the whole exception is not arrested and to satiate the lines of resemblance, this and no more is underdone. The public and pilot, all the shining land and the wind and no neglect, all this does not mean that there is no denial. It has been there the same result of no intended excavation, it has been there and that exception planted no resemblance has a moment, none and the illustration is planted and the time is placed.

So then there is no secret. A secret means that when there is a thing there is nothing and if there is nothing then there is no addition. A sum is not sacrificed.

Handing a lizard to any one is a green thing receiving a curtain. The change is not present and the sensible way to have agony is not precautious. Then the shirting is extreme and there is a lilac smell and no ginger. Halt and suggest a leaf which has no circle and no singular center, this has that show and does judge that there is a need of moving toward the equal height of a hot sinking center and surface. Then there is a space, then there is exception, then there is no reason why a pound should be smaller and all the time there is the courage and the mint and the repeating result that surely if there has been a change there has not been a fire. Surely a fire is famous and a famous fire is in the fire. Surely no more special spending shows anything. And yet if there is no wind there is no haste and if there is no haste why is twenty older than thirty and thirty older than twenty-eight, why is it and why is there no mistake. There is no mistake because there is the time and the accusation is indented and this makes enough so that clouding does not make a cemetery. A surprise is not in sight. This is the sentence present. There is no danger and the silent height is so high that sound rises higher. This does not make sound infamous, it does not shatter a conclusion. Nothing is hollow in water, nothing is high in air, nothing is louder and nothing is perpendicular. The establishment is thorough. A chance shows a bright blue sound, a chance is the same wind out of a window.

A Persian kitten is a purring kitten. The safety that comes is so gathered that there can be news. One oak and more oaks and the training of water this means that a color attracts a signal it means that the result of a certain well is seen by there being no extra example of a kind of closet. In the beginning when there is no rising and resisting and letting a singular section of the whole rise together, in the beginning the imparting actual relation to a time of surfaces does show that there is an origin of originating. In showing this there is no repair. There is a whole half of a turtle and the presence of more is not rope, it is not and certainly is so wise that fever is fainting. This is this. Then there is that and the singular example is not predicted by resting in more contraction. Not very and what is then to be extending is the whole place with filling. Filling is not spreading. The size is not that it is not proportioned to the moon and the lantern, it is fully proportioned together and aroused and interested. This made no measure and no misery and no murder. There is no acute trimming nor trembling. So then there is that thing. This is not that silent thing. This is not the thing that is anything. This is the thing that is that thing.

A large moist blue and a paler color, a large dust rose and no water nearer, a small tall frame and no building finer this makes a prediction that necessity is work and then why is there no question. There is no question because investigation is miraculous.

Mrs. Whitehead

But you like it.

They can't any of them be quite as bad because they learned french but I never did.

He doesn't look dead at all.

The wind might have blown him.

He comes from that direction. That's the way.

They are not knotted. Have you smelt it. What would you suggest, your advice I have come across three or four.

So they are the others.

Separate them.

It does make one come, he is extraordinarily charming and endearing once of twice only twice I think.

He is not staying out that's hard beside that what does he do.

That's long for his mother.

She travelled from this rest. She crocheted from this nest.

She crocheted from this nest. I thought it wasn't ever.

It's one of my favorite ones this.

And yet not this.

Isn't it funny.

It isn't.

Break or breaking, very fair, break or very wanting.

I tried it this way before.

Very difficult to change extra places and yet I can agree. I can agree by that. I rest this piece of it and it's nearly the same climate. I will tell you why they want a real door. They choose it.

They do so and very pure water. They are safe when they take a bath. Oh it is very. Oh it is.

In a way a vest.

I do think you get what you want.

Corrections.

It is eleven weeks from the middle of September. I glance in a way.

It is eleven weeks from the middle of September.

Total recollect others.

I glance at and I can recollect others. I make a division neatly, I close.

What is wrong with not blue. That is right with apples. Apples four. For. Fore.

Before that.

Next stretching.

Next for that leaf stretching.

I do not state leaf.

I like to beg very much stream.

Not exactly in state.

Understate.

All in so.

They expect all the blues to take of all the other families, the whites are extra they are beside all that, they make a little house and through and beside that they live in Paris.

Hardly enough for wood.

Not a color even.

By now a change of grass and wedding rings and all but the rest plan. I don't care I won't look.

I am not sure that yellow is good. I am tall.

Allow that. I don't want any more out in conversation.

I can be careful.

Not within wearing it.

I cannot say to stay.

No please don't get up.

And now that.

Yes I see.

Did you pay him for that whether for a spider and such splendor and indeed quitting. I meant to gather.

I see it I see it.

Please ocean spoke please Helen land please take it away.

I saw a spoken leave leaf and flowers made vegetables and foliage in soil. I saw representative mistakes and glass cups, I saw a whole appearance of respectable refugees, I did not ask actors I asked pearls, I did not choose to ask trains, I was satisfied with celebrated ransoms. I cannot deny Bertie Henschel is coming tomorrow. Saturdays are even. There is a regular principle, if you mention it you mention what happened.

What do you make of it.

You exceed all hope and all praise.

Portrait of Constance Fletcher

When she was quite a young one she knew she had been in a family living and that that family living was one that any one could be one not have been having if they were to be one being one not thinking about being one having been having family living. She was one then when she was a young one thinking about having, about having been having family living. She was one thinking about this thinking, she was one feeling thinking about this thing, she was one feeling being one who could completely have feeling in thinking about being one who had had, who was having family living.

She was one having, she was one who had had family living. When she was a young one she was one having, she was one having had family living.

She was one thinking about having family living, about having had family living. When she was a young one she was thinking about having family living, she was thinking about having had family living.

She was feeling having had family living, she was feeling having family living. When she was a young one she was feeling having had family living, she was feeling having family living.

She was knowing, when she was a young one, that she could be completely feeling in having family living in having had family living. She was knowing, when she was a young one, she was knowing that she was thinking, she was knowing that she was feeling in having family living, in having had family living. She was thinking and feeling having had, having family living.

She could be completely feeling having, having had family living. She was thinking in being one who could be completely feeling having had, having family living. She was feeling in being one who could be completely feeling having had, who could be completely feeling having family living.

She was living in feeling, in thinking having had, having family living. She had had family living. She was having family living. She could be completely feeling having family living, having had family living.

She was then a young one, she was then quite a young one, she was later a little an older one. She was then feeling in being one loving, she was then thinking in being one loving. She was then living in being one loving. She could be then one being completely loving. She was filled then, completely filled then, she was then feeling in being loving, she was then thinking in being loving. She was completely filled then. She was feeling, she was thinking, she was feeling and thinking then in being one loving.

She could be then one being completely loving, she was thinking and feeling in being one who could be completely loving. She was coming then to be a full one, she was coming then to be thinking and feeling in this thing in being one being a completely filled one. She was full then, she was filling in then in being one living in loving, in living in thinking in being loving, in living in feeling being one being loving.

She was full then and was not then losing anything. She was thinking then, she was feeling then, she was thinking then and feeling then in being full then. She was thinking and feeling then in being one not losing anything of any such thing as being one being full then.

She could be one being completely full. She was thinking in being one who could be completely full. She was feeling in being one who could be completely full. She was always living in being one feeling and thinking in being one who could be completely full.

She was full then and she was thinking and feeling, thinking in this thing, feeling in this thing. She was thinking and feeling and being full then. She was thinking and feeling in being one who could be completely full.

She was filling in in all her living to be a full one, she was thinking and feeling in all her living in being a full one. She was thinking and feeling all her living in being one who could be a completely full one. She was all her living a full one. She was completely filling in to be a full one and she always was a full one. She was thinking in being a full one. She was feeling in being a full one. She was thinking in feeling in being a full one. She was feeling in thinking in being a full one.

If they move in the shoe there is everything to do. They do not move in the shoe.

The language of education is not replacing the special position that is the expression of the emanation of evil. There is an expression when contemplation is not connecting the object that is in position with the forehead that is returning looking. It is not overpowering. That is a cruel description. The memory is the same and surely the one who is not older is not dead yet although if he has been blind he is seeing. This has not any meaning.

Oh the bells that are the same are not stirring and the languid grace is not out of place and the older fur is disappearing. There is not such an end.

If it had happened that the little flower was larger and the white color was deeper and the silent light was darker and the passage was rougher it would have been as it was and the triumph was in the place where the light was bright and the beauty was not losing having that possession. That was not what was tenderly. This was the piece of the health that was strange when there was the disappearance that had not any origin. The darkness was not the same. There was the writing and the preparation that was pleasing and succeeding and being enterprising. It was not subdued when there was discussion, it was done where there was the room that was not a dream.

This is all to prepare the way that is not the way to like anything that in speaking is telling what has come that like a swelling is inside when there is yellowing.

There is that liking. That does not shape the way to say that there is not anywhere anything that is resembling. Perfection is not adulteration. There is the substance that has not any defect.

If the program is not despondent and it has that substance then certainly the beginning is the tender blessing that unfolding is not subduing. There is that presentment and the quiet is not so sound but that there can be a change of origin. There can be that elevation. This is not an argument. There is the work that has that place and there is a garden. A little taller bending does not haste the erection of the grotto that has a fountain. That is so soon.

To pardon, that is to have seen that there was a long way to stare when the heat was the same as there was when the voices were together. This was the temptation and so solidly was there when there was there that the whole reception was not filled with more than all every day who had come anywhere and had heard that there was. This did not mean more than all. It meant all and the result of the precious and precise way was that there was that preparation and not the disintegration when there was that distinct evolution. There could be the same if any one was certain that there is not any evolution. This does not make the tedium that is eternal so particular that listening is a blessing. This does not disguise a flower.

Come in and that expression is not that one of waiting. To use a name is not the time that seeing has not been. This is discussion. This is obligation. This is the composition.

Oh sadly has the oak-tree not that sadness. It has not the particular reason. It has not that digression. It has not that penetration. It has that piece that is there where there is all that remains when everything remains. Nothing is all old. That is not the redoubtable repudiation. That has that precious meaning when the hindrance has not that little pain which is not the same as the passing out of what is not about when it is there where there is no care to say that anything is better. Everything has that description. That is not reorganization. The way to say that they went away is the way that the passage has come to be adhered. This is not the token that shows the steering that is not broken. The plea is not that the arabesque has that meaning when the whole thing is exposed. The meaning is that the precious picture is the bargain that has not met the ancient day when there is everything to say. The light is finer. That is not that discrimination. That is the way to have that to keep where there is not any interdiction. She had that name. That was the origin of the penguin. That was not that bird. And because the strong man is the warder when the little ones are sounder so the particular ticket is not limited when there is not the best establishment where all the black and white show that. It is a blessing when there has been falling the heavy way to stay where the regard is what is not all that distance. The breaking of the tame show is not the way to glow because the waste is not there. It is not any where.

Mark the data that tells the merit of having that time to state that not to wait is to say that the door has not been entered. If to wait marks the place where the entrance if it is made comes to be approached then to do what is not done is to do all that and carefully that which is solid does not fill the space. That is not a disclosure. That is not the way for all of them who are looking to refuse to see. That is not at all any such way. It is not a pleasure to be the one when there is the whole of it all and when there where there is no separation there is weeping, quite ostentation, completion, not any compensation, where there is the softening of the published soap. This is not that decree. There is no failure. There is no condition of incision.

Particle of all the color is that which is not white and the black which is open is not older when the time has come back for black to be younger.

The meaning of this is that why the difference is always louder is that that which is above that which is all there is and there is much is that there is all that there has that reason to be which is the reason that is all certain and this which is not mentioned and which does not make that which is lost is the same and has the detail which does not make any escaping remain separate. This does adjoin all and all is enough so that the whole which is not parted has not the place where sticking makes anything that is wet dry. This has not that mistake when softness is union.

The first time.

Winning distinction is discretion and all who are going are the three who have not that distraction. They have not all the hardihood. They are not separated. The two who are not older are not remaining to be interesting. They are not undertaking any beginning. Excellent is the same union. Breathless is not the shade when the opening is not limiting. They did not seem in that place. That was any end.

She.

If three are eager and plainer and having a full temper and if all of them unite in that happy way that makes a garden give the way to be there where there is a way, if there is the last time and a young time is a stolen beauty then the way it has been said that the white flower has not been bled is the way to remember that decision is not the same as crumpling a parting. She did not animate what was mechanical. She has not this to do.

They.

They were the three and they were not employed in looking. They had not every union when they had that education.

To be they and then not be away is not the time and place that makes the whole expression because after all when there is the time and the place and when they are they they are not away and that does not make any more. If they were there they had the time to see which way was older and when they did not feel that stain they had the time to address what they did address when they would address one another. They did not all listen.

No silence.

There was not that hesitation and this was not all there was when the sounds were not so loud but that they might be hearing. They had the quiet and surely if they taught that they were each one not all of any other. This was not the half of all the time. It took a separate ticket.

All the time that there was all the winning of all the wonder that was not under the weather was not passing as the exchange was not lessening. The older was not newer. They had the same description. This does not mean that if there are all three to learn that not any one is there but they have any way to say that not to go away is to stay. They were equal to enough so that all the separation made them remain. They had so much excess.

It was not the only smile the smile that did not come to face the pleasure of there being three and the three were not there to gather together.

One.

If the way to learn is to have that presence then certainly the changes did not balance the description. She had that which was not alarming.

Two.

If the habit of saying all the education is the development of that expression then certainly if there is being pleasant all can be there to not expect that measure of all who are together.

Three.

The one who is a sun is the last flower that is not open when all the petals falling feel the whole of all intention.

So there are then what is not what will not have been when all the seeing that is and is not seen is had and has been having having and having had and meaning. That is some intention and all is enough to complete all the whole.

The delay was not that which separated that separation from the time when all the ones who said something said every thing. It was not so in place.

The change.

There was not any time and all there was was reason. There was all that and if there were all there were there were the ones there were.

That which was pleasing was not all there was if there was all there was of that consideration. Certainly the time was not the present and past flavor and the time was not the future and the present presentation. There was all there and sincerely did the biting that was not bit fill out the strength and explanation. It did not furnish the intention. It did not succeed when there was all that care.

This which did not escape was not the narrow connection that can make a larger blossom and make it take the sea where the ocean is larger and the ships are quicker. The pleasure is the same.

To face that way.

To face the way that each one does say that they have any day which is clearly not away is to say that the time is not there when the color is not lighter and the hair is not redder. This does not make all there is of any invitation. There is not anything of any such suggestion.

If the practice of the present and the practice of the past and there is any practice and the practice of the future then latterly there is not any change. If the way to say the turn is the turn the way that is the way to turn that way then all of the thing is in that thing. There has been all of that painstaking.

Awhile while there is no band, awhile while the train is late, awhile while the town is full, awhile while the sounds have the tone, awhile there is a settled waste and this is not to say that anything that is given away is given away, nothing is wasted that is not given away and anything that is given away is wasted. The appearance is not the only way to say that what is given away is wasted and nothing is given away. It is so remained.

That which is not tiring and that which is not aiding any of that which is not needing tiring, that was the sampler and there was not the sewing which was using any corner. That did not need the same width as all that is solid is using which is not wider. That which is solid is all that is wider and the rest is not that which has that passing odor which is not passing. It does not pass anything. It is not the only primrose. It has the sentence that in placing what is not that care has all that is which is all there where any more care is most care. There where the time is not cruel is the place where the time is what is filling the half and the whole and no passage that has that intention can be intended when that which is solid is not building every house. All houses are open that is to say a door and a window and a table and the waiter make the shadow smaller and the shadow which is larger is not flickering.

A Poem about Waldberg

What I am afraid of is that they will just attract an awful bombardment on themselves in which they will have to be supported. Oh no they won't do that.

I don't think they will do that. What I think is that I will have to reach the country before I ask myself the way to see the city. I don't mean this as a joke. I know very well that I know all about nurses. Who doesn't. And who would like to see children win. I love my boy very much. His mother feeds him. I can smile and think of it. We both laugh together. Altogether I have said to them keep still.

Curtains a japanese curtain.

Complete flowers.

I never use a pass.

Of course you wouldn't.

You wouldn't be careful enough. I don't mean that.

How can I hear him speak. You don't mean a victim. Eugene Paul. What is Waldberg's name.

I don't care for him.

I am not sorry for her.

I do not have flowers here.

California

Let me see. What do you say. They can take care of riches. Kiss my hand. Why. Because Russians are rich. All Russians are valuable. That is what I said.

I wish I could be as funny as he is.

Yes thank you I believe in Russia.

Johnny Grey

What did he say. I was disagreeing with him. He said he didn't have it by his side. He said. Hurry.

Eat it.

I am not going to talk about it. I am not going to talk about it.

Another thing.

This is mentioned. He was silly. He said there would have been many more elevators if it hadn't been for this war.

He was so thirsty.

They asked him.

Please.

If it weren't for them there would be wind.

I said there wasn't.

I said it was balmy.

I said that when I was little I asked for a closet.

This was the way it was written.

I was awed.

It is so injudicious to make plans.

We will not decide about three.

Three is the best way to add.

The bank opens tomorrow.

I was mistaken.

I hope I can continue.

To be a tailor.

The other said nothing.

The other one said he was hindering him and he made that mistake and he would not prepare further.

It is not deceiving.

I can say so gladly.

It's always better.

It's wonderful how it always comes out.

Conversational.

Plants were said to bring lining together. This is not deceived. This is not deceived. Plants.

Plants were said to bring meadows springing. Shattering stubbornly in their teeth.

Plants aid sad and not furniture.

This is it.

Plants are riotous.

Not even.

If you give money.

Plants are said to be left out if you give money.

Join or gray.

Points are spoken. This in one. Picturesque. It is just the same.

I cannot freeze.

I understand a picture. It is to have stop it who does. It is to have asked about it the sneezing bell. Bell or better.

A simple extenuation.

I mean to be fine with it.

A picture with all of it bitten by that supper. Call it. I shall please. Nowadays.

I find this a very pleasant pencil. Do I. I find this a very pleasant pencil. Do I find this a pleasant pencil.

How to give soldiers fresh water.

How do you.

You use the echoes.

Dear Jenny.

I am your brother. Nestling.

Nestling noses.

My gay.

Baby.

Little.

Lobster.

Chatter.

Sweet.

Joy.

My.

Baby.

Example.

Be good.

Always.

Six.

Seven.

Eight.

Nine.

All.

The.

Time.

Me.

Extra.

My.

Baby.

Scenes where there is no piece of a let it go.

No I am not pleased with their descriptions.

This is not their year.

Two of them.

Johnny Grey and Eddy.

Why not however.

It was not polite.

A long way.

I understand and I say, I understand him to say that, I see him I say I see him or I say, I say that I understand. What is it. He doesn't realise. I don't say that he isn't there I don't solidly favor him. I said I was prepared. I was prepared to relieve him. I was prepared to relieve him then or then and I was holding, I was holding anything. I am often for them. They gave it. They were pleased. So pleased and side with it. So pleased and have it. So have it and say it. Say it then. If he was promised, it, he had been left by the belief. He had the action. All old. In it. He was wretched. I do not believe or for it. I do not arouse rubbers. When we went away were we then told to be left with them. Do they or do they do it. Do they believe the truth.

I am beginning. Go on Saturday. I believe for Sunday. We deceived everybody.

I forgot to drink water.

No I haven't seen it.

He said it.

It's wonderful.

Target.

They don't believe it either.

Call it.

That.

Fat.

Cheeks.

By.

That.

Time.

Drenched.

By.

That.

Time.

Obligation.

To sign.

That

Today

When

By

That

Field.

He said he was a Spanish family.

It will make.

A

Terrible

Not terrible.

It will not make that one believe me it is not for my pleasure that I promise it.

No

Neither.

That

Or

Another

Neither

One

Lightly

Widened.

Widened by what.

Not this.

Not left.

Buy

Their

Hedges.

It's not a country.

I told him so.

I wish to begin.

Lining.

Of that thing.

By that time.

It.

Or.

It.

Was.

How.

We don't know whom to invite for lunch. You told me you'd tell me. I don't know.

Either.

I do get wonderful action into them don't I.

Blame.

Worthy.

Out.

Standing.

Eraser.

That was a seat.

Leave it out.

Seat.

Stretch.

Sober.

Left.

Over.

Curling.

Irresistible.

I come to it at last.

I know what I want.

Call.

Tried.

To be.

Just.

Seated.

Beside.

The.

Meaning.

Please come.

I met.

A steady house which was neither blocking nor behaving as if it would for the road.

He looks like it.

A ladder insults.

Me.

I do stem when in.

I don't look at them any more.

Johnny Grey.

What did I say.

I said I would leave it.

He was so kind.

That was lasting.

I am so certain.

Please.

It's remarkable that I can make good sentences.

It reminds me of a play that I remember which is better.

It is better.

Everything.

In.

I am coming.

To it.

I know it.

Please.

Pleased.

Pleased with me.

Pleased with me.

Canvas covers.

I wished to go away.

I asked for an astonishing green I asked for more Bertie.

I asked only once.

Pack it.

Package.

A little leaving.

We went to eat.

I have plenty of food.

Always.

Nearly.

Always.

Certainly.

By an example.

I was never afraid.

He doesn't say anything.

In that way.

Not after.

He was.

Sure.

Of it.

Then.

By then.

We were.

In Munich.

And sat.

Today.

By way

Of

Staring.

And nearly all of it.

In.

That.

Shining.

Firm.

Spread.

Paul.

Slices.

If I copy nature.

If I copy nature.

If I copy nature.

If I copy nature.

For it.

Open.

Seen

Piling.

Left.

In.

Left in.

Not in.

Border

Sew.

Why.

Spaces.

I.

Mean.

To.

Laugh.

Do be.

Do be all.

Do be all out.

If you can.

Come.

To stay.

And.

After.

All.

Have.

A.

Night.

Which.

Means.

That.

There

Is.

Not

This

Essential.

By that way.

It was all out in it.

By this time.

Which was reasonable and an explanation.

We never expected he would tell a lie.

Not this.

For.

More.

To be.

Indians are disappointing.

Not to me.

I was never disappointed in an Indian.

I was never disappointed in an Indian in any way.

How old are you.

Careless.

Heavy all the time.

I know she is.

I am.

Politely.

Finished.

A Portrait of F. B.

A peal is that mountain which makes a ring and is ringing. There is no squeak, there is no touch there is no lump, a light bed is left when it is carried away, it has no temper, it has when it has, it has the bent bedspread, it lies like that left not limply and next to lightly and no mixed more. It is so christened when it is there. It has that space to identify. It is the mending of the beam and it is not clear and shows the courage more of the plentiful timber which is not scattered and put together. It is so lightly clad and furs show it. It is so planter. There is no occasion and the copy is not reversed to so little, there is nothing tiny.

Leave the package will the book use the warmer there, sight the sound that has no platter, season all the simple ginger, make a bucket simpler.

Praise the lion and the rat, see the morsels fairly, show the swimming of the rat show the rabbit winning. Bestow the light and chase it there, see the hall is dimmer, see the lightening everywhere see the lightening dimmer. Make no dinner in the morning, make it in the evening, see the same and see it there, see it in the morning. See the time when there is that, see it in the morning, see it all and say the hat, say it every morning, say no more and undertake what is so ridiculous that there is no time to say that and any how what is the abuse of an intention, why should there be etiquette, why is there every lightening, why if the season is the same is there summer, when is there more night than in winter.

Return after the garden, remain after the tea, single out a timepiece, so hatly and so true there is neither more to do. All the time is the past and piece meal is that meal and a little chicken is a liver, and solitude is enough. A little jerk is no occasion, so supremely is there a category.

Very good the place is rough, the bed is silver and the sheets are there, the little slipper is not organized, the pleasure is obtained and actually there is a garden. In union there is withering. In sunlight there is breakfast.

A turn of the table does not mean that cups are there, it means that there is no loneliness and it means that the copy is not extreme when there is a frame. It does not mean any little thing.

A clatter registered has a calming center. That is the outlasting of a sight of all. If it is possible that there is the result then certainly no one would think so. Every one does. There is no sense in such a history. There is no sense at all. Not a bit of broom has the window open, not a bit.

No borrowing or lending and pearls are sweet. They are the same as a little chain, they have the color early, they see the time and they need no wine and they secure the distaste of pink pepper.

Choose running anyway, that is to say that rolling has more distinction, choose a feather boa and range all the plumes and a yellow one is sweeter.

Bake a table, the rest is empty, see the plate first, the first is distributed, see the arrangement the arrangement is in the curling Christmas.

Bet more than sugar, copy no more principally, restrict more decoration, repeat the needle. There is made.

So to see and so to go and so to turn the list around, so to go and so there is the practice of Nileing. Plainer sheets have simple stripes.

A target is by way of marks. The youngest is shaken. The pleasure is rested.

The length is the laughing dater, there is no challenge in mingling later. There is none, the rate is facing a lender.

All along and in the mind there is a plate and there is meal. There is the rate that makes no more. The stairs are not stumbling.

Sacred Emily

Compose compose beds.

Wives of great men rest tranquil.

Come go stay philip philip.

Egg be takers.

Parts of place nuts.

Suppose twenty for cent.

It is rose in hen.

Come one day.

A firm terrible a firm terrible hindering, a firm hindering have a ray nor pin nor.

Egg in places.

Egg in few insists.

In set a place.

I am not missing.

Who is a permit.

I love honor and obey I do love honor and obey I do.

Melancholy do lip sing.

How old is he.

Murmur pet murmur pet murmur.

Push sea push sea push sea push sea push sea push sea push sea push sea.

Sweet and good and kind to all.

Wearing head.

Cousin tip nicely.

Cousin tip.

Nicely.

Wearing head.

Leave us sit.

I do believe it will finish, I do believe it will finish.

Pat ten patent, Pat ten patent.

Eleven and eighteen.

Foolish is foolish is.

Birds measure birds measure stores birds measure stores measure birds measure.

Exceptional firm bites.

How do you do I forgive you everything and there is nothing to forgive.

Never the less.

Leave it to me.

Weeds without papers.

Weeds without papers are necessary.

Left again left again.

Exceptional considerations.

Never the less tenderness.

Resting cow curtain.

Resting bull pin.

Resting cow curtain.

Resting bull pin.

Next to a frame.

The only hat hair.

Leave us mass leave us. Leave us pass. Leave us. Leave us pass leave us.

Humming is.

No climate.

What is a size.

Ease all I can do.

Colored frame.

Couple of canning.

Ease all I can do.

Humming does as

Humming does as humming is.

What is a size.

No climate.

Ease all I can do.

Shall give it, please to give it.

Like to give it, please to give it.

What a surprise.

Not sooner whether.

Cordially yours.

Pause.

Cordially yours.

Not sooner together.

Cordially yours.

In strewing, in strewing.

That is the way we are one and indivisible.

Pay nuts renounce.

Now without turning around.

I will give them to you tonight.

Cunning is and does cunning is and does the most beautiful notes.

I would like a thousand most most.

Center pricking petunia.

Electrics are tight electrics are white electrics are a button.

Singular pressing.

Recent thimble.

Noisy pearls noisy pearl coat.

Arrange.

Arrange wide opposite.

Opposite it.

Lily ice-cream.

Nevertheless.

A hand is Willie.

Henry Henry Henry.

A hand is Henry.

Henry Henry Henry.

A hand is Willie.

Henry Henry Henry.

All the time.

A wading chest.

Do you mind.

Lizzie do you mind.

Ethel.

Ethel.

Ethel.

Next to barber.

Next to barber bury.

Next to barber bury china.

Next to barber bury china glass.

Next to barber china and glass.

Next to barber and china.

Next to barber and hurry.

Next to hurry.

Next to hurry and glass and china.

Next to hurry and glass and hurry.

Next to hurry and hurry.

Next to hurry and hurry.

Plain cases for see.

Tickle tickle tickle you for education.

A very reasonable berry.

Suppose a selection were reverse.

Cousin to sadden.

A coral neck and a little song so very extra so very Susie.

Cow come out cow come out and out and smell a little.

Draw prettily.

Next to a bloom.

Neat stretch.

Place plenty.

Cauliflower.

Cauliflower.

Curtain cousin.

Apron.

Neither best set.

Do I make faces like that at you.

Pinkie.

Not writing not writing another.

Another one.

Think.

Jack Rose Jack Rose.

Yard.

Practically all of them.

Does believe it.

Measure a measure a measure or.

Which is pretty which is pretty which is pretty.

To be top.

Neglect Waldberg.

Sudden say separate.

So great so great Emily.

Sew grate sew grate Emily.

Not a spell nicely.

Ring.

Weigh pieces of pound.

Aged steps.

Stops.

Not a plan bow.

Why is lacings.

Little slam up.

Cold seam peaches.

Begging to state begging to state begging to state alright.

Begging to state begging to state begging to state alright.

Wheels stows wheels stows.

Wickedness.

Cotton could mere less.

Nevertheless.

Anne.

Analysis.

From the standpoint of all white a week is none too much.

Pink coral white coral, coral coral.

Happy happy happy.

All the, chose.

Is a necessity.

Necessity.

Happy happy happy all the.

Happy happy happy all the.

Necessity.

Remain seated.

Come on come on come on on.

All the close.

Remain seated.

Happy.

All the.

Necessity.

Remain seated.

All the, close.

Websters and mines, websters and mines.

Websters and mines.

Trimming.

Gold space gold space of toes.

Twos, twos.

Pinned to the letter.

In accompany.

In a company in.

Received.

Must.

Natural lace.

Spend up.

Spend up length.

Spend up length.

Length thoroughly.

Neatness.

Neatness Neatness.

Excellent cording.

Excellent cording short close.

Close to.

When.

Pin black.

Cough or up.

Shouting.

Shouting.

Neater pin.

Pinned to the letter.

Was it a space was it a space was it a space to see.

Neither things.

Persons.

Transition.

Say say say.

North of the calendar.

Window.

Peoples rest.

Preserve pulls.

Cunning piler.

Next to a chance.

Apples.

Apples.

Apples went.

It was a chance to preach Saturday.

Please come to Susan.

Purpose purpose black.

Extra plain silver.

Furious slippers.

Have a reason.

Have a reason candy.

Points of places.

Neat Nezars.

Which is a cream, can cream.

Ink of paper slightly mine breathes a shoulder able shine.

Necessity.

Near glass.

Put a stove put a stove hoarser.

If I was surely if I was surely.

See girl says.

All the same bright.

Brightness.

When a churn say suddenly when a churn say suddenly.

Poor pour percent.

Little branches.

Pale.

Pale.

Pale.

Pale.

Pale.

Pale.

Pale.

Near sights.

Please sorts.

Example.

Example.

Put something down.

Put something down some day.

Put something down some day in.

Put something down some day in my.

In my hand.

In my hand right.

In my hand writing.

Put something down some day in my hand writing.

Needles less.

Never the less.

Never the less.

Pepperness.

Never the less extra stress.

Never the less.

Tenderness.

Old sight.

Pearls.

Real line.

Shoulders.

Upper states.

Mere colors.

Recent resign.

Search needles.

All a plain all a plain show.

White papers.

Slippers.

Slippers underneath.

Little tell.

I chance.

I chance to.

I chance to to.

I chance to.

What is a winter wedding a winter wedding.

Furnish seats.

Furnish seats nicely.

Please repeat.

Please repeat for.

Please repeat.

This is a name to Anna.

Cushions and pears.

Reason purses.

Reason purses to relay to relay carpets.

Marble is thorough fare.

Nuts are spittoons.

That is a word.

That is a word careless.

Paper peaches.

Paper peaches are tears.

Rest in grapes.

Thoroughly needed.

Thoroughly needed signs.

All but.

Relieving relieving.

Argonauts.

That is plenty.

Cunning saxon symbol.

Symbol of beauty.

Thimble of everything.

Cunning clover thimble.

Cunning of everything.

Cunning of thimble.

Cunning cunning.

Place in pets.

Night town.

Night town a glass.

Color mahogany.

Color mahogany center.

Rose is a rose is a rose is a rose.

Loveliness extreme.

Extra gaiters.

Loveliness extreme.

Sweetest ice-cream.

Page ages page ages page ages.

Wiped Wiped wire wire.

Sweeter than peaches and pears and cream.

Wiped wire wiped wire.

Extra extreme.

Put measure treasure.

Measure treasure.

Tables track.

Nursed.

Dough.

That will do.

Cup or cup or.

Excessively illigitimate.

Pussy pussy pussy what what.

Current secret sneezers.

Ever.

Mercy for a dog.

Medal make medal.

Able able able.

A go to green and a letter spoke a go to green or praise or

Worships worships worships.

Door.

Do or.

Table linen.

Wet spoil.

Wet spoil gaiters and knees and little spools little spools or ready silk lining.

Suppose misses misses.

Curls to butter.

Curls.

Curls.

Settle stretches.

See at till.

Louise.

Sunny.

Sail or.

Sail or rustle.

Mourn in morning.

The way to say.

Patter.

Deal own a.

Robber.

A high b and a perfect sight.

Little things singer.

Jane.

Aiming.

Not in description.

Day way.

A blow is delighted.

IIIIIIIIII

INCLINE.

Clinch, melody, hurry, spoon, special, dumb, cake, forrester. Fine, cane, carpet, incline, spread, gate, light, labor.

BANKING.

Coffee, cough, glass, spoon, white, singing. Choose, selection, visible, lightning, garden, conversation, ink, spending, light space, morning, celebration, invisible, reception, hour, glass, curving, summons, sparkle, suffering the minisection, sanctioning the widening, less than the wireless, more certain. All the change. Any counselling non consuming and split splendor.

Forward and a rapidity and no resemblance no more utterly. Safe light, more safes no more safe for the separation.

M—N H—.

A cook. A cook can see. Pointedly in uniform, exertion in a medium. A cook can see.

Clark which is awful, clark which is shameful, clark and order.

A pin is a plump point and pecking and combined and more much more is in fine.

Rats is, rats is oaken. Robber. Height, age, miles, plaster, pedal, more order.

Bake, a barn has cause and more late oat-cake specially.

Spend rubber, holder and coal, high, careful, in a pointed collar. A hideous south west is always a climb in aged seldom succeeded flavoring untimely, necessity white, hour in a glaze.

Break, sky blue light, obliquely, in a cut carpet, in the pack. A sound.

COO—GE.

Press in the ink and stare and cheese. Pick in the faint and feather and white. White in the plume.

M—N H—.

No noon back. No noon settler, no sun in the slant and carpet utterly surrounded.

No pressed plaster. None.

No pressing pan and pan cake. Not related exactly. Not related.

Matter in the center of single sand and slide in the hut.

No account of gibberish. No sky lark utterly.

Perfect lemon and cutting a central black. Not such clouding. A sugar, a lame sugar, certainly. No sobriety no silver ash tray.

M—N H—.

A co existence with hard suckling and spoons, and spoons. A co existence with orange supper. A last mending. A begging. Should the assault be exterminated, should it.

M—N H—.

A sound is in the best society. It hums and moves, it throws the hat in no way away and in no way particularly at paving. The meanness is a selection of parts and all of that is no more a handkerchief merely and large.

POINTS.

The exchange which is fanciful and righteous and mingled is in the author mostly in the piece.

CH—N.

A unity is the meantime in a union. A branch case is exactly so anxious and avoided and even then is it in place of blunders, is it in the piece that makes hesitation clear.

The youth and the check board and the all color minutely, this and the chance of the bright flours inward is not in a glance. A check is an instance and more more is indwelling.

PECKED PLACES.

In the unconcise word that is ministered and in the blame extraordinarily the center the whole center is coupled. This is choice.

M—N H—.

Hunger is not hurry and a silence and no more than ever, it is not so exactly and the word used is there.

T—S WH—.

A cut in trusts and in black colors which are not carpets not at all likely carpets and no sucking in substance of the sacking placed only in air outside. This makes a change precious and not odd not odd in place of more use. Not odd in the meaning rapidly.

M—N H—.

The soon estate and established alternately has bright soldiers and peaceable in the rest of the stretch.

J—S B—E.

A regular walking ground is that which shows peeping and soft places between mush and this is most moist in the settled summer. So much wet does gleam and the shutters all the shutters are sober. A piece of cut grass is dangerous dangerous to smelling and to all most.

S—NS.

A dark ground is not colored black mostly and dirtily securely and much exchange is much with a sight and so much to sponge in with speeches to whittle.

J—E B—E.

A tight laundry that is piece meal is in the best astounding. Between, in, on the beside, and no more origin, more in the weed blessed.

M—N H—.

Point, face, canvas, toy, struck off, sense or, weigh coach, soon beak on, so suck in, and an iron.

W—IE C—N.

Point a rose, see a soil, see a saddle, see a monk tree, see a sand tree, trust a cold bit of pickle usefully in an oration.

See the meadow in a meadow light.

The blame is necessarily an interruption perpendicularly.

L—E.

The seam in between is fenceless.

E—E.

The seam in most tight legs are looser and not secure politely.

K—Y.

The separation is a sight.

R—CK.

Chocolate is alarming in old places, chocolate is thunder.

Joining jerked sour green grass is yesterday and tomorrow and alternately.
CH—N.

Kindness is necessary and a spilled iron loan. The best choice is a sucked place readily and much any within the cut spilling.

ALF—.

Jacket in buds and in glasses, jackets entirely in collision.

A triangle is worried with recollected socks and examples.

Peace is in.

No spilling and an argument, no spilling and no spilling is beckoned. A shout is particular.

CH—N.

An heroic countenance justly named and special, special and contained and in eagle.

A mark and a window glass and a splendid chew, altogether a singer.

R—CK.

Secret in a season makes the pining wetter. So much hooding, so best to saw into right pieces the clang and the hush. The held up ocean, the eaten pan that has no cut cake, the same only different clover is the best, is the best.

K—Y.

Caution, caution all, caution the cloud and the oats and the beagle and the clearing and the happy dent and the widow soaking and the climb and the correction.

M—N H—.

Shut the chamber in the door, so well and so weak and so buttered. Shut the chest out, do not shut it in.

ALF—.

Crime, crime is that way to charge safely, crime is a tooth-pick. It is. It has a credit. Any old stick that has a choking in the way that there is leather shows a mean spirit.

An eye glass, a yellow and neck lace person, a special way to date something, any pleasing register means no readily replaced mice.

L—E.

A set cold egg, a set in together is lively.

ALF—.

A barked out sunshine, a better way to arrange Monday, a cloud of neglected Thursdays, all these are together somehow.

E—E.

A white wedding cake means a white thing and so no more left in the bottle, no more water grows.

A very likely told place is that which is not best mentioned, not the very best.

The incline is in classes in coats in whole classes puzzling peculiarly.

The best way to put it all in is a bite, it is so in every way especially.

S—NS.

Cunning, very cunning. Cute, very cute, critical, not only very critical, critical, critical.

ALF—.

Climbing into the most high piece of prepared furniture is no collection. It is part of the winding old glass.

M—N H—.

A sun in shine, and a so and a so helped angle is the same as the whole right.

THE WEDDING

It is not for nothing that the row placed quantity without grinding. Furnishing is something, individual is pointed. Beetles, only aged sounds are hot, a can in ease and a sponge full, a can in case and a wax well come, a can, a single hole, a wild suggesting wood, a half carpet and a pillow, a pillow increasing, a shirt in a cloud, a dirty distress, a thing grey, a thing thin, a long shout, a wonder, an over piece of cool oil, a sugar can, a shut open accident, a result in a feat, a copper, any copper. A cape coat, in bold shutters, in bold shutters shutting and not changing shutters not changing climaxes and feelings and hold over the switch, the binding of a pet and a revolver, the chosen loan, the owned cake in pieces, the way to swim.

B—B—B.

A language in a bath and in a dressing gown to a precision and a likely union and a single persian and a pressing quite not colored and a gloom not a gloom, and a pin all the same, and a pin not to share and a pin with a stone.

W—IE C—N.

A sudden plunge into a forest and a sudden reserve in a cup of water coldly and a dark sunshine and a squeeze, a length in all.

T—S WH—.

A kind of cataract is a hopeless stroke.

CURLS

A choked part of a loud sound in an old piece of glass is happening, it is solid and all that and not by any means noisy. The best way is just to stay any way and to think. The best way is always lively by a kind of a hoarse whisper. A shutter is only light when there is a joke. This is no use.

ALF—.

A birthday cake is in the morning when there is no use in sleeping. Supposing there is time at nine, the less often there is seven the more use there is in lending a joke. Any nice way to remain is longer than was necessary and the temptation the real temptation never happens, there is a cut away and there is a kind of a mellow cheese that has just begun.

Climbing in and climbing are the ways to change and the only hope is what is there, when it is not a difference between all of it every time.

J—S B—E.

A countenance and order and a bite, really a bit and care and receiving and a vacation and a long half mounted hat box and more silver and more in silver in some and the buttons in a hat and a mild market and goats and not coats Thursday and all health and heels in front grasses and light corn cropping, all this is a toiler and much breading and a kind of a cover is the kind unoccurringly.

KEYS

A wild waist and a simple jerk and bloom and best to come in a way, hut, heart, hide, have, within, a study, hard in, all which, black busts, coal car, gold nose, white wood, curly seize, half in, all which, best plant, cold carpet, in the glass.

KEYS

Why are stains silky and old pieces ruddy and colored angels way built. Why are knuckles calmer and pins chunks and bold in heats frightened. Why are the savage stern and old age coming. Why are the best old seem culpable and a decision, decisive.

CH—N.

Enthusiasm, prudence, cold heart and elegant example, a winding alley and a stair case center, a complete poison slip.

CH—N AND R—CK.

A clatter of curious pin cushions softly gathered by the pan that comes.

Wide in the street makes the double engagement stutter, a lean in the roll, a lean in it.

A lean in when and all came but when it was for and the hindrance and it.

A residence.

CH—N R—CK AND M—N H—.

Be advised that really no insolence is in the bicycle shop. Be advised by it.

Be advised that no belgian is strong, be wonderful.

Bet use that come in.

M—N H— AND ALF—.

An occasion to sell all cables all towels and all that is what is met, is not met.

A cold hash that means saw dust and hot enough, hot enough heating. Not cutting furiously.

A single speech is in it, a soil. A single speech. A ham. A cold. A collusion. A count. A cowslip. A tune ditch. A well king. A house to let. A cut out.

B—B—B.

A shudder makes a shake. A bit of green breeze makes a whole green breeze and a breeze is in between. A breeze is canvassed by a week wet and all sold, anything dwelling, in the mist. All the whole steer, all of it.

SHOUT

Best to shut in broken cows with mud and splinters and little pieces of gain and more steel doors a better aches and a spine and a cool school and shouting, early mounting and a best passion and a bliss and a bliss and a bliss. No wide coal gas.

One

Carl Van Vechten

One.

In the ample checked fur in the back and in the house, in the by next cloth and inner, in the chest, in mean wind.

One.

In the best most silk and water much, in the best most silk.

One.

In the best might last and wind that. In the best might last and wind in the best might last.

Ages, ages, all what sat.

One.

In the gold presently, in the gold presently unsuddenly and decapsized and dewalking.

In the gold coming in.

One.

One.

None in stable, none at ghosts, none in the latter spot.

One.

One.

An oil in a can, an oil and a vial with a thousand stems. An oil in a cup and a steel sofa.

One.

An oil in a cup and a woolen coin, a woolen card and a best satin.

A water house and a hut to speak, a water house and entirely water, water and water.

Two.

Two.

A touching white shining sash and a touching white green undercoat and a touching white colored orange and a touching piece of elastic. A touching piece of elastic suddenly.

A touching white inlined ruddy hurry, a touching research in all may day. A touching research is an over show.

A touching expartition is in an example of work, a touching beat is in the best way.

A touching box is in a coach seat so that a touching box is on a coach seat so a touching box is on a coach seat, a touching box is on a coat seat, a touching box is on a coach seat.

A touching box is on the touching so helping held.

Two.

Any left in the touch is a scene, a scene. Any left in is left somehow.

Four.

Four.

Four between, four between and hacking. Four between and hacking.

Five.

Four between and a saddle, a kind of dim judge and a great big so colored dog.

A Portrait of One

Harry Phelan Gibb

Some one in knowing everything is knowing that some one is something. Some one is something and is succeeding is succeeding in hoping that thing. He is suffering.

He is succeeding in hoping and he is succeeding in saying that that is something. He is suffering, he is suffering and succeeding in hoping that in succeeding in saying that he is succeeding in hoping is something.

He is suffering, he is hoping, he is succeeding in saying that anything is something. He is suffering, he is hoping, he is succeeding in saying that something is something. He is hoping that he is succeeding in hoping that something is something. He is hoping that he is succeeding in saying that he is succeeding in hoping that something is something. He is hoping that he is succeeding in saying that something is something.

A Curtain Raiser

Six.

Twenty.

           Outrageous.

Late,

Weak.

           Forty.

More in any wetness.

Sixty three certainly.

Five.

Sixteen.

Seven.

Three.

More in orderly. Seventy-five.

Ladies' Voices

Curtain Raiser

Ladies' voices give pleasure.

The acting two is easily lead. Leading is not in winter. Here the winter is sunny.

Does that surprise you.

Ladies voices together and then she came in.

Very well good night.

Very well good night.

(Mrs. Cardillac.)

That's silver.

You mean the sound.

Yes the sound.

Act II

Honest to God Miss Williams I don't mean to say that I was older.

But you were.

Yes I was. I do not excuse myself. I feel that there is no reason for passing an archduke.

You like the word.

You know very well that they all call it their house.

As Christ was to Lazarus so was the founder of the hill to Mahon.

You really mean it.

I do.

Act III

Yes Genevieve does not know it. What. That we are seeing Caesar.

Caesar kisses.

Kisses today.

Caesar kisses every day.

Genevieve does not know that it is only in this country that she could speak as she does.

She does speak very well doesn't she. She told them that there was not the slightest intention on the part of her countrymen to eat the fish that was not caught in their country.

In this she was mistaken.

Act IV

What are ladies voices.

Do you mean to believe me.

Have you caught the sun.

Dear me have you caught the sun.

Scene II

Did you say they were different. I said it made no difference.

Where does it. Yes.

Mr. Richard Sutherland. This is a name I know.

Yes.

The Hotel Victoria.

Many words spoken to me have seemed English.

Yes we do hear one another and yet what are called voices the best decision in telling of balls.

Masked balls.

Yes masked balls.

Poor Augustine.

What Happened

A Five Act Play

Act One

(One.)

Loud and no cataract. Not any nuisance is depressing.

(Five.)

A single sum four and five together and one, not any sun a clear signal and an exchange.

Silence is in blessing and chasing and coincidences being ripe. A simple melancholy clearly precious and on the surface and surrounded and mixed strangely. A vegetable window and clearly most clearly an exchange in parts and complete.

A tiger a rapt and surrounded overcoat securely arranged with spots old enough to be thought useful and witty quite witty in a secret and in a blinding flurry.

Length what is length when silence is so windowful. What is the use of a sore if there is no joint and no toady and no tag and not even an eraser. What is the commonest exchange between more laughing and most. Carelessness is carelessness and a cake well a cake is a powder, it is very likely to be powder, it is very likely to be much worse.

A shutter and only shutter and Christmas, quite Christmas, an only shutter and a target a whole color in every center and shooting real shooting and what can hear, that can hear that which makes such an establishment provided with what is provisionary.

(Two.)

Urgent action is not in graciousness it is not in clocks it is not in water wheels. It is the same so essentially, it is a worry a real worry.

A silence a whole waste of a desert spoon, a whole waste of any little shaving, a whole waste altogether open.

(Two.)

Paralysis why is paralysis a syllable why is it not more lively.

A special sense a very special sense is ludicrous.

(Three.)

Suggesting a sage brush with a turkey and also something abominable is not the only pain there is in so much provoking. There is even more. To begin a lecture is a strange way of taking dirty apple blossoms and is there more use in water, certainly there is if there is going to be fishing, enough water would make desert and even prunes, it would make nothing throw any shade because after all is there not more practical humor in a series of photographs and also in a treacherous scupture.

Any hurry any little hurry has so much subsistence, it has and choosing, it has.

Act Two

(Three.)

Four and nobody wounded, five and nobody flourishing, six and nobody talkative, eight and nobody sensible.

One and a left hand lift that is so heavy that there is no way of pronouncing perfectly.

A point of accuracy, a point of a strange stove, a point that is so sober that the reason left is all the chance of swelling.

(The same three.)

A wide oak a wide enough oak, a very wide cake, a lightning cooky, a single wide open and exchanged box filled with the same little sac that shines.

The best the only better and more left footed stranger.

The very kindness there is in all lemons oranges apples pears and potatoes.

(The same three.)

A same frame a sadder portal, a singular gate and a bracketed mischance.

A rich market where there is no memory of more moon than there is everywhere and yet where strangely there is apparel and a whole set.

A connection, a clam cup connection, a survey, a ticket and a return to laying over.

Act Three

(Two.)

A cut, a cut is not a slice, what is the occasion for representing a cut and a slice. What is the occasion for all that.

A cut is a slice, a cut is the same slice. The reason that a cut is a slice is that if there is no hurry any time is just as useful.

(Four.)

A cut and a slice is there any question when a cut and a slice are just the same.

A cut and a slice has no particular exchange it has such a strange exception to all that which is different.

A cut and only slice, only a cut and only a slice, the remains of a taste may remain and tasting is accurate.

A cut and an occasion, a slice and a substitute a single hurry and a circumstance that shows that, all this is so reasonable when every thing is clear.

(One.)

All alone with the best reception, all alone with more than the best reception, all alone with a paragraph and something that is worth something, worth almost anything, worth the best example there is of a little occasional archbishop. This which is so clean is precious little when there is no bath water. A long time a very long time there is no use in an obstacle that is original and has a source.

Act Four

(Four and four more.)

A birthday, what is a birthday, a birthday is a speech, it is a second time when there is tobacco, it is only one time when there is poison. It is more than one time when the occasion which shows an occasional sharp separation is unanimous.

A blanket, what is a blanket, a blanket is so speedy that heat much heat is hotter and cooler, very much cooler almost more nearly cooler than at any other time often.

A blame what is a blame, a blame is what arises and cautions each one to be calm and an ocean and a masterpiece.

A clever saucer, what is a clever saucer, a clever saucer is very likely practiced and even has toes, it has tiny things to shake and really if it were not for a delicate blue color would there be any reason for every one to differ.

The objection and the perfect central table, the sorrow in borrowing and the hurry in a nervous feeling, the question is it really a plague, is it really an oleander, is it really saffron in color, the surmountable appetite which shows inclination to be warmer, the safety in a match and the safety in a little piece of splinter, the real reason why cocoa is cheaper, the same use for bread as for any breathing that is softer, the lecture and the surrounding large white soft unequal and spread out sale of more and still less is no better, all this makes one regard in a season, one hat in a curtain that in rising higher, one landing and many many more, and many more many more many many more.

Act Five

(Two.)

A regret a single regret makes a door way. What is a door way, a door way is a photograph.

What is a photograph a photograph is a sight and a sight is always a sight of something. Very likely there is a photograph that gives color if there is then there is that color that does not change any more than it did when there was much more use for photography.

White Wines

Three Acts

1. All together.
2. Witnesses.
3. House to house.
(5 women)

All together.
Cunning very cunning and cheap, at that rate a sale is a place to use type writing. Shall we go home.

Cunning, cunning, quite cunning, a block a strange block is filled with choking.

Not too cunning, not cunning enough for wit and a stroke and careless laughter, not cunning enough.

A pet, a winter pet and a summer pet and any kind of a pet, a whole waste of pets and no more hardly more than ever.

A touching spoon a real touching spoon is golden and show in that color. A really touching spoon is splendid, is splendid, and dark and is so nearly just right that there is no excuse.

The best way is to wave an arm, the best way is to show more used to it than could be expected.

Comfort a sudden way to go home, comfort that and the best way is known.

All together.
Hold hard in a decision about eyes. Hold the tongue in a sober value as to bunches. See the indication in all kinds of rigorous landscapes. Spell out what is to be expected.

Show much blame in order and all in there, show much blame when there is a breath in a flannel. Show the tongue strongly in eating. Puzzle anybody.

Violet and the ink and the old ulster, shut in trembling and a whole departure, flood the sunshine, terrorize the grown didy, mingle sweetness with communion.

All together.
Change the sucking with a little sucking.

Modify the brave gallant pin wheel. Show the shout, worry with wounds, love out what is a pendant and a choke and a dress in together.

Punish the grasshopper with needles and pins are plenty. Show the old chink.

All together.
Put the putty in before the door put the oil glass in with what is green. Put the mellow choice with all the test, rust with night and language in the waist. Praise the cat and show the twine the door, mention every scrap of linen carpet, see the eagle and behold the west, win the day light with the hat unpressed, show it in a shudder and a limp, make a best container with no speed, and a jacket and a choice and beets, beets are what there are when bets are less. Bets are less in summer.

Single Witnesses
(I). A spread out case is so personal it is a mountain of change and any little piece is personal, any one of them is an exchange. No forethought is removed. Nothing, hindrances, butter, a safe smooth, a safe why is a tongue a season, why is a loin large by way of spoiling. There is no cake in front. A choking is an example.

More witnesses.
It is true, it certainly is true and a coat any coat, any dress, all dress, a hat, many hats, all colors, every kind of coloring, all this makes shadows longer and birds, makes birds, just makes birds.

Not much limping is in the back, not much limping is in the front, not much limping is circular, a bosom, a candle, an elegant foot fall, all this makes daylight.

Single Witnesses.
(2). A blunder in a charger is blue. A high pocket not higher than the wrist and the elbow, the pocket is not added.

A clutch, a real clutch is merry and a joke and a baby, a real clutch is such a happy way. A real clutch is so soon worried so easily made the same, so soon made so.

A real white and blue, blue and blue, blue is raised by being so and more much more is ready. At last a person is safe.

More Witnesses.
Pile in the windows, freeze with the doors, paint with the ceiling, shut in the floors, paint with the ceiling, paint with the doors, shut in the ceiling, shut out the doors, shut in the doors, shut in the floors, shut in the floors, shut in the doors.

More Witnesses.
Put the patient goat away, put the patient boat away, put away the boat and put it, the boat, put it, put away that boat. Put away the boat.

Single Witnesses.
(3). An army of invincible and ever ready mustaches and all the same mind and a way of winding and no more repertoire, not any more noise, this did increase every day.

A moon, a moon, a darkness and the stars and little bits of eels and a special sauce, not a very special sauce, not only that.

A wide pair that are not slippers, not a wide pair of slippers, not pressed to be any of that in that particular but surely, surely, surely a loan, surely every kind of a capital.

More Witnesses.

A splendid little charles louis philip, a splendid spout of little cups and colds, a splendid big stir, a splendid glass, a splendid little splinter, a splendid cluster.

Single Witnesses.
(4). Why should wet be that and cut, cut with the grass, why should wet be that and clut with the purse, why should wet be wet and the wet that wet. Why should wet be the time to class. Why should there be solemn cuppings.

The lean bark, that is the round and intense and common stop and in shouting, the left bark and the right bark and a belt, in that belt, in no belt and a corset, in a belt and chores, in a belt and single stitches, in more boys than enough, in all thin beer and in all such eggs, in all the pile and in all the bread, in the bread, in the bread, in the condition of pretty nearly saying that yesterday is today, and tomorrow, tomorrow is yesterday. The whole swindle is in short cake and choice cake is white cake and white cake is sponge cake and sponge cake is butter.

House to house.
(1). A habit that is not left by always screaming, a habit that is similar to the one that made quiet quite quiet and made the whole plain show dust and white birds and little plaintive drops of water, a habit which brightened the returning butter fly and the yellow weed and even tumbling, the habit which made a well choose the bottom and refuses all chances to change, the habit that cut in two whatever was for the use of the same number, the habit which credited a long touch with raising the table and the hour glass and even eye glasses and plenty of milk, the habit which made a little piece of cheese wholesome and darkness bitter and clanging a simple way to be solemn, a habit which has the best situation and nearly all the day break and the darkness a habit that is cautious and serious and strange and violent and even a little disturbed, a habit which is better than almost anything, a habit that is so little irritating, so wondering and so unlikely is not more difficult than every other.

(2). A change a real change is made by a piece, by any piece by a whole mixture of words and likenesses and whole outlines and ranges, a change is a butt and a wagon and an institution, a change is a sweetness and a leaning and a bundle, a change is no touch and buzzing and cruelty, a change is no darkness and swinging and highness, a change is no season and winter and leaving, a change is no stage and blister and column, a change is no black and silver and copper, a change is no jelly and anything proper, a change is not place, a change is not church, a change is not more clad, a change is not more in between when there is that and the change is the kind and the king is the king and the king is the king and the king is the king.

(3). Could there be the best almost could there be almost the most, could there be almost almost, could there be the most almost. Could there be the most almost, could there be the most almost, could there be almost almost. Could there be almost, almost.

Can the stretch have any choice, can the choice have every chunk, can the choice have all the choice, can the stretch have in the choice. Can there be water, can there be water and water. Can there be water. Can there be.

(4). A cousin to cooning, a cousin to that and mixed labor and a strange orange and a height and a piece of holy phone and a catching hat glass and a bit of undertaking. All this makes willows and even then there is no use in dusting not in really redusting, not in really taking everything away. The best excuse for shadows is in the time when white is starched and hair is released and all the old clothes are in the best bag.

House to house.
A wet hurt and a yellow stain and a high wind and a color stone, a place in and the whole real set all this and each one has a chin. This is not a claim it is a reorganization and a balance and a return.

Do Let Us Go Away

A Play

(Theodore.) I don't think it's my fault I don't think I could do it so unconsciously. I think she brings it in every morning.

(Nicholas.) I used to be hurried, now I imagine I will not be.

(Theodore.) It is not necessary to dance or sing. Let us sing that song. Let us call them their names Nicholas. Theodore we will. We are dishonored. We visit one another and say good-bye.

(Nicholas.) I do not like to be teased. It is so easy to kill mosquitoes but what is the use when we are discouraged by the war. We are so are the Japanese. We will never mention them.

(Theodore.) My principle idea is to eat my meals in peace.

> They withdraw. Several people come in. With one of them there is a dog. His name is Polybe. They speak to each other.

100 dollars good-bye good-bye good-bye.

(Jane and Nicholas and Theodore and the lawyer and the children.)

(Jane.) I speak slowly. I do it intentionally.

(Henry.) We have fragments. We call out sometimes. When two bands are playing they play in the distance. Some play in people's houses. We say hush.

(Arthur.) Dishonored. Never believe in September. Never believe in September in the sense of visions.

(Henry.) I do know the chorus. Individual cases do not bring the war home to me. I suddenly remember and I rest in it. I am ashamed. I have patience and earnest feeling. I am liking the new boat. It is still painted white and is enormously disappointing. Some one has been willing. Oh I am disgusted. This is not the conversation.

(Helen.) The same. I am a settled character. I have visions of welcoming them. They do behave so well and eat so regularly and very well too. They grow almonds in their grounds and I like to eat them green or later. I like to eat them. They are willing. Do not disappoint me.

(Nicholas.) Don't cry.

(Nicholas.) I am looking for a candle. I have it. I am putting it in a Venetian box. Please leave it alone. Don't tease me. I have it. I can place it.

(Theodore.) We are altogether.

> Silence and the lights are out. Everybody is laughing. They say (Leave it alone. We like to hear it.) They are very patient. (I cannot spare another handkerchief.)

Anybody can come in. We were surprised to see musicians. There were servants.

(Albert.) Do not repeat it. I tell you I won't have it. I will have a justice of the peace.

(He did.)

Jenny is sick.

(Jenny.) I am sick.

(The lawyer.) I went often to see you and every day I said I love you better I do love you better. That's it.

> They were together and they said John are you going. He said something.

They were altogether.

I often think about it.

Genevieve was patient. She was angry because the water was another color.

She said. He is very good now.

A scene where there are two houses. One on either side and we are in the middle there is a great deal of talking in one of them. In the other they eat a late dinner.

(Nicholas.) Anthony. Henriette open the other door and tell mamma. I'll tell mamma.

Mamma coockcoo.

(Pirate.) What is a pirate not a man who kills and pursues boats but the one who has a family, he is the one who comes home today, he expects to be hated. We don't have that feeling.

A scene.

They all laugh.

Please rent a garden for chickens and a turkey.

I wonder if I like dancing.

I can mention a subject which is agreeable so agreeable and exciting and there are three names two of them are almost alike.

We are there.

The Scene

Conversation. I asked him did he like to hear the dog bark. He said he would shoot at him. I said did he like to hear it. We were ashamed of his servants. They talked together loudly. We hoped he would control them.

He wrote it. So did they together. Please have peace. Say the date. Please have the Fangturm. Please have peace. Please don't fish so near the shore. Please do not be asked to buy it when it is living. It is not disgusting. All of us are not so pleased.

(Nicholas and Jane.) They are old. They have taken the house for the month of September and we do hope that they will go away. We do hope that they will go away.

The proprietor came and took the almonds. We said do not take the grapes, we will not give you the key.

Have we gotten as far as that.

Mallorcan singing.

They are all singing they sing the song about the chicken. Jenny Chicken does not sing a song about the chicken. She says she does not like them small.

I am so bothered.

I am angry.

I am angry at these sounds. They say.

This is Spain and I say. It is not.

(Nicholas.) I have a governess. She tells me to pray. I am not religious.

Servants can speak to each other. Two of them have long hair. They all wear it down their back.

Come in. We are not coming tonight. We hope to see the fire-works. There will also be a procession. Do you believe you will see the procession. We will see the fire-works from here.

(Paul.) Thunder. It will not rain yet. It usually does not at this season. I hope that a war will come. I would like to be interpreter.

(Antonio.) I believe in merrymaking. It has been possible for me to catch fish. I avoided cooking the lunch by leaving two young boys in charge. Their names were Clarence and Emanuel.

(Clarence.) I will see to everything.

(Emanuel.) I will help you.

(Pablo.) I will be of some assistance.

(Antonio.) I will come when called.

(Maggie.) I do not like hot weather.

The part of the house which has windows back and front is cooler.

Coming together.

We move.

I will tell you about Eugenia. She moved the table and hopes to be married. I do not think so because I do not think she is attractive. There is not a family in which some do not embroider. It is a great industry.

The wind.

There is wind every day.

I am so disappointed.

It is difficult to stop now because of annoyances. Now we will tell of the things that were sent together.

We were surprised they had not moved in. Open homes.

Go on. Go on.

Making people better.

The servants. They did say that they were Spanish. I said they weren't.

I said Spaniards were polite.

(Nicholas.) I have seen the consul he is going to get me my passport.

(William.) But he can't he is only consular agent. He has to send to Barcelona.

(Nicholas.) I was not speaking of him. I was speaking of the ambassador.

(William.) Oh that's another matter.

Mr. and Mrs. Clement came in they said that they had lost a friend.

Music.

When they ask for money for the sailors who were drowned they make gay music.

When they say here is some one who refuses to give them something they are impertinent.

(Brothers.) How did we know they were brothers. We knew it because they have the same perplexity. He has lost money in boats and he has in steel cars.

(Officials.) Come together you can fly a kite if you like. We do not like. We like to see others do it. It is not much trouble. It depends entirely on the height of the house.

Nicholas Jane and Anthony and the evening rain. It comes every morning about two and we have the habit of closing up.

Please me. I will.

Three months yes three months.

Piles of initials he made piles of initials. Would any one think that they embroidered the name in Mallorca.

(Stephen.) How much is it.

(Stephen.) Forty-five.

(Stephen.) We will change it to forty.

Older ones have gotten to see that it's dangerous to go to Marseilles.

(The colonel.) He owns this house and he wants the almond crop.

We said we did not know that.

He said it was in the lease. Mr. Clement said he had never heard of such a thing being done.

We met an old frenchman.

We met the people who are going around together and asking for money.

(Genevieve.) Widows should have it.

(Bobbie.) Do as you like.

We asked them not to come in.

The dealer his wife and the servant. Hush don't wake anybody. You must not call out to one another. Everybody does it. We do not ask you to control the others. We have decided not to say anything to you about them.

(The owner of the house.) I am assisting and I am further obliged to come tomorrow. Will you kindly give me the key.

(The servant.) Will you kindly give me some water. Will you show me the way to go.

(The wife.) I will not believe that they are settled. It is a great disappointment to me.

Plenty of time.

Beginning tomorrow can we count a month before they return to the city.

Counting tomorrow can we count a month before they leave the country.

It is a disappointment to me that we have not been able to be rid of that which is bothering us. It is a great disappointment to me.

Two count, we count two.

The one came first.

He eats sweetbreads by preference and he has a wife and a child. I did not mean him.

The one came later and is really not very well pleased.

He does not care for the vegetables which are for sale here.

We know an old man that we like better. We like to see that he is met.

When did the owner of the house decide to write to us. He did not write. He came.

(The owner.) It was agreed that you take it by three months. It will disturb me to come up once a month for the money.

It was agreed that we take it by the month and we will send you your money by mail.

(The owner.) If it is lost it will be at your risk.

It will not be lost.

(The owner.) I am very anxious to have you pleased with the house.

We like the view.

(The owner.) Did the storm do much injury.

A little rain came in.

(The owner.) I meant to the trees.

I do not think so.

What is it.

We went together.

We did not feel too warm.

There is much talk of obligation.

We never have butter.

We are not going to.

The rest of the day was there. He said that he would be pleased if we came again and asked for that which we were to get.

(The older woman.) Do not for one moment think of not receiving back that which is owing to you.

We said that we have made a mistake.

Excuse me. Come in some time tomorrow.

Tomorrow in a week.

A week is over on Sunday.

Come tomorrow.

This evening at four.

Tomorrow too.

Come tomorrow or early not before six.

We will have them to-morrow.

Yes tomorrow.

They had them. They were the kind that lit themselves. We were so careful. We said yes we like the kind that we have had.

By believing in everything we happen to be careful to ask what was paid.

It is necessary to know how the time is arranged.

(William.) Teeth, do not mention teeth. My front teeth are longer.

Is it surprising that every one is fond of mutton.

Is it.

I think it is.

(Monica.) I am careful about turns. I walk up hill.

She is enthusiastic she has gone in whenever there was kite flying.

(Anthony.) Whatever you do don't make a noise.

Please be careful of me.

Let us talk about fowls.

When we went hunting we had eleven dogs. They ran after rabbits. We went there. Ours is certainly not petted. He likes to be able to be told that it is true.

Jenny, sister, Nicholas and Hermann.

Who did he call to.

He did not call me away.

He was hoping for other results. We bowed politely.

To be seventy five.

To be seventy five together.

To be able to see stitches.

To have decided not to stay here.

We will not see to count.

The End of May

The weather in June is like the weather in September. The end of May is cooler.

The bathman is disgusted that the Mallorcans don't bathe in September. The water is warm in September. It is warmer in July and August.

(The War.) Are there German submarines in Spanish waters.

(Signor Dato.) There are no german submarines in Spanish waters.

(Marquis of Ibyza.) I hate the English.

(The King.) Have you any daughters.

(Marquis of Ibyza.) I have.

(The King.) Then leave them all alone.

(The Cuban Boat.) It has sunk.

(The sailors.) They all came from Saint Katherine square.

The sailors were all drowned. A great deal of money was collected for their families.

In speaking of Mallorca we must remember that there is making acquaintance. They make acquaintance with each other.

(Jane.) I will not be old. I have four children. The two servants are man and wife.

(Iphegenia.) To work hard is commendable if one earns money. I do not wish to be married. I wish to be sure of marriage. I have selected my sisters. They do embroidery. I will not copy them. I am not so old. I have a younger brother and sister. I do not pay attention. We do not pay attention to one another. I am in a way disappointed. I do believe in fish. Everybody does in Mallorca.

(Minorca answering in french.) I know the name of Mary Rose.

What is a saint.

Stamp on a flag.

Believe in your country.

Singing at night.

(Paul.) I am going to see John.

(John.) Come when you like. How is your wife.

(Paul.) My wife is tired. We walked too far yesterday. It was beautiful moonlight.

(John.) Remember me to her.

(Paul.) How is your wife today.

(John.) Oh she is all right now.

(Paul.) And Bartholomew.

(John.) Bartholomew is not here just now. He has gone down stairs.

(Paul.) Yes I saw Bartholomew when I came in.

We do not know whether it has anything to do with the weather whether they will go away. It is said by every one that almost every one goes away by the middle of October. They came in July. We hear something.

Yes it's german. They give French music too and one English and one American. They are all there but they do not say it.

I dance.

Keep still.

Do keep still.

They keep our dog still.

We kept our dog still.

We can see signs that they are going away. I do not wish to say this in the manner of Monica.

When do car conductors work.

They work in the evening.

Miss Alice Toklas wishes Roberts to kindly send her by registered mail—under separate cover—1 Ivory soap—and a good face soap that Roberts can recommend.

(Genevieve.) The melon is always warmer in the center when it has been in the sun.

Well then we will have the green.

That's the way our melons are cooled.

They are not going today.

We have decided that we will tell the consul that we were very glad to see him.

(Genevieve.) I am angry. I will not go to the workingman.

(Monica.) I am not angry I am going to lie down.

(Nicholas.) I believe in loud furnaces.

(William.) I am married.

Are you.

To whom.

If they go away they leave suddenly. This is not the way they came. They came unexpectedly. They will not go away suddenly.

> Always sincerely yours.
> Mabel Weeks.

He can do as he pleases with Mary Rose.

He can do as he pleases with Mary Rose.

Not finished yet. When can we come in and bring Mary Rose.

(Monica.) I like Polly. He is so handsome.

(Monica.) And we were right.

(Genevieve.) Why were we not right.

(Nicholas.) Because we felt that it was not true.

(Paul.) Why does the german boat give out oil.

(William.) Because it wishes to feed german submarines.

(The Marquis.) I will express my wishes.

(The landlord.) That is as you wish sir.

(Monica.) I like to feel that if any one falls I fall.

(Paul.) I am going to fix the string with a wire.

Thanks so much when will it be done.

(Paul.) I will do it tomorrow.

(Nicholas.) Saturday does not include Sunday.

Doesn't it.

(Nicholas.) Not in Palma in Mallorca.

You mean that they will all go away.

(Nicholas.) Not right away but they won't stay.

Very well. Good-bye.

(May Mary.) Yes I hear.

When the girl went away we said they had umbrellas. When the rest went away they said good-bye.

Let us wait and see.

We waited for them and they passed. They were all of them old. They had loud voices. We want to know in a neutral country have they servants.

Please be able to finish.

(Nicholas.) Mamma Coockcoo.

(Joseph.) Dolores Dolores.

(Jane.) Jenny give me the keys. Oh yes. I am waiting.

(Nicholas.) Follow me.

(The lawyer.) Stay to play.

The End.

Yes I have a brother.

Sitting at a cafe.

For the Country Entirely

A Play in Letters

Almond trees in the hill. We saw them to-day.

Dear Mrs. Steele.

I like to ask you questions. Do you believe that it is necessary to worship individuality. We do.

Mrs. Henry Watterson.

Of course I have heard.

Dear Sir. Of course I have heard.

They didn't leave the book.

Dear Sir.

They didn't leave the book.

Yes Yes.

I know what I hear. Yes sir.

Dear Sir.

I heard her hurrying.

We all did.

Good night.

Isabel Furness.

I like their names.

Anthony Rosello.

It's easy to name a street like that.

It is.

With a view

Of trees and a hill.

Yes sir.

Herbert.

Dear Herbert.

Come again.

William.

William Cook.

Chapter 2.

Dear Sir. A play.

A great many people ask me in misery.

Have they come.

Dear friends. Say what you have to say.

Dear Whitehead and Paul and Woolston and Thorne.

Why can't you accomodate yourselves and leave me alone. I don't mean to day or yesterday or by counting. Everybody cannot count. An avenue goes through a city and a street crosses it crosses the city. There is no use in pointing out associations. A great many people can read. Not women. Not in some countries. Not in some countries. Oh yes not in some countries.

Caesar.

Caesar isn't a name that is not used. I have known that a great many people have it.

Henry Caesar. A class is full and teaching is difficult. They do not understand. Who does not understand. The Barcelonese.

Color. A country and a cup where they sell water.

Everybody sells water. In this country. Everybody sells water in this country. Is it a hot country. It is not and water is plentiful. Then I do not understand you. You need not question me.

Dear girl.

Grandfathers can not make sacrifices for their children.

It is not expected of them and they are not sacrificed. A great many people are sacrificed.

Oh dear yes.

Helen.

CHAPTER 3.

Why do you play in letters.

Because we are English.

Is it an English custom.

It is not an American.

Oh yes I remember you did mention.

Dear Mr. and Mrs. Eaton.

Can you recollect can you remember what day it was that we promised to go into the wind and not take shelter.

I cannot remember that we ever undertook to do that.

We are going in another direction.

To day.

And day after to morrow.

We often spell together.

We like latin.

How goes it.

Frederick and Harriet Beef.

Do be anxious about me.

We are not anxious about me.

No you were told to be so were you not.

We were not advised.

No indeed you were not.

Dear Mr. Colin Bell.

Do be gracious and come again.

Soon.

As soon as you like.

I do not know how to reply.

No you don't and I am so uneasy.

Not today.

No not at all.

Dear Sir.

      Good night.

Act 2.

Here we come to act two.

Australian papers.

Canadian papers.

American papers.

Dear Miss Millicant.

      Do not be insulting.

You know very well that we have not conscription.

Were you surprised.

In states.

Or in territories.

My dear Milly. I wish you would come and tell me about Rigoletto.

Oh yes handkerchiefs

From Bonnets.

Good evening Mrs.

That is not well said.

Dear Gilbert. Remember me to your mother.

All the time.

Dear Mr. Lindo Webb.

I understand why you are not better liked. A great many people expect you to teach them English. You do so and very well. You might be married and have a wife and son. With these helping you to teach you could teach many more people English.

Then we can expect that you will change your place of residence.

We do not expect you to change your coat. No Englishman does. We understand that.

Young Bonnet.

We have been very much annoyed by the impertinence of Mr. Alfred Bonnet.

Little pieces of paper are suddenly burnt.

In believing a shoe maker you believe his father.

I do not believe his father.

Why because he does not dress well.

Dress well dress well.

Dear Mrs. Cook.

Have you any special wishes. Do you want to know about almond leaves and almond roots. Or do you refer to olive roots. Olive trees have large roots. I do not know about almond trees.

The rest of the time was spent in deploring the tempest.

Dear Mrs. Carlock.

I do not know the name. I have often been told that the easiest way to be believed is to examine every one. I have endeavored to do so but without success. Some people believe that they will be killed. By this I mean that they delight in teaching.

Some teach very well. Some teach in the north. Do not stay away.

Sincerely yours and not carelessly.

Walter Winter.

How do you know my name. I speak three languages spanish french and english.

Dear Mr. Cook.

How do you do. Do you mean that you are able to stay.

The rest of the afternoon.

I do understand a red nose.

Not today.

No not to-day. You see the explanation is this.

We will not be pleased altogether.

Mrs. Cook I ask of you do not come again.

Do you mean it.

I cannot understand Mary Rose Palmer.

I can understand explaining things to one another.

We were there and the almond flowers turned to almond leaves.

Dear Mr. Cook.

Come again.

Sincerely yours

Daisy Clement.

Act 3.

In the country and for the country.

Dear Master. Do not say so.

You mean there is no such address.

I do not mean that I criticize. I do mean that the method used does not agree with me.

Certainly not.

Sincerely yours.

Harmon.

Why do you need a name.

I don't know. I like the point of Inca.

Do not see it everywhere.

I will not.

Dear land.

When I call away I do not mean that I wish the coal to burn. It is not necessary to tell me that the peas will suffer. They certainly will not neither will the pinks.

Thank you for using that word.

Dear me it is windy.

SCENE 2.

Dear Sir. Mr. Cousins told me that they were away when it happened. They recollected being asked if they were well if they had recovered from their emotion. They were also asked if their wives and children were well. They certainly did not know how to say excuse me I do not know who you are. They might have said I would wish to know your name because it would not be right not to be able to give your message and if we do not know your name we cannot say from whom the message came.

This was not done.

Dear Sir. Do not be angry with your government.

Sincerely yours.

William Hague.

SCENE 3.

This was the way to reason. Did he leave after the other came. Was he a sea captain. Was the other one of the same profession although a citizen of another nation. Now as to the word citizen. The use of it differs. Some are inclined to ratify the use of it others prefer to ask what is a citizen. A citizen is one who employing all the uses of his nature cleans the world of adjoining relations. In this way we cannot conquer. We do conquer and I ask how, how do you do.

Dear Sir. When it is necessary to come you will come.

Yes sir.

Dear sir. When it is necessary to be hurried you are not nervous.

Not at all.

Very well.

Dear Sir. Why have you special places for your handkerchiefs.

Because they have been so charmingly embroidered.

You are pleased then.

Yes very pleased indeed.

Scene 3.

Dear Sir.

     Extra dresses.

Oh yes.

See here. Extra gloves.

I do not like the word gloves it has a combination of letters in it that displeases me.

Since when.

Since this evening.

I do not understand your objection.

It is easy to understand if I explain.

Dear Genevieve. Do say where you heard them speak of the decision they had come to not to have masked balls.

I didn't say. They always have masked balls.

Oh so they do.

Yes indeed they do.

There are many of them.

A great many.

Looks.

Looks to me.

Dear Sir. Why have you such splendid olive trees.

Dear Mr. Wilson.

Why have you such plain entrances.

What do you mean.

I mean in Mallorca they do it in such a way that every house has an interesting entrance.

You mean chairs.

Yes I mean chairs.

Act 4.

Scene 1.

Dear Sir. Please do not persist.

The one in the house said it.

Dear Lady Cryst what do you say to that again.

I say nothing.

Indeed you are discreet and timid.

Mrs. Seeman has been disappointed. In Saint Katherine.

Yes because of the children.

How do you mean.

One of them was not bewildering and he blasphemed the saints.

Oh no.

No one could be older.

You mean today.

I mean anyday.

Dear Sir. Come to another conclusion.

Yes I will.

Receive me and Cuba. You mean the name. Yes the name. You always liked hearing noises. Not in France. No indeed not in France.

Not in France.

No indeed.

Really you prepare me. I do. Not today. Today. You prepare me today.

Scene 2.

This is so pleasing.

Dear Sir. How do you pronounce Crowtell.

The land is very near and is seen and nuns fix it.

And the tramway.

Shall I say street car.

Not necessarily here it is more a country road and the electricity is easily had.

Everywhere.

Yes everywhere.

That is such a comfort.

Dear sir. You mean dear Mr. Rossilo do you know my older brother.

Scene 3.

Charles King. Lindo Webb Lindo Webb.

Dear Charles King. You do not mind that I am in distress. I have no means of satisfying myself whether I am obliged to be careful or not.

Careful of what.

Of what I say in public.

Certainly not.

No.

Certainly not.

Dear Mr. Lindo Webb.

Come again will you.

A great many mountains are higher than any on the island.

Do you believe in lessons.

Of course I do.

So does Mrs. Gilbert.

Scene 4.

I am enjoying it.

Dear Mr. Lindo Webb. Why do you wish to win.

In the more readily seen places there is no muttering. You mean no quarreling. I mean neither one or the other.

Oh I understand you.

By that I mean that I am poor.

I see what you mean.

Dear Woodrow. This is a name.

What does anybody mean by interesting.

That is not a word that has that position.

You mean not nicely.

I mean that I am English.

Dear Mr. Henry. What have you been meaning to do.

Scene 5.

Dear Sir. Why do you speak.

Dear Sir. Please me.

How can I be called.

Do you wish to go to market.

Dear Sir. Do you wish me to go to market.

Dear Sir. Do you wish me to have that made.

How do you mean.

Scene 6.

Dear Sir. Remember that when you have no further requests to make you must not blame me.

Dear Sir. I know you do not object to smoke.

Dear Mrs. Lindo Webb How can you break your teeth.

By falling down in the street.

You mean now when the pavement is so dark.

Naturally.

It would not have happened otherwise.

This is because of the necessary condition of lighting.

We all suffer from that.

SCENE 7.

Do you remember Charles Mark. Figs. Especially mentioned figs.

Dear Sir. Will you come today and wear three diamond rings and an officers suit. You have a perfect right to wear an officer's suit. You are a major.

Dear Mrs. English. Do you like a different country.

Do you mean higher up in the hills.

Not so very much higher.

Act 5.

Scene 1.

This is the last time we will use seasoning.

You mean you like it better cold.

No don't be foolish.

Dear Sir. Is there much wisdom in searching for asphodels.

Not if you already know what they are.

We do know now.

Then there is no use in trying to accustom yourself to their beauty. But we don't find it beautiful. I too have failed to find beauty in them.

This is not surprising as they do not grow prettily.

They were a great disappointment to us.

Scene 2.

We all are able to see I don't care a bit about Lena. We are all able to say I don't care a bit about Lena.

Dear Mrs. Landor. How can you cease to be troubled about the rest of the winter. How can you cease to be troubled about the rest of the summer and the beginning of the winter.

Dear Sir. Every evening the snow falls. Red. Yes and so do the asphodels. Asphodel isn't red. I know it it looks so.

Dear friend. Can you give me any pleasure.

Yesterday afternoon was a holiday. You mean a festival. I mean a day of the country.

Do you mean that you understand the country.

No indeed.

Scene 3.

Dear friends. Have patience.

Scene 4.

This has ended very well.

You mean meeting one another.

Yes and asking us to remain here.

You mean that a great many people were troubled.

Not a great many people.

Some are very happy.

So are others.

We all have wishes.

Expressed wishes.

Dear Sir. Will you come again and eat ham.

Not in this country.

Fish.

Not in this country.

Turkey and Bones and Eating and We Liked It

A Play

He was very restless. He does not like to stand while he picks flowers. He does not smell flowers. He has a reasonable liking for herbs. He likes their smell. He is not able to see storms. He can see anything running. He has been able to be praised.

SCENE I.

Polybe and seats.
Straw seats which are so well made that they resemble stools. They are all of straw and thick. They are made with two handles.

Genevieve and cotton.
I do not like cotton drawers. I prefer wool or linen. I admit that linen is damp. Wool is warm. I believe I prefer wool.

Minorca and dogs.
I like a dog which is easily understood as I have never had the habit of going out except on Sunday. Now I go out every day.

Anthony and coal.
I believe that coal is better than wood. If coal is good it burns longer. In any case it is very difficult to get here.

Felix and a letter.
I do not wish to reply to a telegram, not because I find it difficult to explain in it that I wished to see you. I did wish to see you.

Mr. Clement.
It gives me great pleasure to meet you. I am feeling well today and I see that you are enjoying the mild weather. It will continue so. I hope you will

be pleased. I will present myself to you in saying that I am certain that you are deriving pleasure from your winter. I am certainly eager.

William.

He is too difficult. I mean he is too difficult. I don't believe you understand me yet. He is too difficult.

SCENE II.

She would not insist. We were to have a saddle of mutton. We were served first with a not distasteful supply of vegetables. There was ham in it and pork. These had boiling and they were a sauce. Let me tell you about the german.

A little girl.

I can tell blue when I see it.

A German.

Look.

Italians.

We expect to go home.

When

When the cigarettes come. I know these were stale. If I go to the war I will be readily excused because I am lame. You have every reason to be lame. You are a waiter but the out of door life may do you good.

Genevieve.

I could not leave the house as I was expecting the reparation of a mattress.

You did not find it necessary to leave the house.

Not in the morning.

William and Mary.

William is William and he does not use any precaution. He is not very adroit.

She. Will you drink wine.

I do.

I know that but will you take any now.

I don't mind the taste of it.

This is really not wine. It is a concoction of brown sugar and water and fermented juice. I call it wine it is a drink. I did not know it was not wine.

The count.

Why does the count wish for this house. He wishes for it because it has all conveniences. It really hasn't but it is better situated than the one he has now.

Raymond and Jenny.

I do like a Spanish name a Spanish name always begins with a V.

We went together.

We went together and we did not go to the Opera. The opera that was being given was Boris Goudonoff.

SCENE III.

A whole collection of stamps. A family meeting.

Where did you get it.

I got it when I saw the envelope.

Where did you see it.

Don't hold it.

Don't spoil it.

Let me see it.

Thanks.

Thanks so much.

I thank you.

I thank you for your kindness.

Please make a collection of flowers.

Collecting flowers is not a misery. You have to carry something a handkerchief will do and more than that is perfectly selfish.

We are not perfectly selfish.

William. Do be persevering.

Mrs. Clement. I am. I do not leave my house.

Genevieve. Don't you leave your house.

Mr. and Mrs. Clement. We do.

Maud. The hills would be better than water. We like water.

Mrs. Clement. Everybody likes water.

Maud. And fish.

Genevieve. I do not care for the fish here.

William. Radishes.

Maud. Radishes are strong.

Mrs. Clement. I am glad to have seen you.

SCENE IV.

An interlude.

If you were a Breton and read a book and understood Spanish would you be richer than a frenchman who talked in a field. If a man talked in a field and told about papers and contraband and laughed would you see a resemblance in him to a Swiss. I would. This is what happened. He says it is very necessary to be young to be young and unmarried and then you can not do as you please. You can not go where you please. He believed that it was alright. I am certain that he understood talking. He also laughed. I am not convinced that ploughing is safe. Ploughing is done with a plough and under a tree. Dogs bark, little dogs bark the horse and sometimes a mule and sometimes a donkey. The people say leave it to me. I will not.

SCENE V.

Farmer.

Listen to me.

I will not.

Then do not listen to me.

I heard you when you said it. I like to see goats feed.

And so do I like to see them lay the tracks.

They are laying them for the electrical railroad.

Sarah. I don't like him. I don't like his ways. I don't like it and I will not say it. I will do as you do and you do it so nicely. I will do as you do and then we were right. We were right to ask him to come in. He will not come in. I will not go out. We will not stay there. We will say yes certainly, we are not very busy. Yes please see that you have the things you want. You have not been given them. Don't fail to come again when you need them.

A Farmer.

A fisherman.

We don't like to look at a wall.

A Fisherman and a farmer.

They both believe in fish. Fish is a fertilizer. It cannot be found in the bay. You do not have to go out far. You have to have a great many boats.

An English mother.

You make me quite afraid of dogs.

SCENE VI.

A water faucet.

We were very likely to meet one another. None of us have running water. The count Rangle had.

We were all fond of winter. We said we liked summer. The trouble with the summer is that it is too hot. You see I am convinced.

Harold.

Harold is your name. I thought it was Martin.

It is Martin or Mark.

Thank you.

You speak English.

Yes certainly.

And french.

Very nicely.

And Hindustani.

My mother does.

I supposed she did.

We had never thought about it.

SCENE VII.

ACT II.

We are deserted. We are left alone. They are going to Paris. We stay here.

Minorca. And there is such a nice view.

A dinner.

Tomorrow.

Every day.

Yes every day.

In the morning.

We will ride. We will come home. Yes we will. Don't bother. Yes you need to we understand. We will meet you at half past one old time. You need never be drunk. It is an older word.

Do be clear.

Golly Moses it is damp out here.

Any little piece of paper makes a wind.

Yes yes.

Anthony and Cleopatra.
Do you like him. I must go and see the workingmen.

Do you like them they are giving our son a knife.

Whom does he resemble. The son resembles his mother. Don't say it.

Why not.

Because the father does not prefer to hear it. He prefers to hear that the son resembles him.

The son resembles him but he looks like his mother.

They wish him to have every advantage.

Change of scene.
In walking home we did not go that way. I had my reason for not going that way. I did not care about losing a button. As a matter of fact I didn't lose it.

Winnie and William.
How are they today.

They are going away.

We are going away.

I am sorry.

We are not sorry.

No I cannot say whether we are not sorry.

We are not sorry.

Another climate.
The ponds are frozen. We did not read that today.

Mike wrote it.

We were very careful to look at the water.

It was not cold here.

There are a great many times when there is rain.

Oh yes.

All right.

He.

He came in.

What is the name of it.

I cannot say it.

Do not say it.

I do not care to look at any one.

I do.

Then please yourself.

I do not understand electricity.

I do.

I do not understand hail.

I can explain it.

I do not care for history.

I can read it.

I do not care about individual wishes.

I understand it.

Plenty of people do love another.

She.

Loud voices are attractive. When two people talk together they have to talk louder.

I wish you would not talk about summer. Say anything you please but don't say that you are not to stay here altogether. I do not want it known.

Alright. We will stay here altogether.

That is not my wish. We will stay here for the winter. The summer climate is not possible.

I quite agree with you.

Do you.

Yes I do.

No I can't say that.

What.

You know it is the words of a song.

I know what you mean.

Of course you do.

This is the end of this month.

Next month will be shorter.

Why.

Because it is December.

I understand that.

Of course you do.

They have gone away.

William. I am drinking.

Maria. I am so sorry to go.

Henrietta. I cannot understand departure because if you are french you attend mass.

Sarah. I quite agree with you I think it unforgiveable.

Mrs. Clement. And they are.

Mr. Penfield. We are very often forgetful.

Many of us think of things.

How many times have you been defeated.

Sleeping.

Turning.

Turning and sleeping.

What did you say. I said I am closing the door. Very well.

Henrietta. John and I are bewildered.

So are William and Monica.

Henrietta. The difference between us is that we know what we want.

Oh do you.

Henrietta knows.

Henrietta. Why are you shutting the door.

Because it is the habit. It really isn't necessary.

Then why do you do it.

Henrietta. Every one knows William and Monica.

Yes and every one knows how they started.

How did they start.

By quarreling with their landlord.

Indeed yes.

It was not a comfortable house in summer.

They knew this.

No they didn't.

You are quite right they didn't.

SCENE IX.

Go on.

Go on and on.

The day I was settled down to making a fire I found that it came very easily. All I had to do was to be here when the wood came. We had not ordered any water.

Tonight.

Mrs. Chambers. When did you leave him.

I didn't leave you.

I know you didn't then and I am vainly wishing for a postman.

What did you wish of him.

I wish to tell him that I don't want my packages open.

How do you know where they are open.

I know that they are not opened here I mean in this house.

I understand what you mean.

SCENE X.

A mother. Do not listen to a mass.

Another mother. I have left my children at home.

A son. I have no engagement on Wednesday.

A niece. I go out frequently.

Do you.

Oh yes.

Do you go out with your aunt.

We go out together.

Mrs. Hitchcock. I do not understand wishes.

A large time is not a sentence we use.

That I understood.

Two Englishmen have searched for a Polish flag. They found it not the flag of the nation the flag of war and commerce.

Thank you so much.

SCENE XI.

The life of the turkey.

Who is cruel.

Not the little boy he lifts it in his arms.

No the other one. He is a guardian. They are all placing their confidence in them.

The life of the turkies here exist after Christmas. We were surprised to see that. So many of them were eaten that we supposed there were no more.

The life of the turkey.

In church.

Here in church.

Nonsense I will not say I prefer suckling pig.

I don't know but that I do.

I like grouse.

To eat.

And also.

Chicken liver.

Arthur Llynn. Come and rest.

Helen Lewis. We are waiting for the letter carrier.

Is he coming today.

I don't know.

SCENE XII.

Come in Come in

Mary and Susan. Shall we come again.

Andrew. Yes that's the name.

What I want you to know is the origin of it all.

The one is a soldier, the other an admiral the third a gypsy.

We were not pleased.

Captain Rose. You must pronounce after me. A fire in the kitchen not against the outer wall.

Yes we know that.

I have been convinced.

Don't you like it's appearance.

Very much.

I am not satisfied.

With what with it's appearance.

I expected it to be white.

Oh that can be arranged afterward.

Yes I see.

You are going.

May we stay a little while.

SCENE XIII.

It was rarely neglected. Come in Herbert.

I recognise the name Herbert.

Come in.

We are going out.

Do you like walking.

Very much.

Do you like the sound of the waves.

Yes certainly.

Do you like them near or at distance.

The effect is different far and near.

Yes so it is.

Which do you prefer.

I have no choice.

This evening we will have to be cold.

But not at all.

Yes indeed and I mean to speak to my landlord about it.

Good-night.

SCENE XIV.

Clarence for a change.

If you have as vacation one day a month and you take it every six months you have six days vacation. In those six days you can visit your family in the country or you can work in your garden or you can make changes in the position of the wall you can do all this and then there will be six days in six months. If you are not able to be about this will be counted off of the days.

The french language.

Who is it.

What was I saying.

You were saying that you were able to be at home.

Yes I am able to be at home.

Then this is what troubles you.

No it does not trouble me. It makes me realize that I do not wish to leave.

Of course you do not wish to leave.

Yes that was understood.

Did you say that you listened.

Were you speaking what did you wish.

I wish not to be disturbed.

Oh yes we will leave in the spring.

I am not satisfied with what is right.

SCENE XV.

Come again.

Mr. Picard. He was dedicated to him.

Was he.

Do you feel happy.

All the time.

Do not be

Neglected.

I was.

And I saw

That

There are mountains.

And the water.

We are really not interested in the country if there is no water.

You mean salt water.

Yes.

Do not dispute about it.

It is unlucky to wish any one happy new year before the new year.

SCENE XVI.

Do you want me to go on.

Yes I want you to go on.

Where shall we walk tomorrow.

Tonight you mean.

Not not this evening.

Yes I understand.

Where shall we walk tomorrow.

To Fernville.

No not to Fernville.

To Arbuthnot.

No not to Arbuthnot.

In the park.

No not the park.

Well then let's walk along by the water.

No let's not go that way.

Then let us walk to Wintersdale.

Yes let's walk to Wintersdale.

Very well then.

Where are you going this afternoon.

We are going down town.

Oh yes you have a good deal to do.

Yes we have a good deal to do.

Will you go in the morning.

As you like.

SCENE XVII.

Come happily.

Yes we come very happily.

There is very good reason for suspecting Mr. Bournville.

Is there.

Yes very good reason.

What is the reason.

The real reason is that he has been incorrect.

How has he been incorrect.

He has been altogether incorrect as to the necessity of having water.

Do you mean to say that he said it would be difficult to have water.

He said so.

But it hasn't been

No indeed.

That may be because the season is different.

That may be the reason. In any case he is pardonable.

In any case he is pardonable.

You agree with me.

Yes I agree with you.

Do you always agree with me.

You know I always agree with you.

Then that is satisfactory.

To me.

And to me too.

FINIS.

Every Afternoon

A Dialogue

I get up.

So do you get up.

We are pleased with each other.

Why are you.

Because we are hopeful.

Have you any reason to be.

We have reason to be.

What is it.

I am not prepared to say.

Is there any change.

Naturally.

I know what you mean.

I consider that it is not necessary for me to teach languages.

It would be foolish of you to.

It would here.

It would anywhere.

I do not care about Peru.

I hope you do.

Do I begin this.

Yes you began this.

Of course we did.

Yes indeed we did.

When will we speak of another.

Not today I assure you.

Yes certainly you mentioned it.

We mentioned everything.

To another.

I do not wish reasons.

You mean you are taught early.

That is exactly what I mean.

And I feel the same.

You feel it to be the same.

Don't tempt him.

Do not tempt him.

This evening there was no question of temptation he was not the least interested.

Neither was she.

Of course she wasn't.

It's really not necessary to ask her.

I found it necessary.

You did

Certainly.

And when have you leisure.

Reading and knitting.

Reading or knitting.

Reading or knitting.

Yes reading or knitting.

In the evening.

Actively first.

He was very settled.

Where was he settled.

In Marseilles.

I cannot understand words.

Cannot you.

You are so easily deceived you don't ask what do they decide what are they to decide.

There is no reason.

No there is no reason.

Between meals.

Do you really sew.

He was so necessary to me.

We are equally pleased.

Come and stay.

Do so.

Do you mean to be rude.

Did he.

I ask you why.

Tomorrow.

Yes tomorrow.

Every afternoon.

A dialogue.

What did you do with your dog.

We sent him into the country.

Was he a trouble.

Not at all but we thought he would be better off there.

Yes it isn't right to keep a large dog in the city.

Yes I agree with you.

Yes

Coming.

Yes certainly.

Do be quick.

Not in breathing.

No you know you don't mind.

We said yes.

Come ahead.

That sounded like an animal.

Were you expecting something.

I don't know.

Don't you know about it at all.

You know I don't believe it.

She did.

Well they are different

I am not very careful.

Mention that again.

Here.

Not here.

Don't receive wood.

Don't receive wood.

Well we went and found it.

Tomorrow.

Come tomorrow.

Come tomorrow.

Yes we said yes. Come tomorrow.

Coming very well. Don't be irritable. Don't say you haven't been told. You know I want a telegram. Why. Because emperors didn't.

I don't remember that.

I don't care for a long time.

For a long time to pass away.

Why not.

Because I like him.

That's what she said.

We said.

We will gladly come Saturday.

She will go.

Oh yes she will.

What is a conversation.

We can all sing.

A great many people come in.

A great many people come in.

Why do the days pass so quickly.

Because we are very happy.

Yes that's so.

That's it.

That is it.

Who cares for daisies.

Do you hear me.

Yes I can hear you.

Very well then explain.

That I care for daisies.

That we care for daisies.

Come in come in.

Yes and I will not cry.

No indeed.

We will picnic.

Oh yes.

We are very happy.

Very happy.

And content.

And content.

We will go and hear Tito Ruffo.

Here.

Yes here.

Oh yes I remember about that. He is to be here.

To begin with what did we buy.

Scolding.

If you remember you will remember other things that frighten you.

Will I.

Yes and there is no necessity the explanation is not in your walking first of walking last of walking beside me the only reason that there is plenty of room is that I choose it.

Then we will say that it will rain.

The other day there was bright moonlight.

Not here.

No not here but on the whole there is more moonlight than in Brittany.

Come again.

Come in again.

Coming again.

Coming in again.

Come again.

I say I do understand calling.

Calling him.

Yes Polybe.

Come.

Come.

Come again and bring a book.

We meet him so often.

We meant to see about it. You mean the light.

I am proud of her. You have every reason to be and she takes it so naturally.

It is better that it is her hands.

Yes of course.

Nothing can pay for that.

Republics are so ungrateful.

Do you desire to appear here.

Why of course in that sense.

I do not know those words.

It is really wretched.

You do see it.

I don't see it that way.

No you wouldn't you would prefer the words well and tall.

Say it to me.

You know I never wished to be blamed.

An effort to eat quickly.

Did you promise him.

Did I promise him the woods.

The woods.

Not now.

You mean not now.

Captain Walter Arnold

A Play

Do you mean to please me.

I do.

Do you have any doubt of the value of food and water.

I have not.

Can you recollect any example of easy repetition.

I can and I can mention it. I can explain how by twice repeating you change the meaning you actually change the meaning. This makes it more interesting. If we attach it to a person we make for realization.

Do you really mean you have no preferences.

I can not visualise the condition.

By that time I am free to say that we have made offers of finding the right name for everything.

Do you know that you are careful.

Do you see the state of your purse.

Have you been told that I will give you more if you ask for it.

Or do you not care to receive a favor.

Certainly you wish to be helped.

Let me help you.

Do not refuse me.

You can regulate your expenditure.

It is unreasonable.

Not because you do it.

Not because you do not do it.

Standard pieces.

Eating and drinking.

Can you forget Minerva.

I make the mistake.

I mean Monica.

Can you forget Monica.

Or Polybe.

ACT II.

A dazzling dress. We dazzle altogether.

Please Do Not Suffer

A Play

Genevieve, Mrs. Marchand and Count Daisy Wrangel.
(Mrs. Marchand.) Where was she born and with whom did she go to school. Did she know the Marquise of Bowers then or did she not. Did she come to know her in Italy. Did she learn English in Morocco. She has never been to England nor did she go to school in Florence. She lived in the house with the friends of the count Berny and as such she knew them and she knew him. She went to eat an Arab dinner.

How did she come to know the people she has known. I do not understand it.

With whom did she go to school. We are not sure. When did she first know about Morocco. Where did she hear English.

She heard English spoken to children.

(Count Daisy Wrangel.) He speaks English very well. He has an impediment in his speech. He likes cauliflower and green peas. He does not find an old woman satisfactory as a cook. He wishes for his Italian. It is too expensive to bring her down. He does like dogs. He once had eight. They were black poodles. They were living in a garden on a duchess' estate. He trained them to be very willing and he has pictures of them all. He has often written a book. He writes about art sometimes. He also paints a little. He has a friend who paints a picture every morning and paints a picture every afternoon. He is not disagreeable. He did not come with him. He asked to see the dog he thought he had grown.

(Genevieve.) She believes in Fraconville. What is a thunder storm. This is my history. I worked at a cafe in Rennes. Before that I was instructed by a woman who knew knitting and everything. My mother and father worked at gardening. I was ruined by a butcher. I am not particularly fond of children. My child is a girl and is still a little one. She is living in an invaded district but is now in Avignon. I had a coat made for her but it did not fit her very well and now I am sending the money so that it will be made at Verdun. I am not necessarily a very happy woman. Every one is willing. I like knitting and I like to buy provision. Yes I enjoy the capital. There is plenty of meat here. I do not care for the variety. I prefer veal to chicken. I prefer mutton. I understand that it is difficult to have anything.

(Mrs. Marchand.) I do not write often. I say I will mention it if a man pays attention to a woman and so I can and I can say that I have not written. I will do as I like. I find that my baby is very healthy. I hope he will not talk the language spoken here but I can not say this to him. He is too young. He is not walking. If the Dardenelles are not taken perhaps they will open. I hear myself speaking. I have an orange tree that is open. The sun comes in. For ten days during ten days it rains and then until December we will have good weather. There is no fire in the house. I do not like to look at that map. Will you excuse me while I give my baby his luncheon.

(Count Daisy Wrangel.) It is the same name as an island. We were from Courland and some are Russians and some are Prussians and some are Swedes. None are Lithuanians. Mr. Berenson is a Lithuanian. I have a Danish friend who has been married four times. His last wife is a singer. She is a married woman. His first wife has been married to four different men. She has been a good friend to each one of them. They do say this. I have no pleasure in my stay on the Island because I do not eat anything. I would like to have something.

(Genevieve.) The count was here. He wanted to see the dog and he said he would like to see him. He was not very well. He had been suffering. He did not say that his friend would come with him. He said he thought not. I am often told that the french are everything. I ask do you believe that the french are winning. I believe that the french are winning. Do you need butter for cooking.

(Mrs. Marchand.) Let me give you a peach that is softer. Do you like this one. We will come again for an evening. This is the shortest way. Yes I like walking. We say very little when we are worrying. Let us go away. We cannot because my husband cannot go away.

Nellie Mildred and Carrie.

(Nellie.) Handwriting is not curving. It is not a disappointment or a service it is frequently prepossessing.

(Mildred.) It is copied. Six handkerchiefs. Two of one kind four of another.

(Carrie.) She backhands that means she takes good care of herself.

(Mrs. Marchand.) She does not know any of them. She knows Mr. Rothschild.

(Genevieve.) What is the use of being tranquil when this house is built for the winter. The winter here is warm.

(Count Daisy Wrangel.) He will not stay longer than November.

William and Mary.
(William.) He is fond of reading and drinking. He drinks wine. He also drinks siphon. This is water with sterilised water in it. He drinks it with and also without lemon. He is very fond of walking. He does not prefer resting. He is a painter by profession.

(Mary.) Mary is winning. She has a brother who is fighting. He has made a ring for her. She has a mother and another brother. We were asked does she like swimming. She has not a knowledge of swimming.

(Mrs. Marchand.) She is a large woman and rather walking. She walks along. We met her and Mr. Marchand who were walking. We said it was too cold for walking.

(The English Consul.) All right. The dog is too closely muzzled. He can't breathe properly.

(Count Daisy Wrangel.) Why do you all speak to me. Let me tell about it. In coming into the first office I first saw one young lady. I told her she was looking very well. I then went out and came back and went up to the other lady. I said how do you do I was sorry not to see you the other day. You were out when I called. My friend is a bear. I thought he would have come with me to call. I will come soon again.

(Mrs. Marchand.) I don't know him very well that is to say my husband has pointed him out to me and I knew he was here. It will not be a disappointment to us.

(Genevieve.) I prefer a basket to a mesh. It is the one souvenir that I will have. I do not wish to say that I am not pleased. I do not like to spend 35 dollars over again all over again. It is exact enough.

(Count Daisy Wrangel.) There is a great deal to write in a newspaper.

(Michael.) Michael was the son of Daniel. He moved into a house. He had been living at a hotel a whole winter. He has steam heat and light. We have not seen photographs of the place.

(Jane.) I have five children the youngest is three years old. Many of them died.

(Felix.) What kind of wool do you prefer black or in color, heavy or thin and for what use do you desire it. Do you also wish knitting needles and what thickness.

(Alice.) What did we have to eat today. We had very young pork. It is very delicious. I have never eaten it better.

(Genevieve.) I like to choose my meat.

(Mrs. Marchand.) I understand everything better. I like to have to think and look at maps. I hate to see so much black. I do not mean by that that I am sullen. I am not that. I am delighted with surroundings.

(Genevieve.) I wish to spend a little money on some things. I am waiting for the boat. I have nothing to do except sleep. Really not.

(Mrs. Marchand.) I understand Spanish.

(Count Daisy Wrangel.) To please him and to please me I do not dine at home.

(Harry Francis.) It hangs out in the rain and it is not dry what shall I put on underneath.

Anything you like.

(Roger Henry.) Why do you prefer a picture of a boat.

Because it is useful.

(Mrs. Marchand.) I am so disappointed in the morning.

We are all of us disappointed.

(Mrs. Marchand.) I did not meet you to-day.

Yes you did.

Every man swallowing. What.

(Mrs. Marchand.) I told you that you had every reason to expect warm weather and now it's cold.

It won't be cold long I hope. These are equinoxial storms. They last from seven to ten days.

(The English Consul.) He has had some trying experiences but he has a pleasant home. He has a view of the sea and also of the woods. It is natural that he has chosen that house.

(Mrs. Marchand.) I have met her. She is very pleasant. I did not think she was his wife. I thought she was his daughter.

So did we all.

He Said It

Monologue

Spoken.

In English.

Always spoken.

Between them.

Why do you say yesterday especially.

Why do you say by special appointment is it a mistake is it a great mistake. This I know. What are and beside all there is a desire for white handkerchiefs.

You shall have it.

This is what we give. We give it with a hat. Dear me. A great many people are precious. Are they. I do not ask the question.

This is my fright.

Oh dear Oh dear I thought the fire was out.

I consider it very healthy to eat sugared figs not pressed figs I do not care for pressed figs.

I consider it necessary to eat sugared prunes and an apple. I have felt it to be the only advice I could give. It has been successful. I really feel great satisfaction in the results. No one can say that short hair is unbecoming.

What are the obligations of maternity. Reading and sleeping. Also copying. Yes thank you.

Are you pleased.

I am not pleased.

I am delighted.

It has been a very fruitful evening.

It is not very likely she was pleased.

Pleasures of the chase. Do you like flags. I believe in painting them. I also inquire as to their origin. Are they simple in color or have they various designs. Nobody can be as pleased as I am can be more pleased than I am. I am further delighted with the social relation I have established with a great many acquaintances. I began by intending to change to change the method of branching. I do not find it distinguished. Then I found that by choosing and asking other people to supply I could be satisfied. This is history.

Did he see he would kill a rabbit. Many rabbits are troublesome. I do not care to eat the one he was to give us.

You do not care to eat rabbit.

Who is our well-wisher. I see clearly that you have made a mistake. You have answered me defiantly. I have not.

Large spaces of time are filled by my telling how to sing.

How do you sing.

Some sing so well they laugh.

Others sing so well that they are roses.

I was very pleased with embroidery very very pleased with embroidery.

Indeed.

Indeed I think alone.

And make lists.

And make lists.

I do not make lists.

It is no trouble to make lists.

I feel an infinite satisfaction in the thought that I have stopped worrying.

Indeed you never worry.

Who can be willing to leave an American boat.

No one.

This is what I said.

I said it to an Englishman.

Governed. Do be governed.

I speak of this very kindly. I do not tell him about darkness.

Or anybody.

Many people fear distraction and divert themselves with discussion. Not I.

I am singularly adaptable. I have no opinion. When I am asked I say it is distressing not to be right. It is not distressing to me. I accomodate myself to it. I am inclined to be talkative.

Are you.

Yes sir.

This is the way I say it. I ask any one to say a bowl of water. This is not difficult. Then roses in it. I prefer pansies. Do you. Or daisies. No we do not consider wild flowers. This is not the reason. The real reason is the odor. Some people like a strong odor like china lilies or almond flowers or even tube-roses. I like them very much. I like them all very much. Do you.

Yes I do.

The other day we saw a woman knitting she was doing it not so very quickly and then we understood the reason. She was knitting with cotton. That is quite the custom of the country.

Why do you wish to hear it.

I was very pleased with this and now I want to tell you how to do it. This is what to ask. Do you make decorations. Do you please yourself. Are you fanciful. Have you any use for color. Do you ask for strange resemblances. Have you all always been merry. Do you believe in history. Have you authority.

Do you expect to seem selfish. Do you. I wonder about that.

Why do you talk about stretches.

You mean a series.

Yes I mean that. Do you remember that I said that.

What do I feel today. I feel that I do know how to air a woman.

You mean that I make it too cold. Well to be sure I am selfish I sit before the fire. I really ought to give you the best place only I don't like to change.

You dear you are so sweet to me.

A carpet on the floor makes it a great difference.

Indeed there is a granite which is called marble and rightly called marble because it is found here. Do you know where it is made. Yes I have seen it.

Yes so they say.

Go to sleep.

This is my way.

In speaking I have a belief in saying that I said it last.

Some people differ from me.

This is a sentence.

What was it she reminded me of.

It is satisfactory.

There are a great many plans. Will there be a good crises. I don't know. In our affairs. No the nations. Don't speak to her of it.

I am not certain I like liberty.

Don't you.

Of course not.

We go on saying what he said.

I can't understand why you contradict me.

There we are I have a coat over my knees.

There is no way of speaking english. I say there is no way of speaking English. What do you mean. I mean that anybody can begin and go on. And finish. It's easy enough and especially hard when there is a use. Why do you say exchange. I do not know what they say exchange. They say they believe in exchange. I often talk about nothing.

What have I to say.

I wish to speak to you what shall we do about water. The water is everywhere. Imagine me in bed. We were very careful to ask about it.

Not for teeth.

Why do you talk about it not for the girl.

He was of course not able to pay for the concert. He was of course not able to pay for the concert.

I am not talking about myself.

I can supply furs.

In summer.

Today.

It is not very cold.

But it will be.

What did he say. He said it was explanatory. I said it was explanatory. I said I was careful of climbing. Not into bed. Yes into bed. Why. Because you can never tell about the slats. I remember that word.

What did he say today.

A great many mountains have seas near them.

And the moon. The moon has no tide.

When do you say that.

Every night.

Why.

Because I have never seen so much moonlight.

I feel it very much.

A great many people were listening. To your getting angry

Talking about feeling.

This afternoon we went to New York and we spent the day together. We said which way shall we walk.

In reading the papers I am often struck with the different way I am impressed with the news. Should I be cheerful. I should not. Mr. Sandling says that I am. Indeed I am.

We do not expect it today. Let us go to Soller.

All of you hear me.

I like to see the rocks I mean stones.

I didn't mean it about the clock.

Here we are.

Mrs. misses kisses.

Misses kisses most.

I do like to say that.

Do you wish you had said it first. Not exactly. I repeat more often. A great many people hear you. Not now.

All about the swing. Swing where. In a lamp. You mean electricity. Yes I mean electricity. Wax.

Do read to me.

We went down to the town and we met Mr. and Mrs. Somaillard. We drank something there and we said if they would wait we would call for them in a carriage. We had several things to attend to first.

I nearly said it together.

Do I think that they will.

Do little walks tire you.

Dear Sir. This is the end of the day and I am able to explain that a great deal of trouble has been taken.

I feel that there must be a regular time for the oranges.

Oh yes indeed.

Never have I seen so many trees.

It was a surprise to you.

I say that I am certain that a great many things can be said.

Call it a fan love.

I don't care to see pieces.

Don't you.

Indeed you don't.

Leaving stones aside what do you think of the weather and the country.

I think them both delightful.

So do I.

And we enjoy ourselves.

Oh very much.

Yes and what time do you wake up.

At half past seven.

I don't wake up till nine.

What is the date today.

Wishes

He wishes to think.

Do not distress them.

What we do is this we give it to them.

What did he say.

He said he expected to be ill. He said he said he expected not to be very well. Yes Mr. Lindo Webb.

Yes Mrs.

You should always speak the name.

I don't feel that I can mention it.

Do you believe in me.

Are you surprised that you have gone so far.

To me not to me.

Insulting yes she is insulting she asks have we ever heard of a poet named Willis.

Alice has. I have not. She says he belonged to a group. Like Thoreau.

I am not displeased with the remark.

Did we see the festivity. Water is amusing.

Do I want to go away.

No indeed I do not want to go away.

Two months.

In two months.

Politely miss me.

Call what.

Call Milly.

Don't you understand the difference.

He wanted fifty dollars for six days.

We did not refuse a visit.

No one refuses a visit.

I do.

I see.

A little finish. What was that noise.

I am very pleased to have a good fire.

Here are my stars and stripes.

Yes it's the flag.

What time is it.

Day time.

Of course and the morning.

I always go well prepared.

Of course you would.

What do I think.

Is not this certain.

What.

That there are a great many places where one would not be as comfortable.

Where we would not be so comfortable.

Certainly I don't deny that.

We have been so happy here. Yes but that has nothing to do with the people. No it hasn't. But I like to see what I see here. You know perfectly well you will be just as well pleased with something else.

Why do mules go together. Because those people are religious. They are very religious. Were you invited.

Then I will finish it here.

This is very easy to please. Cups and saucers altogether.

We are going to have a picnic. With chicken not today today we are going to have eggs and salad and vegetables and brown bread and what else. False smuggled contraband tobacco. You mean by that that it isn't tobacco. No it's only leaves. I laugh.

Counting Her Dresses

A Play

PART I.

ACT I.

When they did not see me.

I saw them again.

I did not like it.

ACT II.

I count her dresses again.

ACT III.

Can you draw a dress.

ACT IV.

In a minute.

PART II.

ACT I.

Believe in your mistake.

ACT II.

Act quickly.

ACT III.

Do not mind the tooth.

ACT IV.

Do not be careless.

PART III.

ACT I.

I am careful.

ACT II.

Yes you are.

ACT III.

And obedient.

ACT IV.

Yes you are.

ACT V.

And industrious.

ACT VI.

Certainly.

PART IV.

ACT I.

Come to sing and sit.

ACT II.

Repeat it.

ACT III.

I repeat it.

PART V.

ACT I.

Can you speak quickly.

ACT II.

Can you cough.

ACT III.

Remember me to him.

ACT IV.

Remember that I want a cloak.

PART VI.

ACT I.

I know what I want to say. How do you do I forgive you everything and there is nothing to forgive.

PART VII.

ACT I.

The dog. You mean pale.

ACT II.

No we want dark brown.

ACT III.

I am tired of blue.

PART VIII.

ACT I.

Shall I wear my blue.

ACT II.

Do.

PART IX.

ACT I.

Thank you for the cow.

Thank you for the cow.

ACT II.

Thank you very much.

PART X.

ACT I.

Collecting her dresses.

ACT II.

Shall you be annoyed.

ACT III.

Not at all.

PART XI.

ACT I.

Can you be thankful.

ACT II.

For what.

ACT III.

For me.

PART XII.

ACT I.

I do not like this table.

ACT II.

I can understand that.

ACT III.

A feather.

ACT IV.

It weighs more than a feather.

PART XIII.

ACT I.

It is not tiring to count dresses.

PART XIV.

ACT I.

What is your belief.

PART XV.

ACT I.

In exchange for a table.

ACT II.

In exchange for or on a table.

ACT III.

We were satisfied.

PART XVI.

ACT I.

Can you say you like negro sculpture.

PART XVII.

ACT I.

The meaning of windows is air.

ACT II.

And a door.

ACT III.

A door should be closed.

PART XVIII.

ACT I.

Can you manage it.

ACT II.

You mean dresses.

ACT III.

Do I mean dresses.

PART XIX.

ACT I.

I mean one two three.

PART XX.

ACT I.

Can you spell quickly.

ACT II.

I can spell very quickly.

ACT III.

So can my sister-in-law.

ACT IV.

Can she.

PART XXI.

ACT I.

Have you any way of sitting.

ACT II.

You mean comfortably.

ACT III.

Naturally.

ACT IV.

I understand you.

PART XXII.

ACT I.

Are you afraid.

ACT II.

I am not any more afraid of water than they are.

ACT III.

Do not be insolent.

PART XXIII.

ACT I.

We need clothes.

ACT II.

And wool.

ACT III.

And gloves.

ACT IV.

And waterproofs.

PART XXIV.

ACT I.

Can you laugh at me.

ACT II.

And then say.

ACT III.

Married.

ACT IV.

Yes.

PART XXV.

ACT I.

Do you remember how he looked at clothes.

ACT II.

Do you remember what he said about wishing.

ACT III.

Do you remember all about it.

PART XXVI.

ACT I.

Oh yes.

ACT II.

You are stimulated.

ACT III.

And amused.

ACT IV.

We are.

PART XXVII.

ACT I.

What can I say that I am fond of.

ACT II.

I can see plenty of instances.

ACT III.

Can you.

PART XXVIII.

ACT I.

For that we will make an arrangement.

ACT II.

You mean some drawings.

ACT III.

Do I talk of art.

ACT IV.

All numbers are beautiful to me.

PART XXIX.

ACT I.

Of course they are.

ACT II.

Thursday.

ACT III.

We hope for Thursday.

ACT IV.

So do we.

PART XXX.

ACT I.

Was she angry.

ACT II.

Whom do you mean was she angry.

ACT III.

Was she angry with you.

PART XXXI.

ACT I.

Reflect more.

ACT II.

I do want a garden.

ACT III.

Do you.

ACT IV.

And clothes.

ACT V.

I do not mention clothes.

ACT VI.

No you didn't but I do.

ACT VII.

Yes I know that.

PART XXXII.

ACT I.

He is tiring.

ACT II.

He is not tiring.

ACT III.

No indeed.

ACT IV.

I can count them.

ACT V.

You do not misunderstand me.

ACT VI.

I misunderstand no one.

PART XXXIII.

ACT I.

Can you explain my wishes.

ACT II.

In the morning.

ACT III.

To me.

ACT IV.

Yes in there.

ACT V.

Then you do not explain.

ACT VI.

I do not press for an answer.

PART XXXIV.

ACT I.

Can you expect her today.

ACT II.

We saw a dress.

ACT III.

We saw a man.

ACT IV.

Sarcasm.

PART XXXV.

ACT I.

We can be proud of tomorrow.

ACT II.

And the vests.

ACT III.

And the doors.

ACT IV.

I always remember the roads.

PART XXXVI.

ACT I.

Can you speak English.

ACT II.

In London.

ACT III.

And here.

ACT IV.

With me.

PART XXXVII.

ACT I.

Count her dresses.

ACT II.

Collect her dresses.

ACT III.

Clean her dresses.

ACT IV.

Have the system.

PART XXXVIII.

ACT I.

She polished the table.

ACT II.

Count her dresses again.

ACT III.

When can you come.

ACT IV.

When can you come.

PART XXXIX.

ACT I.

Breathe for me.

ACT II.

I can say that.

ACT III.

It isn't funny.

ACT IV.

In the meantime.

PART XL.

ACT I.

Can you say.

ACT II.

What.

ACT III.

We have been told.

ACT IV.

Oh read that.

PART XLI.

ACT I.

I do not understand this home-coming.

ACT II.

In the evening.

ACT III.

Naturally.

ACT IV.

We have decided.

ACT V.

Indeed.

ACT VI.

If you wish.

I Like It to Be a Play

A Play

I liked it to be a play and so cleverly spoken.

Americans are very clever.

So are others.

Yes indeed.

And all men are brave.

Scene I.

Satisfy.

I like to satisfy them.

He likes purses.

You mean silver purses.

Yes gold purses.

Here they have other purses.

All of them are carried in a procession.

Every day.

Not all day.

The martyrs and red carnations.

You mean red geraniums.

No I mean red pinks.

Purses have that word.

Please me.

To please me.

Called me.

She expected a distress.

Daughters.

Or daughters.

The youngest as children

One's said.

Verdun.

We close.

Here.

Stables or motors.

Stables altogether.

Did we know anything about houses in Mallorca.

Scene II.

So you were pleased with me.

Scene III.

Able men. What do you intend to do today.

I have planned to telegraph for an answer,

Oh yes.

What have you said to them.

I said I was delighted with the photographs.

Scene IV.

Will you be sorry to leave Mallorca.

You mean the island.

The sun.

Or the people.

A great many people dislike the people.

Scene V.

Fifth Avenue in Spanish.

Fifth Avenue in Spanish.

Did you say water.

War water.

I have heard it said that a great many people expected another.

One another.

To be one another.

To be fought.

Do not say bright.

It is not a bright day.

Scene VI.

Have we gone so far indeed have we gone so far.

Scene VII.

Don't make a mistake and lose any leaves.

Classes.

Memory classes.

Don't go so far and lose any leaves.

We were really pleased with the leaves. We were really not pleased with the leaves.

I was very pleased with the leaves.

Scene VIII.

You were astonished by me.

All of us complain.

You were astonished by me.

Don't you understand trying.

Don't you understand trying to stammer.

No indeed I do not.

Scene IX.

Were you surprised to see that we were so far long. You mean in stages. No of course not in selections. What have you selected. Very good sponges. But they are expensive. They are not necessarily cheap. We feel that they ask an extraordinary price here. You have every reason to suppose so. We were quite sure of it. It is easily understood they are accustomed to trading. You mean barter. No I don't mean that I mean metal worker. Metal workers have new clothes. In Palma. Yes in Palma. I did not mean to mention that name. Why do you dislike the town. Not at all.

The rest of the day was spent in visiting.

Scene X.

The end of that little plate.

You mean you didn't like the pottery. The brown one you mean. No the yellow. Yes I liked it very much at first. It was too big. This is not the way to say that you will come again. But we don't want it.

Scene XI.

What did she say. She said that she could read Spanish because all the words that were real words resemble french.

I don't mean to say that I am vexed.

Oh no indeed you are not to be blamed.

Not at all

We are very careful to move together. For pleasure. For our pleasure. Oh yes indeed. We need you. More than ever. I am glad we are not cold. Not here. Believe me. Believe in me. I do.

Not Slightly

A Play

Slightly painful and really more satisfactorily stinted and mentioned in long singling birthdays. Shall it seem strange.

Not wintered my dear.

Not wintered my dear.

Not wintered my dear.

     fellows.
Nine shall combine Straichy and purl wilt and borrowed moans. Why will sold meats have mints. They need it.

They need it yet.

They need it yet.

They need it yet they need it yet.

     A longer pause.
When kinds of similar tens that is to say twenty suffering, when similar tens and perhaps fifty kneeling, when similar and jointed and prized and quilted quietly quilted tights quietly quilted tight minds when three innerly expensive shrugs meant more there was a strain and little meaning water spots came to remain. They saw to that.

A particular relief

     In a particular relief.
Not nodding.

Explain looking. Explain looking again. Alice explain looking again.

Another fact.
Not indeed my dear.

Why should I say supper.

Not every running thing my dear. I am sorry to leave another.

Not then.

I have long bands.
I couldn't do it behind it. I couldn't do it behind it. I would never see Lena. I would mean to hoard separately. I would surely sponge what. I would surely sponge enough.

Intermission.
What does that mean.

There is no use in leaving out Friday. There is some sense in that.

Eighteen.
Twenty three.

Times.
When there can be an arrest and I don't mean to go, by the time there had been water, plants are, in between them. Paul's. They came to say that another was faster. They come to specialize. They were in a year and old.

Now I mean to go on.

Stop it. Stop handling monkeys, stop handling birds stop leaning, stop leaning by a companion.

I came to grave gravely see winding and beat in that cautious outside which does make minor difference differences more either. That's the way to pronounce it cautiously.

Second Act.

I meant to wait and I was simple and I did say shelter god give him shelter. I did go away and I did not mutter I did not believe goats I was not delicate I was not careful to release more excellent tons of really sound apples. This was so painful. This was very painful. I meant to do the same yesterday.

Introduction.
Its really doing my hand a lot of good.

When I spoiled every day I made sashes.

I can understand where he did it.

Able corn.
One day any day not to search within the wounded operating sound of miserable stretches. What shall boats say. By this time.

Now I cannot sing.
Now I cannot sing.

Folded.
Biting meant mining.

Shall he find it out.

There is much to say.

An opportunity in sizes.

Further.
I can scratch.

Not it.

Spool.

She meant it again.

Now I can lose money.

Frightened.
There really is no reason to believe that.

What is your name.

As if he felt himself to be one.

I listened to Bertie.

I felt raining.

Rain is what is understood by singling out breathing.

    In the rest of piles of candles.
It is not necessary that there is a table plentifully, it is not necessary that cloth is besieging it is neither necessary that obligations are finally strung together by meaning all pieces, it is beneath shining really beneath shining.

Then there is a pause. There really is more vacancy than ever. There really is horrible horrible horribly mismanagement. I am not pleased with it at all.

When I stood and measured distances when I stood and measured distances I bowed I bowed to the reasonable interpretation of plain stairs bent together and when I meant to go away I did not leave out of that, consideration. I did not leave out of that, consideration. I was speedily neglected on harmony and I was not beside that altered. I was not in altering changing recently. I was not changing recently. Not to act too. Not to act too much. Not to act too much in being horrified. Not to beckon in spaces. Not really to beckon in spaces. Not really to be beckoning in pointed spaces or pointed spaces. Leave as alone we must be right.

    Act Three.
I spent I mentioned I spent that. I do reline most purses. I do so thoroughly. I do not please safer. This is in sailing. Don't be a silly. How can one sail.

    Field equivalent.

I was so surprised to see that at the bottom of the sealskin.

Its really not very active.

That's not what I want to settle about. It really is not.

      There'll be five acts.
Why do I say blows noses.

Alice why do I say blows noses. Alice I hear you.

You are between there. I shall state what I think and study. I study very much. This is not a request.

      I changed my mind.
No there is no example in this. I meant to be cautious. I was restrained. I shall not come to stay. I believe in sermons. It is a fauning thing.

      I do see a resemblance to Claire.
Why in the nature of pleasing where there can be many tall representative not meaning to be still lining.

      Beside him.
Not in front.

      It seems wrong not to answer anybody.
Title.

Really not.

A girdle needs stitches.

Not it.

Title.

Really not.

      Pleases.
I must say I don't wish to go back.

Pleasures.
Shall I feel it.

Its not possible to sing by way of songs, it is not possible to sing by way of songs.

Next time.
The next time that I wished to be taken away the next time I wished to be taken away, in that way the next time I wished to be taken or that way the next time I wished to be taken that way, or the next time. I meant to poison everybody I meant to poison everybody seriously, I meant it seriously I meant complaining seriously, I meant complaining seriously. In the way of peace in that way by a certain chiming of really mountains by a certain wearing heat, by really mounting cars, that is in abundance for abundantly separating heights, any one is tall in feet, that is a twinkling mother. Surely enough.

The longer to stay for but I don't send it.
Once when prints and letters and little violets of satin wood and spreading out centrally, once when upper leather was reaching reaching by far, once when lively older trees had learned restitution, I don't mean to blame anybody. I haven't said luxurious. I meant to believe my aunt. I mean countless pillows. I wish it was windy.

Painful.
It is painful.

There is a kind of sunset, nobody mentions butter. They hate to be grave.

It really is very strange.

Not in cellars. Not in not cellars. Not wanting, not wanting it.

I spent stitching. I did it in again. I spent fastening. I saw likely. I saw very likely.

When sleeping is wild, Cora is not wild. Cora is not wild.

When sleeping is wild Cora is not wild. Mild pleasant breath.

It is very fine that is very fine.

> Instinct.

Instinct or reason.

Instinct or reason.

Instinct or reason.

Round and about.

Round.

About.

Pale.

Pale enough.

Not so in satisfaction, in real satisfaction.

Not so much.

I meant to go home.

I meant to go home.

I meant to go what do I mean by white. I meant to change in it. More methodically. Yes purling. I don't know instances.

> Act Four.

Not in the least pressing.

Two crowns and a half a crown. That's the way they would say it.

Seven one seven five.

Pleasing extras. I said I should wish to go, to go, I said I should wish to go I said I should wish to go.

No blaming, no such blaming, darling no such blaming.

When I mentioned still in mentioning I had to imagine that I did not estimate wild curses. I did not estimate wild curses. I don't like that name. I will not secrete more wishes. I will say I will exactly say that lands are coarse, that lands are chorused that lands are cursed. This comes to them after knitting. This comes to them after knitting.

This comes to them after special winding. This comes to them after winding.

   Even new its pretty.
Do you mind selecting sashes. Do you mind selecting sashes in it. Do you mind selecting sashes by way of reminding, thanks. Do you mind reminding blinds. Do you mind. Edith do you mind.

Edith seems, Edith seems denied. Edith rests colored, not that colored much, not that colored by them.

   When wean in. When wean in school scissors. Scissors are a count. I make it ahead.

Polish.
Its no use mentioning that I killed many who were believed to be localized. Its no good to dictate that. What I do not determine is more recognizable, it is not in a politeness, it has a recent meaning.

Mr. Fairchild Resolute pure and clouded by night and more feelingly, Mr. Fairchild resolute to emperil the whole catastrophe does licence what he has to say.

A sudden peak a sudden peak of gleaming of gleaming hidden stones of gleaming hidden stones thoroughly.

Yes isn't it an example isn't it a wiser relief than was expected. Isn't it Flemish. I know that allusion it is an allusion to a reached heart.

Not in the least not in the least private not in the least privately. Not more than the sum not very granted. Not by that straining not by that merriment. Can one neglect it.

Two in seven
I meant eleven it's shorter.
Commence to sew.

How can eagerness meet it.
I don't indicate that and more nearly standing I don't realize voices.

They said that. I mean to bury please her. Like.

Finding immense glances.

I don't like to place holes real holes really hollow whites. I do not find long hoes.

That's a change. That is like water. That is plenty of all spots. There is plenty of all pints. There is plenty of another word.

I don't like being discouraged.
When the meaning was in the sofa when the meaning was in shouting when the meaning was found found and found. I speak of it.

Act Five.
In a way I don't in a way I don't.

In a way I don't.

Piling.
Politeness requires

Neglecting plows.

Politeness requires neglecting plows.

Politeness requires neglecting plows.

God bless you.

I inquired into the exact celebration of visual memory. I met pleasing examples of amiable solicitude. I measured strength. I mean to go and stay. I shall certainly neglect sets. It is a complete wrinkling nation.

This was no strawberry meaning with colors and blacks black berry indigo shawls.

To begin to complain.

To begin to complain and straggle straggle with mouse stretches. To begin to straggle to begin to straggle and much any sealing any sealing without thimbles. Thimbles are so noisy. They do so suddenly expose spoons.

Splendidly more splendidly.

She saw mentioned birds.

I do not hesitate to understand myself and I do vainly think that pearls are silly. I have a chance to say I sew. I have a chance to say so.

Witness.

      To begin on again.
It was said and well said it was well said and avoiding, it was avoided by instantaneous crowning it was mounted by sullen points it was suddenly anticipated and nearly by a trinket. What is a trinket.

      I was disappointed in eggs.
Sweet oh sweet oh sweet sweet sweet.

      Acting.
An amazing cow. Simply an amazing cow. Not in sobbing. Not in clenching. An amazing cow. So shot. When.

Out.

They've got so many soldiers. No they haven't my pudding.

Catches.

How do I know.
I selected eating and it had to see what called houses.

I shall teach.

Continuation of an Act Five of the Act Five.
Continuation.

Business goes by favor.
Now count.

Forgive colds.

Be separated.

Have colds.

Wilderness.

Compass.

Compass for.

Plants.

Have it essentially.

Have it island.

Have it for.

Only for it.

Have it within ices.

Have it by a case.

Likeness.

If you like likeness.

     Read out by it.
Read out by it supper splendidly.

I met all sight.

Eight.

I either.

Make it leaving.

Make it or believing.

Make it leaving.

     She said choke night.
     She meant it. She did
     buy teams. Night it.

I saw a venture to be do be quiet and make the home a home. Do not see the limp when he is walking. Do not wonder if there is water. Leave it, sell more splendidly. Do kindly stay in a way. Like what is a little sensational. Do be all to be never. Never wet. Wretched creature. I do not dot what is a new tub. Do regret it. I will not satisfy many I will not satisfy many stitches. Why are corsets warm. They are an answer. Little pleasing noises, This is a sum. All of it astonishes. The Bruces have left.

     Act Five.
I made a mistake.

Bonne Annee

A Play

We do not understand why they do not think this a good market.

We do understand our pleasure. Our pleasure is to do every day the work of that day, to cut our hair and not want blue eyes and to be reasonable and obedient. To obey and not split hairs. This is our duty and our pleasure.

Every day we get up and say we are awake today. By this we mean that we are up early and we are up late. We eat our breakfast and smoke a cigar. That is not so because we call it by another name. We like the country and we are pressed people. Do not be upset by anything. No I won't be. Dear one.

We have given you this.

Yes.

I give you this.

Yes.

You give me this.

Yes.

Yes sir.

Why do I say yes sir. Because it pleases you.

What are the letters in my name.

O. and c and be and tea.

Leading a museum not a pearl there.

Take me to Sevres I do not despair.

This must not be put in a book.

Why not.

Because it mustn't.

Yes sir.

Please be rich.

I am.

So am I.

Of course you are my pretty.

Of course you are.

It isn't necessary for me to mention what a good baby.

Happy New Year.

Mexico

A Play

Ernestine.

Have you mentioned tracing out California.

I have.

How big is it.

As big as a boat.

What boat.

The city of Savannah.

Have you succeeded in tracing the origin of the word ugly.

I have.

It means crab.

It certainly means crab.

Crabbed is an instance.

We learn about rocking chairs from them.

Kites are an example.

We learn about peaches from them.

They learned them too.

Were you dreaming badly. No. Then go to sleep again little sweetheart.

Ernestine.

It is easy to see four boats. Boats are a ship. There are English and Danish and other boats. It is hard to tell the Italian flag. Hard almost impossible.

I do not mean to be discourteous.

Ernestine.

Come in.

John.

Did you meet him.

I did and I believed in him.

Did you go away.

No I stayed a long time.

Did you go to another country to earn your own living.

I did not I stayed here for some time.

I am going away.

I have finished everything.

I will expect a selection.

I have dreams of women.

Do dream of me.

I will come to see weather.

I understand what they mean by dirty weather. It's the color.

Act so that you will be spared the necessity of deceiving anyone.

I do.

I will.

Scene II.

They were willing to have table and bed linen and neglect dressing. They were willing to have excellent eating. They did not care about coffee.

Sarah.

Wood is not to be neglected. I will attend to everything.

If he hasn't them send us his name.

What do we do with methods and respect.

Methods and respect serve us for imitation. We imitate pronunciation. Mexico.

Henry Irving.

Neglect me and believe me and caress me.

Say I am careful.

Believe in punishments. Search for many.

Many men are necessary. We are necessary. We mean more and we have faithful truths.

Mexico.

I was so pleased.

ACT II.

A grand opening and many boats. I like them with white sails. I like them to use better coal.

Appreciations.

Mrs. Guilbert.

I understand Welsh.

So do I.

Mrs. Hendry.

I have never been married.

I have.

Mexico.

Mexico is prettily pronounced in Spanish.

Pronounce it for me.

Yes I will.

Say it prettily.

Mexico.

There are many ways of winning a lottery.

Newspaper notoriety.

A grocery store.

A butcher shop.

A silk seller.

Embroidery.

Clothes.

Muffs.

And corduroy.

This is the way we win.

We refuse to go to theater not because we don't like it but because we'd rather go to Penfolds. Penfolds have not a pleasant house we are going there for tea tomorrow.

Mrs. Guilbert.

She has remarkable lace. She teaches English.

We have chosen a handkerchief.

William Guilbert.

He is very young. He has been here altogether. He is not older than Allan.

How old is Allan.

I do not know I think he is seventeen.

Fairly reorganized they are loading from one boat into another.

I have my foot.

Genevieve.

I do not mean to know her.

Yes you do.

I mean I have not met her.

Well that's possible.

Madeleine.

My name is Victoria.

Yes the Captain told me.

We do not address him.

He speaks English.

Yes of course he does.

Why of course we do.

We are going to begin.

Listen to one another.

We are all together.

This is a song.

Mrs. Childs.

I am decided we must not expose ourselves to the cold.

Thank you very much.

ACT III.

Now let us understand each other. We have more time than we had. Let us begin now.

A cab stand.

Who is restless.

We all are not we are not willing to go.

Very well do not go.

If there are many of you I will ask another.

He agreed to go.

He was very pleased.

I knew he would be content.

It was a mistake we should not have come at that hour.

We have to come when we can.

Quite right.

This is the right city of Mexico.

Or street of Mexico.

Street of Mexico.

SCENE II.

Mark Guilbert.

Yes sir.

It's only a habit.

What is only a habit.

To read the autobiography of Edward Lincoln.

Who is he.

He is the man that recognized the principle of two ships.

Which two.

The Bolton and the Meadow.

Are they both here.

They are.

What are they doing.

They are taking off cargo.

Are they removing it from one ship to the other.

They are.

Genevieve.

I saw a wedding today.

The bride was dressed in black. Her veil was black.

That is because she was a widow.

Oh is that so.

What is the custom in your country.

In my country they always wear white veils.

Even widows.

Yes but unless you are rich you have a black dress.

Yes that is more economical.

And useful.

Yes certainly.

At twelve o'clock.

The fifth and sixth and seventh of January.

Fair fat and a hundred and twenty.

I was right.

Mark Guilbert.

I am free on Wednesday.

With whom do you talk.

I can do that easily.

Of course you can we wish to compliment you.

I am pleased to hear it.

SCENE III.

A play. Mexico.

This evening he mentioned that they were neglected and that they were easily disturbed.

I can understand that.

Mark Guilbert.

Do you know Bird.

No I do not that is to say I have met him and knew about him.

He is very interesting.

A little Mexico.

Do say.

What.

When you have your teeth fixed you use rubber.

Do you.

Yes all the dentists do.

How do you manage it.

Very easily.

And very successful.

Yes indeed.

We have been singularly fortunate with electricity. It was only in the beginning that we were afraid of thunderstorms.

A little kindness.

We do not wish to invite them. When they come they ask pleasant questions.

Who is a watcher.

We are.

In that case do not forget the clock.

And a note.

And a drawing.

And you had better leave me some writing.

Do you mean to do.

No.

Very well then.

Flowers are pretty.

So are fruits.

So are meats.

So are sugars.

So are cheeses.

I like a joke about cheese.

Gilbert Ferdinand.

Why do you make a noise.

Because we are isolated.

Have you not a watchman.

Certainly sir.

SCENE IV.

ACT IV.

First second third and fourth bird.

Do you like it.

All the time.

There is no use asking me that. We never expected to ask any one for flowers.

That is perfectly natural.

Of course it's perfectly natural.

When you settle.

You settle with

Him.

Do you care to do it.

You care to do it if you are visited.

Everybody is visited on an island.

Ermine.

What is influence.

Influence is the pleasure some have in reminding us of villages.

Herbert.

Are villages near a city.

Not if you use the word correctly. Villages are the country. To go to a village is to leave a city.

Augustine.

Is that her name.

It is.

Why does she speak of her employer.

Because she is a servant and cooks.

Does she cook well.

Very well.

Mr. Standish.

What do you say.

You are pleased with the weather.

Yes I am pleased with the weather.

SCENE V.

We were agreed that we would not be angry.

Mr. Murchison.

How often have I been mistaken.

You were mistaken about the length of time that foreigners would stay on the island.

Yes indeed I was.

And can anybody be obedient.

Yes it is not difficult.

Were we mistaken about the president.

Yes we were in a fashion of speaking.

How did we know.

By becoming aware of some facts with which we had not been acquainted.

Yes that is correct.

We do not need to be careful.

No indeed.

Mrs. Giles.

Why do you not state the difference between steps and road.

I have often.

What is it then.

The difference between steps and road is that one is disagreeable and the other isn't.

Certainly.

We have often noticed it.

Now we avoid the steps.

So do we.

Yes I find it is the common practice.

The steps are steep.

So is the road.

Indeed it is.

Why are you late.

I am not very late.

No you are not very late.

We have often met before.

Indeed we have.

Henrietta Fountain.

Dear me have you been here before.

Yes and seen the almonds in flower.

Yes certainly every day.

Yes indeed and with great pleasure.

Yes and some pleasure in exercise.

Yes in exercise and variety.

Yes in that continually.

Yes in that very much.

Did you happen to hear of the city of Georgia.

I did not know there existed a city of that name.

I had reference to a steamer.

Then I can certainly agree with you.

I hoped you could.

It will be a pleasure to meet again.

ACT V.

SCENE VI.

A great many plays are better than another.

Gilbert.

Come in.

Henry.

Do come in.

Francis.

A great many people come in.

Philip.

Do a great many people come in.

Sebastian.

Yes indeed.

James Morey.

Do I have to give permission to everybody.

You have to give permission to every one you think responsible.

Do I have to choose.

You had better be careful whom you choose.

I will be very careful.

We are all very careful.

SCENE VII.

A great many houses are standing.

And some boats.

A great many boats.

Yes a great many boats have not been lost.

Yes a great many boats are useful.

Do you hear them.

I hear about them.

So do we.

SCENE VIII.

It is not necessary to have a saint.

Why not.

Nobody can answer.

Some do.

What do they answer.

They say that they expect repetition.

Some roses which are here look like winter roses. That only means that they are bought Sunday instead of Friday that only means that they are bought Sunday instead of Friday.

ACT V.

SCENE IX.

Did you mean to be astonished.

The servant.

Did she mean to be astonished.

What is Peru.

A republic.

What is engraving.

Commercial.

What is it likely to lead to.

A competence.

Who enjoys food.

A nervous person.

A mother.

No not a mother

A wife.

Yes a wife.

When do they meet very well.

When they believe in what they have in their house.

Was it all made by them.

Not the things they bought.

No certainly not.

Mr. Morton.

How do you do Mr. Morton.

The whole family.

How can you walk about the country.

Quite easily if you don't mind hills.

One gets accustomed to it.

Why is there a difference between South America and North America.

There is no difference he meant to go there.

After all he was very pleased.

Certainly he was and the results were good.

Excellent.

Mr. Clement.

He went away.

Did he.

Yes and I need a dry climate.

Do you.

I am very well content where I am.

And do you mean to stay.

No I think not.

But you did like Peru.

Very much.

MEXICO

PART II.

Loud voices heard by me.

Did we come back.

All the time that we were saying clouds moon they were feasting.

Rice and everything.

Mr. Gentian.

What are the rest.

I don't know.

There are plenty of early dates. Do dates grow in Mexico. They do somewhere. Not the edible kind. No not the edible kind.

Mr. Hawthorne.

What are the changes.

There are very many of them in some states.

Do you see that.

You mean the house.

Yes I mean that house there.

Yes I see it very well.

In the midst of plenty of separation there is always some one having lawns. Do you like lawns. Of course I do.

There is plenty of time.

In that case let us go quietly.

Yes we will go to see one another.

Another.

Not that today.

By this time we are very weak. Strict. Yes strict. There are a great many calls. Yes there are for that matter.

Many of us have places.

There are said to be five thousand oats eaten daily.

Yes there.

We have no occasion to admit phrases.

We do not admit that thing.

Why not.

Because we have a feeling.

Do be told about a fire.

SCENE II.

Change again. We do not change again.

Easily careful. Say the words. Easily careful today.

Martha. Come in.

All the time of merchant marine is taken up with wood. A great deal of wood and then there is no dissatisfaction none at all.

Pearl. What did you say.

The time to suggest winter is when you are very happy. Winter is so pleasant.

I understand advertisements.

All the time.

SCENE III.

That's a very good scene.

Yes sir.

If you want to be respectable address me as sir.

I am very fond of yes sir.

Mildred. Mildred is your name isn't it.

I do not mind anything very much.

Millicent Millicent is your name is it not.

Yes.

I do not wish to make anything too short.

I will make it as long as you wish.

Will you.

Yes.

Dear you are so kind.

Kind you don't like that kind.

Yes I do.

Horace. Have you ever heard of Fernville.

Yes indeed it is in the country.

West of Edite.

Yes.

Oh yes.

There was resemblance.

Wasn't there.

Yes indeed there was.

Many flowers. Are there many flowers.

We have a great many.

ACT II.

Tall boys are fourteen.

Or sixteen.

We saw that and it was not a mistake to connect them with feeling pears so that they might know that they could answer very well. They were perfectly satisfactory. Millicent Millicent Foster.

I do believe I find Captain Foster more interesting.

There is no mistake to be made attacks are spoken of and well spoken of and hesitation is not blameable. No one can say that Catholics are proud.

I do not wish to discuss the matter here.

Miss Millicent Wynne.

Why do you sell your name so.

I do not.

Of course you do.

You mean to.

You ask every one about a train.

We were ashamed about the train.

Were you.

Yes we had reason to be.

I can understand. You can understand everything.

A Spanish lesson.

Begin now.

By leaving the room.

No by mentioning why you have been hesitating.

I have not been hesitating and besides I wish to learn English.

Do you.

Yes.

To read.

To read.

But you read very well.

This cannot be said.

You mean we admire you.

You can do so.

Were they ashamed of their water.

Nobody has any water.

This is what they told us.

Mexico.

SCENE II.

Mexico tide water. I meant not to spell it so.

Mexico tied water.

Mexico border.

I love the letters m and o.

Mr. Gilbert. I do not know that child.

He speaks to you.

Yes he does.

And what does he say.

He asks me what I bequeath to the English.

Does he.

Mrs. Nettie Silk. Have a good time.

We will.

When you say that you pass this way.

You do naturally.

Why don't you return my books.

Do you want them.

Not just at present. You can lend them.

All of them.

Yes all of them.

Thank you so much.

Mrs. William Lane. We found that house.

Yes and we have been accepted.

For what.

For always.

Oh you don't mean to say you won't change your mind.

William will.

So he will.

Yes sir.

The rest of the day.

He wrote about it.

Do you believe him.

I do.

Very well.

Very well.

It doesn't make any difference.

It doesn't make any difference.

Do remember it any way.

Yes I will.

Can I trust you.

Yes Madame.

We will go away.

There is a way.

I know the way.

I know that way.

Yes I know that way anyway.

Don't mean it.

You don't mean it.

Yes sir.

SCENE III.

What's the matter.

Bouncing barley I learn it quickly.

All about corn-meal.

This was so curious we thought she had added an egg.

Herbert Guilbert. This is the name. We are pleased with everything. We like birds and curves and I do not mind saying that we like presents.

We are so disappointed.

About what.

About the iron of course.

Mrs. Henry. Do come to see me at my hotel.

I don't think we will.

Good-night.

The light did come up.

At midnight.

No a little after.

We thought it was not difficult.

A little more difficult.

John Beede. I made a mistake.

Harry Shirley. Leaves and leaves of grass and trees.

Oh yes.

SCENE IV.

Is this the way to begin.

Another page. Does she hear me. Does she hear you what.

Turn the page.

Not if you don't do it.

Oh yes.

Alphonse Nester. What's his name.

Didn't you hear it. It came everywhere.

So it did.

A great many people were blamed.

A great many people were blamed.

Robert Nestor. I have heard of him.

Of course you have.

Be careful.

Be very careful.

There is no danger.

There is no danger.

Not to me.

Not for me.

Oh yes.

Say it.

I've said it.

We can say.

Yes.

Tell the young king not to bother.

What do you mean by young king.

I mean that I am willing.

To do what.

To say everything.

He should not have told him.

Well he told Mr. Doux.

Did he.

Of course he did.

I say stop and think.

I say that.

No I don't change it.

Do you like repetition.

Yes I like repetition.

ACT III.

Don't please me with Mexico.

Mr. and Mrs. Bing. They had a book. Yes Miss.

Mr. and Mrs. Guilbert. I mention that name.

Of course you do.

Of course you do to me.

Don't cry.

SCENE II.

This is the end of the day. Tomorrow we will leave early. We meet everybody. Some all well fed. Will we be. Well I guess yes. It's foolish to be so abstemious. Are they really. I haven't noticed it.

Mexico.

When you come to choose dishes you should remember that they cure the ham themselves that is smoke it.

Oh yes.

So you should be careful in cooking the fat.

You mean on the island.

She was right. Not about the whole. She knows nothing. Well then why ask her about wood.

In their country they celebrate Sunday.

God bless us I say God bless us all day and all night too.

Do not mention it to me.

When this you see remember me.

SCENE III.

I wonder if there is a mistake.

Horace Lewis I can't imagine such a name.

Horace. It is my name.

A great many people are there.

Who says it.

The woods the poor man's overcoat.

We can pronounce everything.

An old man works harder to be eating than a rich one.

Come to me mother.

Don Jose. Have you sold the dog.

Not at all I gave it away.

Don Jose. Where is your dog.

It is in the town.

Don Nicholai. How do you pronounce my name.

So as to go with sow.

That means to sit down.

That means a pig.

Not in this country.

Donna Pilar. Is that cheese.

Yes it's very good cheese.

How do you prepare it.

With cognac.

You mean brandy.

One might not call it wine.

Mrs. Gilbert. I will not insult them again.

Why on account of the lunch they gave you.

No.

Do you know Mr. Bell.

Mr. Henry Bell.

No Mr. Paul Coles Bell.

Oh yes. He teaches English.

Certainly he does.

I would like to teach Spanish.

So would I.

Don Miguel. I believe in a man and wife.

So do I.

And in many children.

And in a new post-office.

We have no opinion about that.

ACT IV.

Do please me.

And the sunshine.

Tomorrow.

We hope so.

We have every reason to expect it.

But we may be disappointed.

Peggy Chambers. She went away.

Did she go away.

She deceived him.

How.

She was not educated.

You mean not well educated.

She was not educated to travel.

Does it take an education to travel.

It does if you wish to take part in the conversation.

Bird never took part in the conversation.

You are greatly mistaken.

Mark Baldwin. What is your name.

Australia. Did you mention Australia.

Oh yes you mentioned Australia.

We believe in Mexico.

SCENE II.

Mexico.

Come to see me in Mexico.

I don't believe in waiting and eating.

That's what we said.

Mark Guilbert. How often I have mentioned his name.

Lindo Bell. I have not mentioned his name before.

Oh yes you have.

Charles Pleyell. This is a name we all know.

My pen is poor my ink is pale my hand shakes like a little dog's tail.

Dorothy Palmer. Where is Ibizza.

Frank Jenny. I do not believe that he is home.

At home.

Yes at his home.

I do not believe that he's out.

Mark Guilbert. He is a young man.

We know three on the island.

Mark, Allan and their mother.

That is not what I meant when I said that she looked American.

SCENE III.

I don't quite understand what I have done.

Wintering and rain it is not raining. It rains every day. Oh yes it makes the wood wet. We prefer it so. Thank you you will come to lunch. At what hour. One o'clock. John Russel. If there is a Mallorcan name if Mallorca gave the missionary who converted the California settlers if the Mallorcans have a little town of their own near New York then we will believe in Spanish influence in Mexico. The Spaniards are not liked in Mexico.

John and Maria Serra.

Foundations.

The middle of the day. Why do you not come in the day time. You mean to listen. No I don't mean to listen.

This is very well said.

Dorothy Palmer Come in and rest.

We are coming in.

A great deal.

A great many mistakes.

Maria Serra. I understand you wish to show me what you have.

Yes.

Will you come tomorrow.

Tomorrow would suit me better.

Or today.

Today would suit me.

Would you be disappointed if Fernando Orro only sang twice.

Of course not.

You mean you would be willing to change your mind.

Of course.

Yes that's it.

Of course a great many people are there and they do not mean to say anything.

You mean praiseworthy.

Yes be glad to meet me.

Yes a diamond.

All the way to come.

Home.

SCENE IV.

Mexico begins here.

You relieve here.

Here we have star-fish. You mean little ones. Yes little ones.

Mark Gilbert. I wish to tell you about mines.

Yes.

Or would you prefer to hear there were meteors.

I would surely prefer to hear there were meteors.

Any one can refer to it.

So they can.

In the meantime the wind this evening is not nearly in that locality.

Do you think one can say that.

No perhaps not.

Mrs. Penfold. Mrs. Penfold sees no one.

ACT V.

The act of coming is pitiful.

Butter is pitiful.

All of it is enough.

She said it is pleasanter now when there is enough so that there can be a change.

Mr. and Mrs. Leland Paul.

Do you know that name. Do you know being called Mr. Paul. Do you hear me telling you that a great many people hear opera.

A great many soldiers in the streets.

This means that there is wood to prevent traffic.

Not plenty of wood oh no.

Dear Mrs. Amos.

      I letter this B because it is very dangerous.

A great many dogs are very dangerous too.

Do you mind. Lilie do you mind.

Yes I do mind.

SCENE II.

John Quilly. Do you recollect him.

You mean the color.

Or the effect.

Why yes of course they were beautiful.

So they were.

Will we get some more Tuesday.

I rather guess yes.

A great many.

As many as we can.

All of that one kind.

Yes.

SCENE III.

Neglected.

Who has neglected Chinese lillies.

Nobody has. They grow so profusely that there is no necessity to cultivate them.

But the season is so short.

Yes but the wild ones have a finer quality than the others.

SCENE IV.

I said that we were delighted.

If they were blue flowers and grew where chalk is they would be blue.

Clay makes them dark.

Stones make them purple and blue.

This is the color described by the time.

We were not disappointed

Indeed no.

John Quilly. Why do you rest.

We were so disappointed in the electricity. Of course it was not our fault.

John Quilly. John Quilly John Quilly my babe baby is prettier than ever John Quillys are.

So they selected to do it in two hours.

I can do it in one hour.

I have known it to be done in five hours and a half

SCENE V.

Have you been relieved.

I should not have mentioned it in the other book.

Oh it doesn't make any difference.

You mean it doesn't matter.

Yes that is what I wished to say.

You have said you believe in delay.

Everybody believes in delay.

Don't annoy me.

ACT VI.

SCENE I.

This is the end. Do you remember the sixth act. I do. It always interested me.

Milly. I thought so.

You mean you thought of a collection.

Mrs. Penfold. Mr. Penfold.

Mr. Lindo Howard. I will not be able to be well. I will explain to Harold.

This is what he said.

Mexico is never a disappointment.

Goats. Goats are Western. You mean in excuses. No of course not in feathering.

I do not use that word.

I was so pleased with Mr. and Mrs. Penfold's voices.

Before to-day.

You mean that as a question.

Tito Ruffo.

Tito Ruffo yes.

SCENE II.

Tito Ruffo. No.

That's the way they say it.

They said I like to be separated.

Do you really mean that.

Really and truly.

Mr. Crowell. How do you pronounce it.

We call it well.

Do you mean to say that that is the way you pronounce it.

Yes are you surprised.

Of course I am surprised.

Do you never read the papers.

Not in the morning or evening.

You mean on account of bad news.

No I like flags.

SCENE III.

Alright Mexico.

We did not call for Peppe. This is short for Joseph.

We did not call Pablo.

We did not call Peppe.

We did not have the pleasure of hearing Rigoletto.

William King. Are you pleased with everything.

Certainly I am the news is good.

Marcelle Helen. How do you do I have been in a bombardment.

So you have.

And were you evacuated.

We did not leave our village.

We asked the consul to tell us what he thought.

He said that there was nothing to fear.

Nothing at all.

So he said.

Very well today.

Oh yes the wind.

SCENE IV.

I do not make a mistake.

Oh yes indeed.

My mother.

You mean your mother.

I mean to say that I think the government should send her to her home.

We will see.

A Family of Perhaps Three

When they were younger there may have been three of them sisters, and a mother. When they were younger there may have been three of them one of them a brother, and a mother. When they were younger there were certainly two of them, sisters, and a mother. There was not then any father. There may have been a father living but certainly he was not then living with them. Anyway there were when they were younger two of them, two sisters, and a mother.

Perhaps the sister who was older then supported her sister and her mother. Perhaps she earned a living then for all of them. She was much older than her sister, enough older so that she could be quite certain that all her living her sister was much younger, that all her living her sister was a young one, that all her living she was earning her living, that all her living her sister was not earning her living.

The sister the younger one was earning her living and certainly then the older one, the one who was much older than her sister who was much younger was certain that the younger one would have been earning her living all her living if she had been one commencing to earn her living. The younger was earning her living, she was not listening then to the story which was distressing of the older sister then almost not earning any living. She would listen sometime to this thing but certainly she would not listen then to this thing.

The older sister had not then any longer any mother. The younger sister then had not then any longer any mother. The older sister then had not then any longer any mother. The younger sister was not then hearing about this thing about the older sister having then not any longer any mother. Not any one then was listening to this thing to the older sister not then having any longer any mother. The older sister was then quite an old person. The younger sister was then not a young person. The younger sister was not then hearing anything about this thing about the older sister having then not any longer any mother.

They were then being living and very many knew them then, two of them, they were sisters, one was older, much older, the other was younger, some younger. They were living together then. The older was then earning some living, the younger was then sometimes hearing this thing, the younger was then not such a young one, she was quite completely hearing this thing, hearing that the older was almost earning a living, they were both living then, the younger was hearing then that the older one was almost earning a living. The younger was not listening, any more then, the older one was not earning any more of a living then. The younger one was almost not listening then.

The younger then earned her living. She was not at all a young one. The older one was not a very old person then, she was an old person then, she was almost not earning a living then. The younger one was not listening then to anything about any such thing then. She was not listening then and certainly the older one was not listening then and certainly neither of them was listening then. The older was almost not earning a living then and she was quite old then and she was not listening then. The younger one was earning a living then and was not listening then and she was not at all a young one then.

The older one was protecting the younger one from knowing where they had been when they were young ones. They both knew where they had been when they were young ones. The younger one was protected for this thing for not knowing where they had been when they were young ones.

The younger one was protected. She was protected from knowing that they were ones having been living when they were young ones, she was protected from knowing that they were not ever completely earning a living, she was protected from knowing that they were not going to be succeeding in earning a living. She was protected from these things, really she was protected from these things. Certainly every one knew everything, both of them and every one knowing them knew everything. That was a natural thing that every one should know everything. In a way they were succeeding in living. In a way the older one was succeeding in living, in a way the younger one was succeeding in living. Everybody knew everything, anybody knowing them knew everything, everybody knowing them knew it again and again, knew everything again and again, the older one knew everything knew it again and again. The younger one knew everything knew it again and again. Certainly every one knew everything. Certainly every one knew everything again and again.

The older one succeeded very well in living. The younger one succeeded very well in living. The older one was successful in being living. The younger one was successful in being living. The older one came to be certain that she was not successful in being living, that she was not succeeding in living, she came to be certain that the younger one would have been successful in living if the older one had not been one protecting the younger one from knowing this thing. The older one came to be certain that she had been successful in living, that she would not be succeeding in living. The older one came to be certain that the younger one would not really be succeeding in living. The younger one came to be certain that the older one could have been succeeding in living. The younger one came to be certain that the older one would not be succeeding in living. The younger one came to be certain that she could be succeeding in living. The younger one came to be certain that it would not be an easy thing to keep on being succeeding in living. The younger came to be certain that the older one never had been keeping on succeeding in living. The younger one was certain that one could keep on succeeding in living but that this was not an easy thing.

The older sister was not ever married. The younger sister was not ever married. This is quite common, not being married. The older sister was one whom some were certain could have been married very often. Certainly if she had been a little different she might have been married again and again. Certainly she was never married. Certainly she was not needing that thing, needing being married, needing being married again and again. She certainly was talking about any such thing, talking very often about any such thing about any being married, about any being married again and again. She certainly was one knowing very many men. Certainly very many men liked this woman. Certainly she was talking about this thing about being married very often, certainly she was very often talking about this thing. Certainly she was not ever completely needing this thing, needing marrying, she certainly was not ever completely needing marrying again and again. She was never a married one. She was not ever completely needing this thing. Certainly she could think again and again of this thing, of marrying. She certainly did think about this thing about marrying. She certainly did talk about marrying again and again. She certainly did feel something about this thing about marrying again and again.

The younger sister was never married and she might sometime have come to be married and she did not come at any time to be married. She was never married. She might talk about this thing about marrying. She might feel something about this thing about marrying. She might completely need this thing, need being married. She might have come to be a married one. She did not come to be a married one. Her sister was not ever certain that she would come to be a married one, that she would not come to be a married one. Her sister was not certain about either of them that they would never come to be married ones. They were never married neither the one nor the other and certainly each one of them knew this thing that neither one of them had come to be a married one.

Certainly the older one had done something and certainly every one was content to tell about this thing about her having done something and being one every one knowing her was remembering as having been one doing something. She certainly had done something and certainly any one knowing her remembered that thing remembered that she was one having done something. She was one going on doing that thing and certainly every one knowing her knew that thing knew that she was going on doing that thing. She was one having done something and doing that thing and certainly any one knowing her remembered that thing. It was a natural thing to remember that thing, any one, every one remembered that thing.

She was one doing something and certainly in a way she was not getting old in doing that thing and certainly in a way she was completely old in doing that thing, she was not doing that thing she was so old in doing that thing. In a way she was not old in doing that thing, in doing anything and certainly then she was completely old and not really to any one doing that thing. She was not old in doing that thing, that is to say she was doing that thing, that is to say if not anything had been changing she would not have been old in doing that thing. In a way somethings are not changing and so in a way she was not old in doing that thing. Certainly to those being then doing that thing and not being old then anything is a changed thing and certainly then she was old in doing that thing.

She was not old in being living that is to say as not anything is changing she was completely not old in being living. She was pretty nearly old in being living that is to say she was not young in being living that is to say some were old in being living and she was talking to them and they were understanding and some were young in being living and they were telling something and she was certain they were not telling any such thing. She certainly was not old in being living. She certainly was not young in being living.

The younger one was certainly not an old one. She certainly was not such a young one. In a way she was certainly a young one and certainly she was such a one in not hearing some things and in telling some things and certainly this did not astonish any one and was a natural thing and certainly she was not then a young one.

She was an older one and she was certain of this thing and this was not an astonishing thing to any one and not to her sister who was not astonished at her being a younger one at her being an older one but was certainly hoping to have had this thing happening that the younger one would have been going on being a younger one and being an older one and not be remembering anything of any such thing. Certainly the younger one came to be one almost liking to be remembering something and then again she certainly came to be quite tired of doing this thing of remembering anything, of remembering being an older one and remembering being a younger one and then she came to going on being one remembering being an older one, she was then remembering being a younger one. Certainly she came to be remembering pretty nearly everything and to going on in this thing, keeping going on in this thing, steadily enough going on in this thing.

They could both of them, they did, both of them, they would, either of them, know that they were ones having been together and they were ones having been alone. The older one certainly was one having been alone, being alone, going to be alone and certainly this thing was something that she was certain she was completely needing, was something she was certain she was completely regretting, was something that certainly she was one certain she could be feeling and certainly she was feeling this thing and certainly she would be one having been feeling this thing and certainly she could never be not feeling that this was something that was a thing she was needing, she was regretting, in which she was suffering, in which she was glorying, in which she was believing, in which she was despairing, in which and by which she was really being living.

The younger one was alone and not feeling about this thing that it was an important thing, she was feeling about this thing that it was a thing that she was needing to be changing. The older one was quite certain that the younger would never be changing anything. The younger one was not certain whether she would or whether she would not be changing anything but this was not to be an important thing, the important thing for her was to be one living where she wanted to be living and to be working if she needed to be working. Certainly her sister was one to whom any such thing was an important thing and so the younger one did not tell her sister anything about this thing until she had changed everything, that is gone to where she wanted to and working because she had to.

So each of them were ones being not living with any one and certainly the older one had that then as an important thing in being one being living.

Certainly any one could know that having been being living was an interesting thing in knowing the older one. Any one could know this thing could know that the older one had been one being living and that that was an interesting thing. She certainly had been one being living and that certainly was an interesting thing. She had been being living and this had been going on a very long time and it was all that time and later then a very interesting thing. She was being living and this was then to her then an important thing and not then so completely interesting. The younger one had been being living and this was to some an important enough thing and was to some quite an important thing and was not to any one a very interesting thing not to the older one either or to the other one herself who was one doing that living. They certainly had been both being living and were then being living. Certainly having been being living was an important thing was a completely interesting thing, any one could know that thing, certainly the older one could know that thing, certainly the younger one was not remembering that thing.

They had been together, they were together, they were not together. When they had been together the older one was almost completely succeeding in being one naturally needing that the younger one was something any one would be protecting. The older one was then going to be one being completely interesting in having been living. The older one was then almost completely brilliantly this thing being one being completely interesting in having been living. The older one was completely then succeeding in this thing in being one going to be interesting in having been living, in being one needing that any one would have been protecting the younger one. They had been together. They were together. When they were together the older one was almost needing that any one would be certain to be doing that thing certain to be sometime protecting the younger one. The older one was then certainly completely interesting in having been living and certainly then was completely interesting. She was almost then, was almost brilliantly succeeding in this thing in being completely interesting in having been living. Certainly they were both being living then and they were together then. Certainly then the older one was going on in being interesting in having been living, she certainly was then quite completely interesting. She certainly then was being living and certainly then she was almost certain that any one would be one to protect the younger one. They were together then and certainly some were not certain of this thing that any one would sometime protect the younger one. They were together then and every one was certain that the older one was completely interesting in having been living. They were together then and some were not certain that the older one was certain that any one would be protecting the younger one. Some were certain then that the older one was interesting in having been living. They were together then and any one could be certain that not every one would ever protect the younger one when the younger one would be needing any protection. Some were certain that the older one was not certain that any one would protect the younger one when the younger one would need protection. The older was almost certain that some one would protect the younger one when the younger one would need protection. The older one was almost quite certain. The older one was almost quite completely interesting in having been one being living. They were together. They were not together. The older one was certain that some one would have been protecting the younger one when they younger one would be needing protection. The older one was certain that sometime the younger one would be needing that thing would be needing protection. The younger one was not with the older one. The younger one was remembering that she was not with the older one. The younger one was remembering that she was not with the older one and was needing that the older one would be one coming sometime to remembering that thing. The older one was pretty nearly interesting in having been one being living. She was pretty nearly certain that some one would have been protecting the younger one when the younger one would have been needing that thing. They were not together then. The older one was pretty nearly interesting in having been one being living. She was quite certain that any one could have protected the younger one when the younger one would have needed that thing. She was almost remembering that they were not together then. She was almost quite remembering that thing. She was quite interesting in having been one being living. She was almost quite interesting in having been living.

Advertisements

I was winsome. Dishonored. And a kingdom. I was not a republic. I was an island and land. I was early to bed. I was a character sodden agreeable perfectly constrained and not artificial. I was relieved by contact. I said good-morning, good evening, hour by hour. I said one had power. I said I was frequently troubled. I can be fanciful. They have liberal ideas. They have dislikes. I dread smoke. Where are there many children. Where are there many children. We have an account. We count daisy. Daisy is a daughter. Her name is Antonia. She is pleased to say what will you have. Horns and horns. Nicholas is not a stranger. Neither is Monica. No one is a stranger. We refuse to greet any one. We like Genevieve to satisfy us. I do not like what I am saying.

How can you describe a trip. It is so boastful.

He said definitely that they would. They have. It's a little late. I hope the other things will be as he states them. I have confidence. I have not eaten peaches. Yes I have. I apologize. I did not want to say the other word that was red. You know what I mean.

Why can I read it if I know page to page what is coming if I have not read it before. Why can I read it. I do.

I didn't.

Let me see. I wish to tell about the door. The door opens before the kitchen. The kitchen is closed. The other door is open and that makes a draft. This is very pleasant in summer. We did not expect the weather to change so suddenly. There seem to be more mosquitoes than ever. I don't understand why I like narrative so much to read. I do like it. I see no necessity for disclosing particularity I am mightily disturbed by a name such as an English home. An English home is beautiful. So are the times.

A dog does not bark when he hears other dogs bark. He sleeps carefully he does not know about it. I am not pained.

This is the narrative. In watching a balloon, a kite, a boat, steps and watches, any kind of a call is remarkable remarkably attuned. A resemblance to Lloyd George, bequeathing prayers, saying there is no hope, having a french meeting. Jenny said that she said that she did not believe in her country. Any one who does not believe in her country speaks the truth. How dare you hurt the other with canes. I hope he killed him. Read it. I believe Bulgaria. I have pledges. I have relief.

I AM NOT PATIENT

I am interested. In that table. I like washing gates with a mixture. We get it by bringing up melons. White melons have a delicious flavor.

I am not patient. I get angry at a dog. I do not wish to hear a noise. I did not mind the noise which the client made. I wished to see the pearls. How easily we ask for what we are going to have. By this we are pleased and excited.

The hope there is is that we will hear the news. We are all elated. Did you see her reading the paper. I cannot help wanting to write a story.

A woman who had children and called to them making them hear singing is a match for the man who has one child and does not tell him to play there with children. Heaps of them are gambling. They tell about stitches. Stitches are easily made in hot weather and vegetation. Tube roses are famous.

I could be so pleased. It would please me if Van would mention it. Why is an index dear to him. He has thousands of gesticulations. He can breathe.

White and be a Briton. This means a woman from the north of France. They are very religious. They say blue is not a water color. It should be a bay. We are pleased with her. She washes her hair very often.

Do not tremble. If she had an institution it is the one excluding her mother. Her native land is not beautiful. She likes the poet to mutter.
He does. The olive.

We had that impression. Do speak. Have they been able to arrange matters with the proprietor.

I will not please play. I will adorn the station. It has extraordinarily comfortable seats.

TO OPEN

Not too long for leading, not opening his mouth and sitting. Not bequeathing butter. Butter comes from Brittany. In the summer it smells rancid. We do not like it. We have ceased use of it. We find that oil does as well. We can mix oil with butter but we have lard. We use lard altogether. We prefer it to butter. We use the butter in winter. We have not been using it before the winter. We mix lard and oil. We will use butter.

DO LET US BE FAITHFUL AND TRUE

I do not wish to see I do not wish to see Harry I do not wish to see Harry Brackett I do not wish to see Harry Brackett.

A GRAPE CURE

What did we have for dinner we had a melon lobster chicken then beet salad and fruit. How can you tell a melon. You tell it by weight and pressing it. You do not make mistakes. We are pleased with it. Do we like a large dog. Not at all.

BATTLE

Battle creek. I was wet. All the doors showed light. It is strange how Brittany is not attractive as Mallorca and yet butter does make a difference. We are perfect creatures. What is a festival. Saturday to some. Not to be dishonored. Not to be tall and dishonored they usually aren't but some are, some are tall and dishonored. By this I mean that coming down the mountain faces which are shining are reflecting the waving of the boat which is there now. I distrust everybody. Do sleep well. Everywhere there is a cat. We will leave by boat. I am not pleased with this. I will get so that I can write a story.

FASTENING TUBE ROSES

I understand perfectly well how to fix an electric fan. Of course it makes sparks but when the two black pieces that do not come together are used up you get this. I do it without any bother. I am not certain I could learn it. It is not difficult. We do not find that it does away with mosquitoes. We use it in the night. Sundays there is no electricity.

THEY DO IT BETTER THAN I DO

I can. I can be irritated. I hate lizards when you call them crocodile. She screamed. She screamed. I do not know why I am irritated.

IT IS A NATURAL THING

Do not do that again. I do not like it. Please give it away. We will not take it to Paris. I do not want the gas stove. It has a round oven. It does not bake. We use coal by preference. It is very difficult not to bathe in rain water. Rain water is so delicious. It is boiled. We boil it.

LOUD LETTERS

Look up and not down.

Look right and not left.

And lend a hand.

We were so pleased with the Mallorcans and the wind and the party. They were so good to offer us ice-cream. They do not know the french names.

Isn't it peculiar that those that fear a thunder storm are willing to drink water again and again, boiled water because it is healthy. All the water is in cisterns rain water. There are no vegetables that is to say no peas. There are plenty of beets. I like them so much. So do I melons. I was so glad that this evening William came and ate some. It would not go back as if it hadn't been good.

PLEASURES IN SINCERE WISHES

I wish you to enjoy these cigarettes. They are a change from those others. I understand that you had some very good ones. You are not able to get these any more. I have tried to get them. They tell me that they cannot say when they will come. They do not know that about them. We sleep easily. We are awakened by the same noise. It is so disagreeable.

AN EXHIBITION

I do not quite succeed in making an exhibition. Please place me where there is air. I like to be free. I like to be sure that the dogs will not be worried. I don't see how they can avoid crickets. They come in. They are so bothersome. We must ask Polybe to wish.

THE BOAT

I was so disappointed in the boat. It was larger than the other. It did not have more accomodation. It made the noise which was disagreeable. I feel that I would have been willing to say that I liked it very well if I had not seen it when it was painted. It is well never to deceive me.

THREADNEEDLE STREET

I am going to conquer. I am going to be flourishing. I am going to be industrious. Please forgive me everything.

PRESENT

This is a ceremonial. When you are bashful you do not think. When a present is offered you accept it you accept the bracelet worn by the nun so that it rusted. You do not know what to do with it. You describe its qualities. It is a pleasure to have it. You will give it. You are steadily tender. You say the beginning is best. Why do you say Englishman. You say Englishman because he wished it. Do not hurry.

EVIAN WATER

Evian water is very good. Sometimes I am not sure it is put up by them at least now when there is a war. I say it is fresh. When I do not like a bottle I throw it away. I throw the water away.

Pink Melon Joy

My dear what is meat.

I certainly regret visiting.

My dear what does it matter.

Leaning.

Maintaining maintaining checkers.

I left a leaf and I meant it.

Splintering and hams.

I caught a cold.

Bessie

They are dirty.

Not polite.

Not steel.

Not fireless.

Not bewildered.

Not a present.

Why do I give old boats.

Theresa.

Exchange in bicycles.

It happened that in the aggregate and they did not hear then, it happened in the aggregate that they were alone.

It is funny. When examples are borrowing and little pleasures are seeking after not exactly a box then comes the time for drilling. Left left or left. Not up. Really believe me it is sheltered oaks that matter. It is they who are sighing. It really is.

Not when I hear it.

I go on.

This is not a dear noise. It is so distressing. Why was he angry. Did he mean to be laughing.

I was astonished besides. Oh do go on.

He was a ruffian.

Especially made. Why does she satisfy it.

It was a beautiful hat anyway it looked like that or by the way what was the handkerchief. Good.

Now I neglected him.

I made mention of an occasion. I made mention of a syllable. I mentioned that. I was reasonably considerate. I undertook nothing.

Why were birds.

When I decided not to look twice I felt that all three were made of the only distinct changeable brown. I did not mean foxes. This is why I shall not visit. Do go gladly. Do be willing.

What an accident.

What a horrid thought.

What a decent ribbon.

That is why I answered.

No please don't be wakened. Do think it over. Do mind what I say. Do breathe when you can. Explain whites for eggs. Examine every time. Do not deceive a brother. What is perfect instigation. I make I go across.

Instances.

Violences.

Not any whirl.

Not by all means.

Don't you think so.

Fourteen days.

I meant to be closeted.

I should have been thin.

I was aching.

I saw all the rose. I do mostly think that there is politeness. All of it on leather. Not it. I shall speak of it. I so mean to be dried. In the retracting glory there is more choice. There is what was threaded. I don't mean permitting.

Webster.

Little reinforced Susan.

Actual.

Actual believe me.

I see it all.

Why shouldn't I.

Lizzie Make Us.

I believe it.

Why shall I polite it. Pilot it.

Eleven o'clock.

Pillow.

I meant to say.

Saturday.

Not polite.

Do satisfy me.

This is to say that baby is all well. That baby is baby. That baby is all well. That there is a piano. That baby is all well. This is to say that baby is all well. This is to say that baby is all well.

Selling.

She has always said she was comfortable.

Was the water hot.

Hymns.

Look here let us think about hospitality. There is more said and kindness. There are words of praise. There is a wonderful salad. There can be excellent excellent arrangements. There can be excellent arrangements. Suddenly I saw that. I rushed in. I was wise.

We were right. We meant pale. We were wonderfully shattered. Why are we shattered. Only by an arrest of thought. I don't make it out. Hope there. Hope not. I didn't mean it. Please do be silly. I have forgotten the height of the table.

That was a good answer.

I have been going on in a little while.

I am going to take it along. Lena says that there is a chance.

I don't mean to deny it.

That's right.

I shall be very tired I shall be extraordinarily pleased, I shall settle it all presently.

Very likely.

I have to look at her all the time. I never see fruit now unless I pick it in my garden. Put it in my garden. Don't put too many. Because it's so much looser. All right. Oh no. I haven't. Chalk. Great Portland Street. I'll mention it. I have resisted. I have resisted that excellently well. I have resisted that I have resisted that excellently. Not a disappointment.

I don't understand, why hasn't she been there before. I know why. I will not have a selection again. It is too many horribly. Is it any use.

I do want to meet pearly. Now I am forgetting I will begin. She had a jewel. She was in that set.

It meant so much.

I wish I had a little celebration.

It meant so much.

The wise presentation comes from saying north, the best one comes a little way, it comes because she wanted to try breads. Why are pansies so stringy, why do they have heaps of resemblance. I said she was anaemic. I meant to coincide. I did certainly. It was so. Not in Paris.

Not in Paris very likely.

I do not mention that for a name. I mention it for a place. I mention it for a please do not consider me. I mention it for that.

Did she mind my saying that I was disappointed. I was not in that way out in that way. I was not in that way a circumstance which counted for it. She did not meet me. She did not observe clouds. She did not say that we were in the window. She did not like it before it was mentioned.

Come in.

I don't mean to antagonize the present aged parent. That is a strong present leaf.

Line.

Line line line away.

Line.

Lining.

I don't care what she mentions.

It will be very funny when I don't mean to say it.

I can forgive that is to say chopping.

Not any more.

Will I be surprised with Jane Singleton. I will not if I meet her. I will say not yet. I will say that. I am determined. It is so much. Good bye.

I did do it then.

Come back to me Fanny.

Oh dear.

Come back to me Fanny.

That's a picture.

When I remembered how surprised I was at certain places which were nearly in the way I cannot doubt that more accumulation is needed. I cannot doubt it.

All recovering.

James Death is a nice name.

I am breaking down I suppose he said when he arrived.

Forbade any communication with him.

He did say when he arrived I suppose.

It was a bright warm spring Sunday morning.

This egg for instance.

She was dressed in dark blue set off by red ribbons.

Except that of custom perhaps.

If you prefer it I will go.

The only lady who had been saved.

He was not hungry and he knew that there would be nothing to eat.

He was aware of a desire to eat and drink now that it was quite impossible for him to obtain anything.

Thanks I chew.

Jakins thinks me a fool I know sometime maybe I'll be able to prove I'm not.

You're busy.

His excitement was gone.

With mouth and muscle.

When used for male voices substitute bless for kiss.

Shall rest.

Shall rest more.

Shall in horror.

Shall rest.

Shall rest more then.

This is it mentioning.

Why do richness make the best heights.

Why do richness make the best heights.

Enough to leave him for ever and to live in another country

I don't see anything any more do I. Yes you do.

Are you pleased with them darling.

I meant to guess later.

I do not please.

Thanks so much.

Yes.

Yes.

Yes.

Please remember that I have said I will not be patient. Please remember that which I have said.

Do not put in a hot water bottle. Thanks so much.

Feeling mounting.

What did she do. She did not sit she was standing. She was standing and filling with a pepper thing and she had a collar not on her head but because she was shining. She was shining with gloves. This is a new destination. I never was surprised before.

What is the matter with it.

Nothing is the matter with it.

I mean to cough.

She said it was a wish.

You are not angry with me.

It's infamous. To put a cold water bottle in a bed. It is steering.

I meant to mention it and it is astonishing that there is a sentence.

Silence is southern.

I will not especially engage to be sick. I will not especially engage to be sick.

Why is Ellen so attractive.

Willing.

Willing, willing.

Willing willing, I met a kind of a clock. It was deepened.

I am not pleased. I am not satisfied and pleased. I am not pleased and certainly I am not more pleased. I am so repressed and I can state it. I can say. It was bitter.

I do not like her.

Fancy a miserable person. Repeat flowers.

A section.

Breathing.

Polite.

Politeness.

Absolutely.

Not a curl.

I come to say.

Winding.

Place.

Wheat.

Or not.

Come in.

Splashes splashes of jelly splashes of jelly.

Weather.

Whether he was presented.

I meant to stay.

Easy or blocks.

Do not be held by the enemy.

All the time.

Now line or them.

That's an established belt or tooth. Really not. I didn't mean to bellow. I won't be a table. I regret it. I shall be very likely to be walking. I shall introduce myself fairly. I do mind it.

Not again.

I do say not again.

I mean to be heavy.

It stands up against as much as it stands up for. That's what I object to. I don't want to be unflattering to us but I think it has been entirely forgotten.

Furs.

Perhaps you will. Then she wrote a very warm letter and sent these furs.

Shall ill.

I don't like it and in neglecting cherishing songs I am so pleased with all and by settling chalk. I am satisfied. We are neglected immensely. Not resting.

Shall it be continuous the liberty of sobriety. The dear thing. Little tremors. I ask the question.

With a wide piano.

Come.

Neglecting cherishing says shall I mistake pleases. In mistakes there is a salutary secretion. What. I said it.

Now and then.

War is Saturday and let us have peace.

Peace is refreshing, let us bear let us be or not by that mine.

Mended.

Now I come to stay away.

Answer.

I shook a darling.

Not eating Oh it was so timely.

Why should pitchers be triumphant. Does it proclaim that eleven, eleven, eleven, come across, speak it, satisfy a man, be neat, leave off oxes, shine flies, call spoken shouting call it back call it by little dotted voices and do be sweet, do be sweet, remember the accoutrement. No I will not pay away.

What a system in voices, what a system in voices.

I met a regular believe me it is not for the pleasure in it that I do it. I met a regular army. I was not certain of that, I was not certain of paper. I knew I was safe. And so he was. Shall I believe it.

I can't help mentioning that I was earnest. In that way there was a reason. I can destroy wetter wetter soaps. I can destroy wetter soaps.

I do.

I do not.

Leave it in there for me.

Leave it in an especial place. Do not make that face. Show it by the indication. I do mean to spell. I am. Believe me.

Pink Melon Joy.

II.

It pleases me very much.

Little swimming on the water.

I meant to mention pugilism. Pugilism leaning. Leaning and thinking. Thinking.

I meant to mention pugilism. Pugilism and leaning.

Leaning and thinking. I think.

I meant to mention that it was a resemblance that was not by way of exceeding the kind thought.

Pugilism. Pugilism and leaning.

I saw a door not that exactly, I saw a lamp shade. Certainly that. I will not stir. Pugilism and leaning.

Leaning.

Pugilism and leaning.

The reason I mention what is happening is not by way of concealing that I have babies. I don't mean to leave so and I shall speak in silence. What is a baby.

Now I know what I say.

I had loads of stationary.

Not pink melon joy. Pink melon joy. Pink melon joy.

I had loads of stationary.

Pugilism and leaning.

The little keys trembling. Why do they spoil a part. They were noisy.

Go to Mudie's first.

Go slowly and carefully and love your dearest.

That's a good idea.

Reconcile is a plain case of wretched pencils.

I cannot see what I shall a bit.

My one idea is to place cloth where there is cloth and to paper where I have hotter water, to place paper where I have hotter water.

I don't determine selfishness. I point it so that always I can always I do, I do always mean to get about.

Shall I be splendid.

Baby mine baby mine I am learning letters I am learning that to be sent baby mine baby mine I arranged it fairly early.

Complete cause for handles.

Complete cause for not tightening that.

I won't say it again.

This is the place to water horses.

I like to be excellently seized.

I made a mistake.

I like to be excellently seizing.

North north I went around and went in that minute.

I like to be excellently searching.

I like to be excellently chimes.

Chiming.

It isn't very good.

Deep set trustworthy eyes dark like his hair

Lips close fitting and without flew.

Blue should have dark eyes.

Light brown flesh color amber shades black nose, ears, legs, good sized feet rather.

Color dark blue, blue and tan, tan and liver, sandy, sandy and tan.

Height about fifteen to sixteen inches.

He wondered if she had ever thought of him as she sat in the chair or walked on the floor.

Islands.

I came to say that I like some things better.

Actual likenesses.

Of course I need large plates.

Standing alone.

She doesn't like it.

She likes to walk on the floor.

She might as well be pretty.

I don't blame Carrie.

No

What do I see when I like to be tall.

I see when there is a platter.

I was not mistaken with violets.

It was no pleasure.

Can you believe me.

Can you not be thoughtful.

Can you be aghast.

I mention most things regularly.

I do not wish whispers.

This makes mining such a loud noise.

I do not forget a war.

It isn't easy to please everybody.

Teeth are perfect.

No.

There is no influence.

Scattered.

Nine times twenty.

Crowded.

Crowded in.

Cups white.

I am solemn.

All taste.

Do you excuse me.

It was a stir.

Please state it please deny it please mean to be right. I am intending.

      Able to mingle pennies.

A penny is not a cent.

      Why do I see sisters.

It's rice.

      Wheat.

I couldn't imagine gladder or more perfect shapes, I couldn't imagine others.

He was really interested in the fluttering deftness of her twinkling hands.

I don't care too.

Likely.

I meant pearls.

Shall I be pleased.

Wire cakes.

      In time or.

Not so far back.

Please.

When I came to stay.

Old places.

When a girl speaks.

Shall you.

Not pleasing.

It is a time for that.

Formidable.

Amiable.

Amiable baby.

Fan.

Fanning.

There is no way of stretching.

Plan.

It is a good pitcher it is a good pitcher and a black pitcher.

It is a circle.

It is a circular.

I beg of you not to.

Bring in the fruit.

She was very comforting.

I wonder what he is doing. If he saw, well he couldn't see him because he is not here, if he saw him he would not ask him any questions, he would beg him to give him all the pictures and in any case he would ask him to arrange it.

What is a splendid horse. A splendid horse is one that is spread and really makes a lot of noise really makes an agreeable sound and a hoarse. This is not an interchange of rapid places by means of tubs.

I know you don't know what the pins are. I know you suspect much more. I know that anything is a great pleasure. I know esquimaux babies, that is to say tender.

I know what I am hearing. I am hearing accents. Not by any means placarded. Not by any means placarded. So that I met everybody.

What is the meaning of photographs.

Yes I mean it.

I believe that when there is a collection and tall pieces are missed and guided, I could have said it.

Let us take boats.

Boats are ships.

We will not take ships.

Ships are doors.

That's the way to be perfect.

I sell hats.

That's a kindness.

Please powder faces.

I have little chickens.

That doesn't mean anything.

When I said water I meant Sunday. Dear me it was Monday. No Tuesday. I don't care I shall please neatness. Then I calculated I did not see arithmetic I saw feathers, any two of them are thicker. What was the principle coughing, it went by way of dishes.

To be binding is to mean Sunday Saturday and eight o'clock. To be eight o'clock oh how heavenly singing. Leave Leave Leave oh my leaving and say why say, say I say say say go away go away I say. I say yes.

Plans.

I was able to state that I believed that if targets if targets not if targets.

Shall I be restless.

I could not eat buttons. I could not eat bundles. I couldn't, I might be why was I seen to be determined. I was surprising. Wasn't I silly.

Please miss me.

Not spider.

I saw a spider there.

Where.

I saw another.

Where.

I saw another and there I saw a pleasing sight.

I saw a waiter.

A spider.

Yes.

Not by left out.

Will you be faithful, will you be so glad that I left any way. Will you be delighted Saturday. Do you understand colors. It was my sister.

Why.

I cannot mention what I have.

I have.

Guess it.

I have a real sight. This is so critical.

Alice.

Put it in.

Put it in.

Nestles.

I wish I was a flower.

Were.

Were when.

Towers.

That is.

That is astonishing.

Mother.

I meant it.

When the moon.

I don't like it.

A million and ten.

Ten million and ten.

Ten and ten million.

Oh leave it to me.

Brutes.

I said whisper.

Anyway Pink melon or joy.

Is that the same.

Pink melon and enjoy.

Pink melon by joy.

Is that in him.

Is that in.

Positive.

At night.

Please be cautious and recalcitrant and determined to be steady. Please be neglectful. Please be ordered out.

Please be ordered out.

Franz Joseph was Emperor of Austria before gold had been discovered in California.

I do not.

Their thoughts were of one another.

The maid a very pretty girl somewhat showily dressed in a costume composed of the royal colors fixed curious eyes down a long passage and a short one. Presently the girl in blue returned.

Blue and white.

Returned.

Food and wine.

How could it be how could it be.

Blue and white, not an especial pinching.

I wish I was may be I am.

This isn't good.

Short erect ears and bold intelligent faces.

He seemed to like it.

Who are you.

Safety in comfort.

A flower should never lack an admirer in its namesake.

Unfortunately.

Unfortunately our weeks in London were full up so that I did not get a felt hat.

Unfortunately before.

Oh dear what did I do with them.

Here is a key for the house painters.

Glove stretchers.

Not any more begging.

Please have it ready.

She did not move.

She was not going to move.

It guards the life the health and the well-being of each user.

Parents encourage its use.

You can be the subject of wild admiration in ten days if you care to.

The skin has the tint of purity.

Very pleasant to use.

A freshly blown rose.

I can't be feeling badly.

I prefer water.

I like no I don't like it.

I fill a free uniform black instantly.

Those features are peculiar to a construction.

Please be dark.

Straws.

Please be straws.

I wish yes.

Plates.

And plates.

When do you gather together.

By ways of extra pages which mean colored places.

I read about the war.

I said that I didn't know Geoffrey Young. I said I believed in boys. I said I was enthusiastic.

I said little more.

To be able to spread water.

To be able to spread water.

There is a difference between kitchen coal and bedrooms.

What pleases you.

What Eugene said.

Eugene said that she would have a different expression from her sister. He did not say anything about her hair. She mentioned a wedding. Oh it was sinful.

Eugene said that there were straits. He did not stop for plates. She said she could cook. He was violent. He never was moved by birthdays. He liked Saturday. He was clean. He was not annoyed.

Consider a pleasant time.

All the time that there is commotion there is powerful autocracy.

Nicely said.

I do mean to win.

Pages and pages.

I don't care about lists.

I don't care about lists.

Pointed or why do you.

When I used that expression I was nervous. Don't take it too seriously James is nervous.

Plans.

Six fires.

Two lights.

Four lights.

Eight lights.

Eighty days.

I wish I was restless.

Out of four.

Out of four.

Six.

Sixty.

Little cats not all gone.

Little dove little love I am loving you with much more love. Parlor.

I saw an extraordinary mixture.

By nearly leaving out gloves and washing them.

By nearly leaving out gloves and washing them and towels, by nearly leaving out towels and all of it by way of reminding every one of every time, by leaving out invitations, by passing some day, let us say Tuesday, by passing Tuesday together and eating, by leaving out all the powder, by leaving out all the powder, Nellie made a mistake. Was it a week Monday. Not with the carelessness. It was carelessness. I meant to do it.

Pink Melon Joy.

III.

Thanks so much.

Do not repeat the miracle.

Thanks so much.

War.

I wish I was in the time when all the blame was feelingly added to mercies. I wish I could ask what's the matter now.

By believing in forms by believing in sheds by more stationing by really swimming as usual, no shell or fish. Pray.

I can hear extra rabbits, I can hear them and I mean beats. What is it.

It is not any use. It's no use. I do believe it. I shall select. I relieve officers. I sell potatoes. That is what clergymen sing.

Singing. What is singing quietly. We are singing quietly. I wish chimneys were old. They sound alike. They bother me.

All the day.

I was disappointed.

Going up.

Good night Mildred.

Good night dear.

They bother one so.

The cause of receding the cause of receding more, the cause of receding is in me. In me by me, for the rest. All of it organ. Take out a name. He did it.

Anything.

Anything to drink.

Anything to think.

Anything.

Very resistant.

I meant to spell teeth.

This is the way to pay.

Why should old people be vivacious. Thumbs do it.

They poison everything. They manage six.

I wish anger.

I wish religion.

I wish bursts.

I do wish fancies.

Fancy balls.

Blue dresses.

Other color cushions.

Points.

Disappoints.

Why should eating be agreeing.

Why should darkness turn colors.

Why should peddling be honorable.

Why should another be mother.

Mother to all.

Mother to some.

I say.

I say it.

He laughed.

He laughed believe me.

I do believe you.

He did not bother to sob.

I do not relegate that to the reverberation.

Please me.

It is not polite.

Cleaning silver.

Colored sack.

If I meant weather and I do mean to be obeyed, if I meant whether I was better I would not say bitter I would speak to every one.

Public character.

Stems.

Stems are caught by better seats they need watches.

I don't mean to be so finished.

Let us consider the french nation, let us watch its growth its order its humanity its care, its elaboration its thought its celebrated singing and nearly best nearly best with it. Let us consider why we are in authority, let us consider distribution, let us consider forget me nots.

Pensive.

By land.

By land.

By land.

By land.

I mentioned gayety.

I mentioned gayety.

No.

Not willing.

By pleasure.

Leading songs.

The moon is as round as a button.

All buttons aren't round said Alfy.

Plated onions.

I wish matches.

I wish all right.

I wish coal.

I do wish.

I wish I may.

I wish not a bird.

I wish when I make it.

I wish again.

I wish more than that.

Carving.

I didn't complain Susie.

If I really believed it I wouldn't be able to know.

But why the sitting was not the bed room he could never understand.

I am just gradually beginning to get to look around.

We were using the end that is by the fire and now that we have good coal I am beginning to separate expenses. I do see shell fish. It is a mistake to recollect all of it very nearly. I had better undertake to measure out a real wood and to borrow little pieces. It was chosen by me. I spoke to a man. He said he would come at once. I said no wait until you finish dinner. He mentioned that the soup was so hot he would prefer that it should cool. I said I would not allow it, that I would be uncomfortable and that there was no hurry I left no one. I never see fire, Mr. Matisse, Mr. Julian, Mr. Meininger, Mrs. Walter and Miss Howard without thinking of it. By nearly wishing for a country by nearly wishing for a country, by this you will spoil her. Do you. Do you ask for Greek. Do you deny Spain. Do you not praise England. Do you prize England. I said that I believed in the country and that I was silent in the city. I said I was silent about the city, I said I believed in the country. He asked me why I reigned. I said I did not deny rain. I said he could promise his mother. When the whole arrangement was mentioned leaving out pieces of plaster, when the whole thing was mentioned and he did not recommend oil, he did not say that he had not made an attempt, he said it was useless at this time to ask a minister to serve an individual. He said they were too busy. He said he would not speak to one another. He said I will ask.

I am trying a new one.

Believe two names.

I am really surprised.

In my surprise I shall stammer.

I do not stammer ordinarily.

Widening putty is not lonesome. It makes a door. I was wondering if the door was wide enough and if not whether the double door would be broken. It certainly would be and now if it were there would be no reparation. Not by reason of not inclining to mend it but because of the time that is only shown by the absence of women. It is astonishing. Really it is astonishing and its true. We have found it out. The day that we asked we heard it. We were surprised. If I wanted the door there is yet to be found the man who makes plaster. Plaster, cement. We say cement.

I am disappointed in women. No I cannot say that. There are ten days. I will be so pleased. I am so pleased. Do you credit me with hearing. I am so pleased.

It's been a success, it's been a perfect success.

Harnessing on or another. Harnessing another.

Harnessing on or another. Harnessing on or another is a great success. I offer. I offer. I offer. I do need it. Please be careful. Harnessing another is a great success. I was surprised when I looked at the picture to see that I could recognise everybody. I had been perfectly right in saying that they were stupid. It is chance. An accident. A resemblance. An offspring. An intuition. A result. A repetition. Repeat. I knew I wanted four hundred. I forgot to ask if he had seen an electrician. If he had was he at Versailles. A silver designer that is a name, Emile. I wanted to laugh. The voice was loud. I did not understand English. I am beautifully rich.

Once when I was fastening a drawing, I fastened it with decision. I did not like it there. We have decided not to have an umbrella stand. I don't think either that we will put everything away, I think what we will decide is this, to meet the train, to insist on paying, to give four eggs, bread, butter, water, meat and pears. Then we will go away and after that I don't think there is any need to notice noise. It is so silvery. I mentioned a fork. We were astonished by all languages. I meant to be told.

This is the light. I can not see plainly. I make a difference.

When are brothers.

By times.

Do old age missions sing.

They do choose choirs.

Why are mistakes late. Because they pleased us and we shall be late.

Render yourselves further. This means servants.

Render yourselves together.

Render together.

I saw a team running. I saw plenty of lamps.

It was lighter than London.

Do you think so.

To be dangerous mother.

We were so tired from sheer pity.

I wish we had loaned another.

Please be a buyer.

I shall spoil.

Not he.

Not he or hurry.

Not he. Not she. For her. Not very good.

The rebellion of Esther.

In a rebellion of Esther or with a study of a sheepdog. What is a police dog.

There may come a pause.

His task accomplished he may feed. It was seldom that increase or decrease in accordance with the one who welcomes first of all the incoming ill-natured purpose showed lightly conscienced boys bribed for the purpose. These exclaim. Do not for a moment fall into the error of considering them as to what becomes of them after they are fifty years of age. Had they been they would have succumbed to earlier opportunities. The sun set upon a curious scene

I went faster.

The infant's face being uncovered the helpless little thing opened its eyes. Although this separation was unavoidable it is I who am never permitted who have never permitted any one to ask me to interfere.

Pears.

Leave me leave me by way of pointing.

Believe me see me by way of dealing out plans.

Believe me believe me be careless, lead it by permission. Is Henner going to Paris.

By me I see sounds of dirt. I can hear something. I listen best. I am willing.

With no plan.

Have you said yes. I think it would be best to ask a baker. He sent her. He meant to hear me. He was loud. He had an unexpected spelling.

Hear me hear me I do.

Plainly.

If I carry you. If you carry, what will you carry.

Carrie.

Carrie.

If you carry me.

Seating.

Little manners.

When I asked everybody to sit down they were annoyed.

Please be at wax matches.

Please beat.

Please beat.

I cannot express emotion.

Any house is a home.

Two hands.

I heard today that it was appalling. I believe what is said and why it is said. I believe that lights are normal. I believe that separate stones coming together count as forty. I believe in two horses. I believe that.

When I heard the description of mud and shouting when I saw him and it was a surprise then I said I would stand. It was pleasant. It was not gentle. It was black and hopeful. It was principally very shapely. Anything can astonish a citizen. I was cautious. I believe in the best.

Not a mile.

When I say that introductions mean that, when I feel that I have met them, when I am out aloud and by spacing I separate letters when I do this and I am melancholy I remember that rivers, only rivers have suppressed sounds. All the rest overflow. Piles are driven. Ice is free. Changes are by little spools, and toys are iron. Toys are iron whether or not they are Italian. This is so far. Please be at rest. I shall. I shall not speak for anybody. I shall do my duty. I shall establish that mile. I shall choose wonder. Be blest.

When she said six and meant seven I made her leave it more than she chose to revise. I made her please me. Do be careful.

I cannot help it. I cannot expect places. I can see that there is some obligation in deciding on straps and in lessening tails. I can see what I come to mention. But do not deceive anybody, do not be churlish. Do place exercises in a book. To be excellently winning, to be exclaiming and really I don't see any use in leaving yet when really there is no moon. I do believe in some. I shall suggest it. Very likely there is cause. I don't say I neglect to mention it. I forgot to place any of it higher. I meant to relive eyes. I saw wealthy boys. I shall judge then. Do not go away. This is this call. I edged it. I mean to say goodness. Don't be a worry. Don't resemble mother. I saw the oldest boy sneeze. It is a calamitous poison. Not when it is old. Not by nearly so much as yesterday. I do believe I hear whether I do see knives. Indeed I do.

What was she going to do Monday morning.

There are plenty of rubber wheels of a kind. The mischief lies in getting the wrong ones. They are remarkable in many shapes and when you ask for hurrying see that you get it.

I think this will be enough.

Closets are cleaner.

We came to be rosy.

Prayers.

I mentioned it satisfactorily.

Do not be careful.

Do not be careful.

She said she would not have displeased her by herself. I will mention it to another. Be quick.

Quickly.

I don't know why emigration has been stopped.

Maps.

I am thinking.

I will not say that.

This is the way I feel about it. He said that. He did not say he was reluctant. He went to the place in front of the same thing. Any one is not tired.

To believe me it is necessary to have a resumption. To resume is war. I say it in the morning. I don't say it in the morning. This is not mischief. I do not believe in fancies in respect to bread. This was mentioned with coal. But not with the same authority.

He goes and he does not believe in draughts. He is invited.

It seems a splendid day.

I said he knew this thing. I said everybody knows something. I was winding stockings. This is the day to pray.

Please be restless.

I cannot count.

I looked for the address.

There was plenty of time in softening.

He said he was surprised and he said laughing is coughing.

There is one such in my company. I am impatient. I believe in crops.

I do not care about the same thing in another way.

Would you have another.

What.

Kiss.

If You Had Three Husbands

If you had three husbands.

If you had three husbands.

If you had three husbands, well not exactly that.

If you had three husbands would you be willing to take everything and be satisfied to live in Belmont in a large house with a view and plenty of flowers and neighbors, neighbors who were cousins and some friends who did not say anything.

This is what happened.

She expressed everything.

She is worthy of signing a will.

And mentioning what she wished.

She was brought up by her mother. She had meaning and she was careful in reading. She read marvelously. She was pleased. She was aged thirty-nine. She was flavored by reason of much memory and recollection.

This is everything.

Foreword.

I cannot believe it.

I cannot realize it.

I cannot see it.

It is what happened.

First there was a wonder.

Really wonder.

Wonder by means of what.

Wonder by means of measures.

Measuring what.

Heights.

How high.

A little.

This was not all.

There were well if you like there were wonderful spots such as were seen by a queen. This came to be a system. Really it was just by a treasure. What was a treasure. Apart from that.

Surely.

Rather.

In their beginning what was a delight. Not signing papers or anything or indeed in having a mother and two sisters. Not nearly enough were mentioned by telegraphing. It was a choice.

I ramble when I mention it.

Did she leave me any money.

I remember something.

I am not clear about what it was.

When did I settle that.

I settled it yesterday.

Early Life.

They were not miserably young they were older than another. She was gliding. It is by nearly weekly leaning that it comes to be exact. It never was in dispute.

They were gayly not gaily gorgeous. They were not gorgeous at all. They were obliging. If you think so. If you think so glow. If you believe in light boys. They were never another.

It came to be seen that any beam of three rooms was not showy. They were proud to sit at mother. Slowly walking makes walking quicker. They have toys and not that in deceiving. They do not deceive them. No one is willing. No one could be cool and mother and divided and necessary and climatical and of origin and beneath that mean and be a sun. It was strange in her cheek. Not strange to them or that.

A young one.

Not by mountains.

Not by oysters.

Not by hearing.

Not by round ways.

Not by circumference again.

Not by leaving luncheon.

Not by birth.

It doesn't make any difference when ten are born. Ten is never a number. Neither is six. Neither is four.

I will not mention it again.

Early days of shading.

Make a mouse in green.

Make a single piece of sun and make a violet bloom. Early piece of swimming makes a sun on time and makes it shine and warm today and sun and sun and not to stay and not to stay or away. Not to stay satin. Out from the whole wide world he chose her. Out from the whole wide world and that is what is said.

Family.

What is famine. It is plenty of another. What is famine. It is eating. What is famine. It is carving. Why is carving a wonderful thing. Because supper is over. This can happen again. Sums are seen.

Please be polite for mother. Lives of them. Call it shall it clothe it. Boil it. Why not color it black and never red or green. This is stubborn. I don't say so.

No opposition.

If you had a little likeness and hoped for more terror. If you had a refusal and were slender. If you had cuff-buttons and jackets and really astonishing kinds of fever would you stop talking. Would you not consider it necessary to talk over affairs.

It was a chance that made them never miss tea. They did not miss it because it was there. They did not mean to be particular. They invited their friends. They were not aching. It was noiseless and beside that they were clever. Who was clever. The way they had of seeing mother.

Mother was prepared.

They were caressing.

They had sound sense.

They were questioned.

They had likeness. Likeness to what. Likeness to loving. Who had likeness to loving. They had likeness to loving. Why did they have a likeness to loving. They had a likeness to loving because it was easily seen that they were immeasurable.

They were fixed by that, they were fixed, not licensed, they were seen, not treasured, they were announced, not restless, they were reasoning, not progressing. I do not wish to imply that there is any remedy for any defect.

I cannot state that anyone was disappointed. I cannot state that any one was ever disappointed by willingly heaping much confusion in particular places. No confusion is reasonable. Anybody can be nervous.

They were nervous again.

This is wishing.

Why is wishing related to a ridiculous pretence of changing opposition to analysis. The answer to this is that nearly any one can faint. I don't mean to say that they don't like tennis.

Please be capable of sounds and shoulders. Please be capable of careful words. Please be capable of meaning to measure further.

They measured there.

They were heroes.

Nobody believed papers.

Everybody believed colors.

I cannot exercise obligation.

I cannot believe cheating.

I cannot sober mother.

I cannot shut my heart.

I cannot cherish vice.

I cannot deceive all.

I cannot be odious.

I cannot see between.

Between what and most.

I cannot answer either.

Do be left over suddenly.

This is not advice.

No one knows so well what widening means. It means that yards are yards and so many of them are perfect. By that I mean I know.

This is not so.

I am not telling the story I am repeating what I have been reading.

What effects tenderness.

Not to remember the name.

Say it.

The time comes when it is natural to realize that solid advantages connect themselves with pages of extreme expression. This is never nervously pale. It is finely and authentically swollen by the time there is any rapid shouting.

I do not like the word shouting. I do not mean that it gives me any pleasure. On the contrary I see that individual annoyances are increased by it but nevertheless I am earnestly persuasive concerning it. Why soothe why soothe each other.

This is not at all what is being said.

It happened very simply that they were married. They were naturally married and really the place to see it was in the reflection every one had of not frightening not the least bit frightening enthusiasm. They were so exact and by nearly every one it was encouraged soothed and lamented. I do not say that they were interested.

Any years are early years and all years are occasions for recalling that she promised me something.

This is the way to write an address.

When they were engaged she said we are happy. When they were married she said we are happy. They talked about everything they talked about individual feeling. This is not what was said. They did not talk about disinterested obligation. They did not talk about pleasantness and circumstances. I do not mean to say that there was conversation. I do not organize a revision. I declare that there was no need of criticism. That there was no criticism. That there was breathing. By that I mean that lights have lanterns and are not huddled together when there is a low ceiling. By that I mean that it was separate. The ceiling was separated from the floor. Everywhere.

I could say that devotion was more merited than walking together. What do you mean. I mean that we all saw it.

When not by a beginning is there meadows and music, you can't call it that exactly, when not by a beginning, there is no beginning, I used to say there was a beginning, there is no beginning, when there is no beginning in a volume and there are parts, who can think.

This pencil was bought in Austria.

Length of time or times.

He agreed. He said I would have known by this time. I don't like to think about it. It would have led to so much. Not that I am disappointed I cannot be disappointed when I have so much to make me happy. I know all that I am to happiness, it is to be happy and I am happy. I am so completely happy that I mention it.

In writing now I find it more of a strain because now I write by sentences. I don't mean that I feel it above, I feel it here and by this time I mention it too. I do not feel the significance of this list.

Can you read a book.

By the time artificial flowers were made out of feathers no pride was left. Any one is proud if the name of their house is the name of a city.

I remember very well the time I was asked to come up and I said I did not want to. I said I did not want to but I was willing not quite to understand why after all there need be poison. Do not say more than a word.

No this is wrong.

Cousins and cousins, height is a brother. Are they careful to stay.

If you had three husbands I don't mean that it is a guess or a wish. I believe finally in what I saw in what I see. I believe finally in what I see, in where I satisfy my extreme shadow.

Believing in an extreme dream. This is so that she told her mother. I do not believe it can be mentioned. I do not believe it can be mentioned.

Astonishing leaves are found in their dread in their dread of that color. Astonishing leaves can be found in their dread not in their dread of that color. Astonishing leaves can be found in their dread in their dread of that color.

When it came to say I mean a whole day nobody meant a whole day. When it came not to say a whole day nobody meant a whole day. There never was a single day or a single murmur or a single word or a single circumstance or sweating. What is sweating. Not distilling. Distilling necessitates knowing. Knowing necessitates reasons and reasons do not necessitate flowers. States are flowers.

Brother to birthdays.

Twenty four days.

Not a beginning.

By politeness. It is not really polite to be unworthy. Unworthy of what unworthy of the house and of the property adjoining.

Let me describe the red room. A red room isn't cold or warm. A red room is not meant to be icy. A red room is worthy of articles.

He pleased she pleased everybody. He pleased her.

He pleased her to go. She was attracted by the time. I do not remember that there were any clocks.

I don't wish to begin counting.

All this was after it was necessary for us to be there all the time. Who were we. We were often enlivening. By way of what. By way of steps or the door. By way of steps. By way of steps or the door.

I remember very well the day he asked me if I were patient. Of course I was or of course I was patient enough, of course I was patient enough.

When it was easy to matter we were all frames not golden or printed, just finely or formerly flattered. It was so easy easy to be bell. Belle was her name. Belle or Bella. I don't mean relations or overwhelming. I don't even mean that we were fond of healthy trees. Trees aren't healthy by yesterday or by roots or by swelling. Trees are a sign of pleasure. It means that there is a country. A country give to me sweet land of liberty.

One can easily get tired of rolls and rows. Rows have one seat. Rolls are polite. In a way there is no difference between them. Rolls and rows have finished purses. Rows and rolls have finished purses.

It isn't easy to be restless.

If sitting is not developed.

If standing is not open.

If active action is represented by lying and if piles of tears are beside more delight, it is a rope.

By that we swim.

Capture sealing wax not in or color.

Ceilings.

I like that dwelling.

All the same sound or bore.

Do it.

Try that.

Try.

Why.

Widen.

Public speaking is sinister if cousins are brothers. We were a little pile.

Buy that.

There is no such sense.

Pleasant days.

So to speak.

Sand today.

Sunday.

Sight in there.

Saturday.

Pray.

What forsooth.

Do be quiet.

Laugh.

I know it.

Shall we.

Let us go ten.

One must be willing.

If one loves one another by that means they do not perish. They frequent the same day and nearly that it was six months apart.

Three and three make two.

Two twenty.

I was not disappointed.

Do as you please, write the name, change it, declare that you are strong, be annoyed. All this is not foolish.

She was doubtless not old.

Pleasant days brother. I don't mean this thing. I don't mean calling aloud, I never did so, I was not plaintive. I was not even reached by coughing. I was splendid and sorrowful. I could catch my breath.

I don't feel that necessity.

They came home.

Why did they come home.

They come home beside.

All of it was strange, their daughter was strange, their excitement was strange and painfully sheltered. Quiet leaning is so puzzling. Certainly glasses makes cats a nuisance. We really have endured too much. Everybody says the same thing.

I do not see much necessity for believing that it would have occurred as it did occur if sun and September and the hope had not been mentioned. It was all foolish. Why not be determined. Why not oppose. Why not settle flowers. Settle on flowers, speak cryingly and be loath to detain her. I don't see how any one can speak.

I am not satisfied.

Present Homes.

There then.

Present ten.

Mother and sister apples, no not apples, they can't be apples, everything can't be apples, sounds can't be apples. Do be quiet and refrain from acceptances.

It was a great disappointment to me.

I can see that there is a balcony. There never was a sea or land, there never was a harbor or a snow storm, there never was excitement. Some said she couldn't love. I don't believe that anybody said that. I don't mean that anybody said that. We were all present. We could be devoted. It does make a different thing. And hair, hair should not be deceiving. Cause tears. Why tears, why not abscesses.

I will never mention an ugly skirt.

It pleased me to say that I was pretty.

Oh we are so pleased.

I don't say this at all.

Consequences are not frightful.

Pleasure in a home.

After lunch, why after lunch, no birds are eaten. Of course carving is special.

I don't say that for candor.

Please be prepared to stay.

I don't care for wishes.

This is not a success.

By this stream.

Streaming out.

I am relieved from draught. This is not the way to spell water.

I cannot believe in much.

I have courage.

Endurance.

And restraint.

After that.

For that end.

This is the title of a conclusion which was not anticipated

When I was last there I smiled behind the car. What car showed it.

By that time.

Believe her out.

Out where.

By that.

Buy that.

She pleased me for. Eye saw.

Do it.

For that over that.

We passed away. By that time servants were memorable. They came to praise.

Please do not.

A blemish.

They have spans.

I cannot consider that the right word.

By the time we are selfish, by that time we are selfish.

By that time we are selfish.

It is a wonderful sight,

It is a wonderful sight to see.

Days.

What are days.

They have hams.

Delicate.

Delicate hams.

Pounds.

Pounds where.

Pounds of.

Where.

Not butter dogs.

I establish souls.

Any spelling will do.

Beside that.

Any spelling will do beside that.

If you look at it.

That way.

I am going on.

In again.

I am going on again in in then.

What I feel.

What I do feel.

They said mirrors.

Undoubtedly they have that phrase.

I can see a hat.

I remember very well knowing largely.

Any shade, by that I do mean iron glass. Iron glass is so torn. By what. By the glare. Be that beside. Size shall be sensible. That size shall be sensible.

Fixing.

Fixing enough.

Fixing up.

By fixing down, that is softness, by fixing down there.

Their end.

Politeness.

Not by linen.

I don't wish to be recalled.

One, day, I do not wish to use the word, one day they asked to buy that.

I don't mean anything by threads. It was wholly unnecessary to do so. It was done and then a gun. By that stand. Wishes.

I do not see what I have to do with that.

Any one can help weeping.

By wise.

I am so indifferent.

Not a bite.

Call me handsome.

It was a nice fate.

Any one could see.

Any one could see.

Any one could see.

Buy that etching.

Do be black.

I do not mean to say etching. Why should I be very sensitive. Why should I matter. Why need I be seen. Why not have politeness.

Why not have politeness.

In my hair.

I don't think it sounds at all like that.

Their end.

To end.

To be for that end.

To be that end.

I don't see what difference it makes

It does matter.

Why have they pots.

Ornaments.

And china.

It isn't at all.

I have made every mistake.

Powder it.

Not put into boxes.

Not put into boxes.

Powder it.

I know that well.

She mentioned it as she was sleeping.

She liked bought cake best. No she didn't for that purpose.

I have utter confusion.

No two can be alike.

They are and they are not stubborn.

Please me.

I was mistaken.

Any way.

By that.

Do not refuse to be wild.

Do not refuse to be all.

We have decided not to withstand it.

We would not rather have the home.

This is to teach lessons of exchange endurance and resemblance and by that time it was turned.

Shout.

By.

Out.

I am going to continue humming.

This does not mean express wishes.

I am not so fanciful. I am beside that calculated to believe in whole pages. Oh do not annoy me.

Days.

I don't like to be fitted. She didn't say that. If it hadn't been as natural as all the rest you would have been as silly as all the rest.

It's not at all when it is right.

I wish for a cake.

She said she did.

She said she didn't.

Gloom.

There was no gloom.

Every room.

There was no room.

There was no room.

Buy that chance.

She didn't leave me any money.

Head.

Ahead.

I don't want to be visible or invisible.

I don't want a dog named Dick.

It has nothing to do with it.

I am obliged to end.

Intend.

My uncle will.

Work Again

Fasten it fat we say Aunt Pauline.

Not snow now nor that in between.

Now we are bold.

All the weights are measures.

Splendid.

Are they plateful.

Girls are.

Women.

Treasures in song.

I see a mountain wheeler

I see a capstan.

I see a straight.

I see a rattle.

All things are breathing.

Can you see me.

Hurrah for America.

A day's sun.

In this miss.

Yes indeed our mat.

We can thank you

We thank you.

Come together.

Come to me there now.

All of it is bit.

Bitter.

In the meaning of bright.

Bright not light.

Light to me.

Then say the essence.

Not a nightingale.

Wild animals are not fierce neither are sponges.

Can you see her dressed or him.

In this way we cough.

What can a mayor do.

In this new school. In this new school they are ladies. And now you mention gifts.

And lists.

Can you believe.

Then then.

All the leaves.

All the hotels.

All the boils.

Cooks cook.

We are so happy.

In the land.

You mean a lady.

Can we have imagination.

They ask have we a stocking.

Did he die to drink.

We have to.

It is not a joke.

A vicar is not a joke.

Did he die there because he was mortal and we leave Rivesaltes.

Be nice to me.

In the kiss.

Laps indeed.

Can you say lapse.

Then think about it.

I think kindly of that bother.

It is not a bother to be a soldier.

Indeed it is yet.

We are so pleased.

With the flag.

With the flag of sets.

Sets of color

Do you like flags.

Blue flags smell sweetly.

Blue flags in a whirl.

The wind blows

And the automobile goes.

Can you guess boards.

Wood.

Can you guess hoops.

Barrels.

Can you guess girls.

Servants.

Can you guess messages.

In deed.

Then there are meats to buy.

We like asparagus so.

This is an interview.

Soldiers like a fuss.

Give them their way.

Yes indeed we will.

We are not mighty

Nor merry.

We are happy.

Very.

                    In the morning.

We believe in the morning

Do we.
                    Please be an interview.

Please be an interview with dogs.

Please comfort me.

Please plan a game.

Please then and places.

In the meantime.

In the meantime we are useful.

That is what I mean to say.

In the meantime can you have beds.

Kindly call a brother.

What is a cure.

I speak french.

What are means.

I can call it in time.

By the way where are fish.

In that case are there any wonders.

Many wonders are women.

And men too

We smile.

In the way sentences.

He does not feel as we do.

But he did have the coat.

He blushed a little

Cook.

In the tenth century chateau.

Who they are we do not know.

But we know they tell us so they tell us that in that way.

Why do we believe in Cook.

We do not hear from him.

In a Casino.

Waiting tomorrow yes yet.

And then we think.

We think often of pens.

Near silk.

In times of peace.

In times of peace

Prepare meals.

This is what was said to us

But we do not believe.

We wait.

We come.

In that way we feel.

And is it useless

It is not useless

Saturday.

Statuatory.

In that case.

In that case what.

Are you satisfied.

Certainly with me.

Then we have the use of it.

Indeed yes.

We are agreed.

In the case of mothers.

Aunt Pauline.

How did you pronounce it.

It was in doubt.

In this way we mention this.

This is the story of it.

He was her uncle and nervous.

In their way they had a black police dog.

In his way he had neither relief nor expeditions.

In this thing he was not patient.

If they gave him the money to clean the gutters need they shut the tobacco shops.

You don't understand that

If they gave him money for the cleaning of city pipes need he have orders to close butchers.

We can understand the universal. This is universal.

What is the difference between one order and a reading. A great many read in a park.

Words question it bakeries threaten it but really hotels receive it. Do we hear about books. Do we. And catalogues. And catalogues. Farmers for speech. A great many vines are said to be sold. In France. And in wealthy homes too. We do not understand the weather. That astonishes me.

Can you think of me.

Confess it confess it weather burns and in that case there is plenty of sausage.

Can you think of me at.

In all cases keep afraid.

And then what happens.

Nothing.

Are you sure nothing.

Of course not.

You are not just saying it.

You know you have your wish.

Thank you in smiles.

Then we see

Very well.

You did not mean to say so.

No but I know I am right

You always are.

This is a paragraph.

Then it will be well

Yes and a fit.

You mean fitly.

Yes slowly.

And then no worry

Not at all

Thank you for saying that.

Many cases are fine.

In that way we wish.

We think.

We recover.

In that way we swim. Camelias finish when roses begin.

Let me tell you about this. We were disappointed in cards. And yet we need not be. We will have them.

In the beginning pinks you mean flowers yes smell.

And pansies too.

Sacred heart pansies.

These are the best.

Can we wonder about cookies. Not those that have no flour.

Sacred heart doughnuts.

Pansies I said.

Camelias.

Camelias.

I do not care to mention it again.

I do it.

How do I not.

It is astonishing that those who have fought so hard and so well should pick yellow irises and fish in a stream.

They have mistaken their doctor.

He was an oculist.

And then there were

And then they were

Please spell a dish.

I do not like called a flower,

Repeat cuckoo

She always makes a mistake

In french.

Castle anew.

And then the sister.

Can you feel a home.

When I see it.

See it with them.

And then a pansy.

I did not ask for it.

It smells.

A sweet smell

With Acacia

Call it locusts

Call it me.

Barrels.

In comparison what are horses.

Compared with that again what are bells.

You mean horns. No I mean noises.

In leaning can we encounter oil.

I meant this to be intelligible.

We were taking a trip. We found the roads not noisy but pleasurable and the shade there was pleasant. We found that the trees had been planted so as to make rows. This is almost universal.

In coming to a village we ask them can they come to see us we mean near enough to talk and then we ask them how do we go there.

This is not fanciful.

In advance we have spoken, of what, can you imagine obedience as a subject. It is. It is laughable when there is no need of any backing. Can you understand that in two ways.

We mean to be lean. Lean to me. And then what a girl. No girl and Emil. We like fresh cooking. So does anybody.

No everybody doesn't.

The right spirit. There are difficulties and they must be met in the right spirit.

This is an illustration of the difficulties we have in many ways.

Then we go on.

I have made up my mind not to be excited.

In speeding I speed.

In neglecting I do not offer anything.

In reason I reverse the car and in this way we are successful.

We have no worries.

What can you think of a bone.

It is useless to think.

Digestion.

In that way we do not prey.

We write of fish.

And then I have been careful.

It is all imagination.

Can you sing rightly.

A trunk locked up in Perpignan.

In this way we pass the hay.

I have reasoned.

I am convinced.

I do not argue.

Or play the piano.

As the daughters of the banker do.

This is now the book in which I write and receive.

Can you guess Beziers.

Was I right.

You are.

Indeed there are barrels.

Tourty or Tourtebattre

A Story of the Great War

Tourtebattre came to visit us in the court he said he heard Americans were in town and he came to see us and we said what is your name and what americans have you known and we said we would go to see him and we did not and we did not give him anything.

Then when we went out to see the hospital we did not take him anything. We asked to see him. Then when the new things came we did take a package to him and we did not see him but he came and called on us to thank us and we were out.

Reflections.

If I must reflect I reflect upon Ann Veronica. This is not what is intended. Mrs. Tourtebattre. Of this we know nothing.

Can we reflect one for another.

Profit and loss is three twenty five never two seventy five.

Yes that is the very easy force, decidedly not.

Then Tourtebattre used to come all the time and then he used to tell us how old he was when he was asked and he took sugar in his coffee as it was given to him. He was not too old to be a father he was thirty seven and he had three children and he told us that he liked to turn a phrase.

China. Whenever he went to the colonies his sister was hurt in an automobile accident. This did not mean that she suffered.

Some one thought she was killed. Will you please put that in.

His father's watch, his wife gave all his most precious belongings to a man who did not belong to the town he said he belonged to. We did not know the truth of this.

Reflections.

We should not color our hero with his wife's misdeeds. Because you see he may be a religion instead of a talker. Little bones have to come out of his hand for action this was after his wound. A good deal.

He was wounded in the attack in April right near where he was always going to visit his wife and he saw the church tower and then he was immediately evacuated to an american hospital where every one was very American and very kind and Miss Bell tried to talk french to him and amuse him but overcome with her difficulties with the french language she retired which made him say she was very nice and these stories that he told to us you told to Sister Cecile which did not please her and she said we must come and hear from every one else the stories they all told of the kindness they had received in the American hospital before they came to her and she said to them what did the major do, and they said he played ball. He did. And you too and all of them said, no sister but you were wounded in an attack. We were both wounded, said the soldier.

Reflections.

Reflections on Sister Cecile lead us to believe that she did not reflect about Friday but about the book in which she often wrote. We were curious. She wrote this note. This is it. Name life, wife, deed, wound, weather, food, devotion, and expression.

What did he ask for.

Why I don't know.

Why don't you know.

I don't call that making literature at all.

What has he asked for.

I call literature telling a story as it happens.

Facts of life make literature.

I can always feel rightly about that.

We obtained beads for him and our own pictures in it.

Dear pictures of us.

We can tell anything over.

We gave him colored beads and he made them with paper that he bought himself of two different colors into frames that we sent with our pictures to our cousins and our papas in America.

Can we say it.

We cannot.

Now.

Then he told us about his wife and his child.

He does not say anything about them now.

Some immediate provision was necessary.

We said in English these are the facts which we are bringing to your memory.

What is capitol.

He told us of bead buttons and black and white. He answered her back very brightly.

He is a man.

Reflections.

What were the reflections.

Have we undertaken too much.

What is the name of his wife.

They were lost. We did not look forward. We did not think much. How long would he stay. Our reflections really came later.

The first thing we heard from her was that the woman was not staying and had left her new address.

How do you do.

We did not look her up.

Her mother and her mother.

Can you think why Marguerite did not wish Jenny Picard to remain longer.

Because she stole.

Not really.

Yes indeed. Little things.

This will never do.

And then.

I said we must go to see her.

And you said we will see.

One night, no one day she called with her mother.

Who was very good looking.

She was very good looking.

And the little boy.

Can you think of the little boy.

They both said that they were not polite.

But they were.

Reflections can come already.

We believed her reasons were real reasons.

Who is always right.

Not she nor her eleven sisters.

No one knew who was kind to her.

What is kindness.

Kindness is being soft or good and has nothing to do with amiable. Albert is kind and good.

And their wives.

Can you tell the difference between wives and children.

Queen Victoria and Queen Victoria.

They made you jump.

And I said the mother you said the mother. I did not remember the mother was in Paris but you did.

Next

Life and Letters of Marçel Duchamp

A family likeness pleases when there is a cessation of resemblances. This is to say that points of remarkable resemblance are those which make Henry leading. Henry leading actually smothers Emil. Emil is pointed. He does not overdo examples. He even hesitates.

But am I sensible. Am I not rather efficient in sympathy or common feeling.

I was looking to see if I could make Marcel out of it but I can't.

Not a doctor to me not a debtor to me not a d to me but a c to me a credit to me. To interlace a story with glass and with rope with color and roam.

How many people roam.

Dark people roam.

Can dark people come from the north. Are they dark then. Do they begin to be dark when they have come from there.

Any question leads away from me. Grave a boy grave.

What I do recollect is this. I collect black and white. From the standpoint of white all color is color. From the standpoint of black. Black is white. White is black. Black is black. White is black. White and black is black and white. What I recollect when I am there is that words are not birds. How easily I feel thin. Birds do not. So I replace birds with tin-foil. Silver is thin.

Life and letters of Marçel Duchamp.

Quickly return the unabridged restraint and mention letters.

My dear Fourth.

Confess to me in a quick saying. The vote is taken.

The lucky strike works well and difficultly. It rounds, it sounds round. I cannot conceal attrition. Let me think. I repeat the fullness of bread. In a way not bread. Delight me. I delight a lamb in birth.

Land of Nations

[Sub Title: And Ask Asia]

After these introductions I wish to say something I wish to say that I am entirely agreed that the best way to meet together is to deny that you wish to spend money. We don't want to spend the money.

They went to spend their money. We all spend our money in this way I spend my money and what do I have. I have a car. That is to say I have spent my money. I do spend my money but not in this way. I do not spend my money in this way. I spend my money. Did you say you had the money. Indeed indeed I believe you there. This is a country. A fine country. This is a fine country. Let us begin with this one which is this country entirely and in this order.

Then we have the country. Let us imagine the country. A country with a wait and wait by me and wait by me and always always always always wait and always wait and always wait and always always wait and wait by me. This is the country I have mentioned. It means to be with us. Then there is a very late country and we wish to embark we wish to embark it altogether. In the midst of money we are whistling.

Continuation.

Jessie

I am angry. Have you been.

I am angry with a din.

I am angry so you see.

Egypt and for Syrie.

I am angry as you hear.

I am angry for the bier.

I am angry for the waist.

I am angry in the taste.

I am angry to the touch.

You can make me see that much.

I am angry and I sigh.

England will be going by.

Going to buy not going to buy.

I am angry and I sigh.

And then in the midst of smoke there was Fiume. I can never make a poem about Italy. About Italy you do, you address, bless and say adieu. Adieu Italy beautiful Italy adieu.

A great many countries have a name.

Let me think of the house and the best.

A house a boat a victory and an alert. In the way of rhyming. I can think of so much. Dirt, flirt and spurt. Do you see any difference. I do. Discourage England, and say you mean well.

Here is a poem.

Amber.

Ambler Curran.

Amber is found on the shores of the Baltic.

Like wild asparagus you must have an eye for it.

All animals howl.

All animals or a barnyard fowl.

All animals are stars

All animals and bars.

Please pay a monkey a dear or a sweet.

Please pay a lion a pheasant or a street.

Please recognize a mother a head or an owl.

Please recognize a feather a heather or a soul. Please recognize the weather. What do you live for.

Climate and the affections. Jews quote that.

Accents in Alsace

A Reasonable Tragedy

Act I. The Schemils.

Brother brother go away and stay.

Sister mother believe me I say.

They will never get me as I run away.

He runs away and stays away and strange to say he passes the lines and goes all the way and they do not find him but hear that he is there in the foreign legion in distant Algier.

And what happens to the family.

The family manages to get along and then some one of his comrades in writing a letter which is gotten hold of by the Boche find he is a soldier whom they cannot touch, so what do they do they decide to embrew his mother and sister and father too. And how did they escape by paying somebody money.

That is what you did with the Boche. You always paid some money to some one it might be a colonel or it might be a sergeant but anyway you did it and it was neccesary so then what happened.

The Schemmels.

Sing so la douse so la dim.

Un deux trois

Can you tell me wha

Is it indeed.

What you call a Petide.

And then what do I say to thee

Let me kiss thee willingly.

Not a mountain not a goat not a door.

Not a whisper not a curl not a gore

In me meeney miney mo.

You are my love and I tell you so.

    In the daylight

    And the night

Baby winks and holds me tight.

In the morning and the day and the evening and alway.

I hold my baby as I say.

Completely.

And what is an accent of my wife.

And accent and the present life.

Oh sweet oh my oh sweet oh my

I love you love you and I try

I try not to be nasty and hasty and good

I am my little baby's daily food.

Alsatia.

In the exercise of greatness there is charm.

Believe me I mean to do you harm.

And except you have a stomach to alarm.

I mean to scatter so you are to arm.

Let me go.

And the Alsatians say.

What has another prince a birthday.

Now we come back to the Schemmils.

Schimmel Schimmel Gott in Himmel

Gott in Himmel There comes Shimmel.

Schimmel is an Alsatian name.

Act II.

It is a little thing to expect nobody to sell what you give them.

It is a little thing to be a minister.

It is a little thing to manufacture articles.

All this is modest.

The Brother.

Brother brother here is mother.

We are all very well.

Scene.

Listen to thee sweet cheerie

Is the pleasure of me.

In the way of being hungry and tired

That is what a depot makes you

A depot is not for trains

Its for us.

What are baby carriages

Household goods

And not the dears.

But dears.

Another Act.

Clouds do not fatten with teaching.

They do not fatten at all.

We wonder if it is influence

By the way I guess.

She said. I like it better than Eggland.

What do you mean.

We never asked how many children over eleven.

You cannot imagine what I think about the country.

Any civilians killed.

Act II.

See the swimmer. He don't swim.

See the swimmer.

My wife is angry when she sees a swimmer.

Opening II.

We like Hirsing.

III.

We like the mayor of Guebwiller.

IV.

We like the road between Cernay and the railroad.

We go everywhere by automobile.

Act II.

This is a particular old winter.

Everybody goes back.

Back.

I can clean.

I can clean.

I cannot clean without a change in birds.

I am so pleased that they cheat.

Act 54.

In silver stars and red crosses.

In paper money and water.

We know a french wine.

Alsatian wine is dearer.

They are not particularly old.

Old men are old.

There are plenty to hear of Schemmel having appendicitis.

Scene II.

Can you mix with another

Can you be a Christian and a Swiss.

Mr. Zumsteg. Do I hear a saint.

Louisa. They call me Lisela.

Mrs. Zumsteg. Are you going to hear me.

Young Mr. Zumsteg. I was looking at the snow.

All of them. Like flowers. They like flowers.

Scene III.

It is an occasion.

When you see a Hussar.

A Zouave.

A soldier

An antiquary.

Perhaps it is another.

We were surprised with the history of Marguerite's father and step-father and the American Civil War.

Joseph. Three three six, six, fifty, six fifty, fifty, seven.

Reading french.

Reading french.

Reading french singing.

Any one can look at pictures.

They explain pictures.

The little children have old birds.

They wish they were women.

Any one can hate a Prussian.

Alphonse what is your name.

Henri what is your name.

Madeleine what is your name.

Louise what is your name.

Rene what is your name.

Berthe what is your name

Charles what is your name

Marguerite what is your name

Jeanne what is your name.

Act 425.

We see a river and we are glad to say that that is in a way in the way today.

We see all the windows and we see a souvenir and we see the best flower. The flower of the truth.

An Interlude.

Thirty days in April gave a chance to sing at a wedding.

Three days in February gave reality to life.

Fifty days every year do not make substraction.

The Alsations sing anyway.

Forty days in September.

Forty days in September we know what it is to spring.

Act in America.

Alsatians living in America.

February XIV.

On this day the troops who had been at Mulhouse came again.

They came in the spring.

The spring is late in Alsace.

Water was good and hot anyway.

What are you doing.

Making music and burning the surface of marble.

When the surface of marble is burned it is not much discolored.

No but there is a discussion.

And then the Swiss.

What is amiss.

The Swiss are the origin of Mulhouse.

Alsace or Alsatians.

We have been deeply interested in the words of the song.

The Alsatians do not sing as well as their storks.

Their storks are their statuettes.

The rule is that angels and food and eggs are all sold by the dozen.

We were astonished.

And potatoes

Potatoes are eaten dry.

This reminds me of another thing I said. A woman likes to use money.

And if not.

She feels it really is her birthday.

Is it her birthday.

God bless her it is her birthday.

Please carry me to Dannemarie.

And what does Herbstadt say.

The names of cities are the names of all.

And pronouncing villages is more of a test than unbrella.

This was the first thing we heard in Alsatia.

Canary, roses, violets and curtains and bags and churches and rubber tires and an examination.

All the leaves are green and babyish.

How many children make a family.

The Watch on the Rhine.

Sweeter than water or cream or ice. Sweeter than bells of roses. Sweeter than winter or summer or spring. Sweeter than pretty posies. Sweeter than anything is my queen and loving is her nature.

Loving and good and delighted and best is her little King and Sire whose devotion is entire who has but one desire to express the love which is hers to inspire.

In the photograph the Rhine hardly showed

In what way do chimes remind you of singing. In what way do birds sing. In what way are forests black or white.

We saw them blue.

With for get me nots.

In the midst of our happiness we were very pleased.

The Psychology of Nations

or

What Are You Looking At

We make a little dance.

Willie Jewetts dance in the tenth century chateau.

Soultz Alsace dance on the Boulevard Raspail

Spanish French dance on the rue de la Boetie

Russian Flemish dance on the docks.

Bread eating is a game understand me.

We laugh to please. Japanese.

And then to seize. Blocks.

Can you remember what you said yesterday.

And now we come to a picture.

A little boy was playing marbles with soldiers, he was rolling the balls and knocking down the soldiers.

Then came a presidential election.

What did he do. He met boys of every nationality and they played together.

Did they like it.

In the middle of the presidential election they had a bonfire.

A policeman stopped them.

What can a policeman do, they said.

What is older than that.

Any baby can look at a list.

This is the way they won Texas

Let us go to the right.

It is wonderful how boys can fill.

Water.

Water swells.

We swell water.

To be lapped and bloated.

With urgency and not necessity and not idiocy.

All men are intelligent.

Please beg a boy.

Then they all danced.

How can a little Pole be a baby rusher.

PART II.

Readings in missions.

Who can neglect papers.

When boys make a bonfire they do not burn daily papers.

It was pleasing to have some mutton.

Suppose a presidential election comes every fourth year.

Startling, start, startles jump again.

Jump for a feather.

A feather burns.

Indians burn have burned burns.

A boy grows dark.

He can really read better better than another.

I cannot decline a celebration.

Do you remember the Fourth of July.

And do you.

Read readily and so tell them what I say.

Jump to the word of command.

Jump where

In there

Not eating beans or butter.

Not eating hair.

Not eating a little

When the presidential election is earnest we are only a year.

A year is so far in May.

Can you love any September.

The little boy was tall.

Dear me.

I have asked a lady to burn wood.

The boy touches the wall.

The boy is tall.

I am thinking that the way to have an election is this. You meet in the street. You meet. You have the election.

That is why horses are of no use.

We do resist horses when we are not afraid of them.

Can one expect to be a victory.

Three long thousands.

Expect to be met.

The boy is satisfied to be steady.

Study me.

Why can't we have a presidential election.

LAST PART

The boy grows up and has a presidential election.

The president is elected.

Why do the words presidential election remind you of anything.

They remind us that the boy who was in the street is not necessarily a poor boy.

Nor was he a poor boy then.

EPILOGUE

Veils and veils and lying down.

Lying down in shoes.

Shoes when they are new have black on the bottom.

We saw today what we will never see again a bride's veil and a nun's veil.

Who can expect an election.

A boy who is the son of another has a memory of permission.

By permission we mean print.

By print. Solution.

Settle on another in your seats.

Kisses do not make a king.

Nor noises a mother.

Benedictions come before presidents.

Words mean more.

I speak now of a man who is not a bother.

How can he not bother.

He is elected by me.

When this you see remember me.

FINIS.

CPSIA information can be obtained
at www.ICGtesting.com
Printed in the USA
LVHW040434030123
736277LV00004B/154